DOUBLE NEGATIVE

DOUBLE NEGATIVE

The Black Image and Popular Culture / RACQUEL J. GATES

Duke University Press / Durham and London / 2018

© 2018 DUKE UNIVERSITY PRESS
All rights reserved
Printed in the United States of America on acid-free paper ∞
Cover designed by Heather Hensley
Interior designed by Courtney Leigh Baker
Typeset in Whitman by Westchester Publishing Services

Library of Congress Cataloging-in-Publication Data
Names: Gates, Racquel J., [date] author.
Title: Double negative : the black image and popular culture /
Racquel J. Gates.
Description: Durham : Duke University Press, 2018. | Includes
bibliographical references and index.
Identifiers: LCCN 2017059815 (print) | LCCN 2017061591 (ebook)
ISBN 9781478002239 (ebook)
ISBN 9781478000419 (hardcover : alk. paper)
ISBN 9781478000549 (pbk. : alk. paper)
Subjects: LCSH: African Americans in mass media. | African
Americans in popular culture. | African Americans and mass
media. | Race in mass media. | African Americans—Race identity.
Classification: LCC P94.5.A372 (ebook) | LCC P94.5.A372 U554 2018
(print) | DDC 305.896/073—dc23
LC record available at https://lccn.loc.gov/2017059815

Cover art: Flavor Flav. Photograph by Jesse Frohman © 1990.

To Luke and Solomon,

The two of you inspire me to be
better in all things, in all ways.

Mommy loves you.

CONTENTS

As someone who watches the Academy Awards with a level of passion that most people reserve for events like the Super Bowl or a papal mass, I have often fantasized about the kind of acceptance speech that I would make if given the opportunity. Therefore, I am delighted to have the chance to publicly recognize the many people who have supported this project, and who have supported me, throughout its development.

I could not imagine a more fitting home for this book than Duke University Press. When aspiring singer Erica Mena first met entertainment manager Yandy Smith on *Love & Hip Hop*, she earnestly told Smith, "I want to be on your roster." While I was tempted to quote this bit of dialogue to my editor, Ken Wissoker, during our first meeting, I erred on the side of caution. However, I can now freely admit that I have aspired to be on Ken's roster since I first started thinking about what I wanted this book to be. My heartfelt thanks go to Ken for his enthusiasm for my book and for his steadfast support. Ken understood what I wanted to do with this project even before I was perfectly clear on it, and he pushed me to go bigger and bolder. *Double Negative* is an infinitely better book due to his guidance. I am immensely grateful for Elizabeth Ault's early encouragement and for all of her help, beginning with the proposal stage and throughout all aspects of the publication process. Finally, two anonymous readers provided their thoughtful comments on the manuscript, and I am thankful to them for their perspectives, insights, and criticisms.

This project began in graduate school, and while it has shifted away from that earlier form, I am still indebted to my professors at Northwestern University who helped me to develop these ideas and how I engage with them. Jacqueline Stewart, E. Patrick Johnson, Lynn Spigel, Jeffrey Sconce, Mimi White, and Harvey Young provided me with the best possible training in graduate school, and I hope that they recognize their influence throughout this book. My cohort in the Screen Cultures program provided me with many years of friendship and intellectual stimulation. Thank you to Robert Cavanagh, Max Dawson, Quinn Miller, and Meghan Sutherland. Meghan once told me to write about the things that I love rather than about the things that I hate, and I have never forgotten that valuable piece of advice.

I began transforming this project into its current form in earnest when I joined the Department of Media Culture at the College of Staten Island, and I am thankful to be surrounded by truly remarkable students, faculty, and staff. My sincere thanks go to my research assistant, Jean-Claude Quintyne, who helped me at a particularly crucial time in the book's development, and to my teaching assistant, Hitomi Kato, who provided me with the time to work on the book as my manuscript deadline and pregnancy due date collided toward the end of 2015. My departmental colleagues have been wonderfully supportive as I developed this project while navigating the first few years on the tenure track. Thank you to Christopher Anderson, Cynthia Chris, Bang Geul Han, Michael Mandiberg, Tara Mateik, Edward Miller, Sherry Millner, Reece Peck, Jason Simon, Valerie Tevere, Cindy Wong, Bilge Yesil, and Ying Zhu. I am especially grateful to Edward Miller for putting together the 2017 Faculty Research Symposium that allowed me to present excerpts from the introduction. My heartfelt thanks go to David Gerstner for his ceaseless encouragement in all things. I must also give special recognition to Jillian Baez for her invaluable friendship.

Over the past few years, I have been fortunate to present parts of this book at various conferences, symposia, and events. Thank you to Jane Gaines at Columbia University for inviting me to present sections of the book at the "Policing the Crisis" Stuart Hall conference and at the Sites of Cinema seminar. Thank you to Aswin Punathambekar for organizing the Television and Television Studies in the 21st Century conference at the University of Michigan, where I presented my concept of negativity for the first time. Thank you to Cathy Davidson for generously inviting me to participate in the Media Blackness symposium at the City University of New York's Graduate Center. I am grateful to the following individuals and institutions for providing me with opportunities to present ongoing research: Shanté Smalls and the English Department at St. John's University, Dale Byam and the Africana Studies Department at Brooklyn College, Mobina Hashmi and the Department of Television and Radio at Brooklyn College, and Ellen Hunter and the Ethnic Media Collective at Queens College. I am also grateful to the organizers and selection committees of the following conferences, where I presented work that would eventually form this book: the American Studies Association, Console-ing Passions, Crossroads in Cultural Studies, and the Society for Cinema and Media Studies. I am also grateful for the opportunity to publish earlier sections of the introduction and chapter 4 as "Activating the Negative Image" in *Television & New Media* 16, no. 7 (2015): 616–630; and as "You Can't Turn a Ho into a Housewife: *Basketball Wives* and the Politics of Wifedom" in *In Media Res* (September 26, 2011).

I am thankful to my friends in the field who kindly agreed to read drafts of the chapters in this book. Allyson Field, Hollis Griffin, Elizabeth Nathanson, and Kristen Warner generously provided their thoughtful feedback, taking time out of their own busy schedules to help me flesh out my ideas and organize them in a cohesive manner. I want to extend a very special thanks to Michael Gillespie, who gave me multiple rounds of feedback on the introduction and indulged my steady barrage of texts and phone calls about all things related to this project: the big, the small, and the random.

While academia can be an isolating and lonely place, particularly as one struggles with the daily challenges of balancing personal and professional responsibilities, I am thankful that I have had the friendship, love, and support of people whom I count as both colleagues and friends. I want to thank Courtney Brannon Donoghue, Allyson Field, Alfred Martin, and Samantha Sheppard for their camaraderie. And, thank you to Bambi Haggins, Miriam Petty, Beretta Smith-Shomade, and Jacqueline Stewart, for everything.

I would be remiss if I did not acknowledge and thank Maria Aviles, Carol Broadus, Stacey-Ann Douglas, Andrea John, Beatrice St. Valle, Carolyn Wynter, and the teachers and staff at Hanover Place Daycare and Child Development Center. These women's labor made it possible for me to do the labor of completing this book. I thank them for taking such good care of my babies and for putting an anxious new mother's mind at ease.

As a Chicago native who has called Brooklyn home for the past decade, I deeply appreciate having a family who has showered me with the kind of love that spans geographic distance. I am also immensely grateful for the friends who have become my chosen family here in New York and across the country. In particular, I am thankful for the support of the following people: Jennifer Jackson, Tamela Blalock, Hollis Griffin, Elizabeth Nathanson, Vicky Davis, Toni and Amuche, Katy and Shiju, Breagin and Andre, Vicky and Pat, Krisha and Dexter, Danae and Guambi, Annie and Michael, Chris and Jessica, the Carey family, the Ebie family, and the myriad Johnsons and Gateses who have offered their support in endless ways. I want to thank my grand-mothers, Mattie Gates and Janet Shields, for serving as sources of inspiration. I also need to extend a special thanks to Chelsea Bullock and Kristen Warner for their unwavering support, encouragement, counsel, and friend-ship over the past years. They talked me down off of countless ledges and told me time and time again that it was going to be all right, whatever "it" may have been on any given day.

Thank you to my parents, Susan and Raymond Gates, for their unwavering love, support, and cheer throughout the many stages of writing this book. I credit them for teaching me what critical analysis was before I had a name for it and for instilling in me a never-ending love of movies and television. Some of my fondest memories are of the three of us going to the movies at Burnham Plaza, or watching television together when we lived at 2901. Those themes of joy, pleasure, and togetherness serve as inspiration for how I approach my research, and I hope that my attempt to capture that comes through in this book.

My sons, Luke and Solomon, were born during the writing of this book, and their arrival left an indelible mark on the finished product. I thank them for giving me a newfound sense of purpose as I endeavored to complete this project and for providing me with a deeper understanding of the concepts of work and labor. They are, quite simply, the best little boys in the entire world, and I am thankful for them every day.

Finally, I want to thank my partner, Kenneth Ebie, for his never-ending efforts to bolster me—personally and professionally—from the earliest stages of this project through its completion. Thank you for always taking as givens the things that I worried about the most. You never doubted that I would complete this book or that it would be published, and your confidence in my abilities sustained me when self-doubt inevitably crept into my mind and spirit. It is a joy and a privilege to be the Lisa to your Akeem.

NEGATIVITY AND THE BLACK POPULAR IMAGE

In order for black people to truly reach the Promised Land, Flavor Flav has to be shot. These are important times. We got a black man running for president. We don't need a nigger running around with a fucking clock around his neck and a Viking hat on his head. —**CHRIS ROCK**, *Kill the Messenger*

All I did was get on the tube and be myself, man, now I got the whole world climbing down my back. All because I was too black. And too strong. But that's all right, man. Yo, they're going to want me back one day. —**WILLIAM DRAYTON, AKA "FLAVOR FLAV,"** *Fight the Power*, B-side

If them motherfuckers was going to call you a crispity, crackly, crunchity coon *anyway*, you might as well get them motherfuckers for everything. Everything? Everything. —**KATT WILLIAMS**, *It's Pimpin' Pimpin'*

Few media figures have elicited as many accusations of "negative representation" as Public Enemy's hype-man-turned-reality star William Drayton, better known by his stage name Flavor Flav. Part of the popular 1980s and 1990s rap group Public Enemy, Flav is perhaps best known for the oversized clock necklaces that he wears and his theatrical behavior, a marked contrast from the more activist intellectual demeanor of Public Enemy's front man, Chuck D, and the militant Black Power vocals of fellow member Professor Griff. Though Flav was actually responsible for writing a large amount of Public Enemy's music, he is primarily known as the group's "hype man," or the one to excite the crowd. Within the context of the group, therefore, Flav's boisterous antics have typically served as a means to prep the audience for the more serious messages delivered by the rest of the group.[1]

Flavor Flav's onstage persona, however, took on a very different context when he made the jump to reality television in the early 2000s. After a period of inactivity marred by several run-ins with the law, the former hype man made his triumphant return to public attention when he appeared on a series of VH1 reality shows created by the producing team of Cris Abrego and Mark Cronin (51 Minds Entertainment): *The Surreal Life* (2003–2006), *Strange Love* (2005), and *Flavor of Love* (2006–2008). Though the shows were huge hits for the network and resuscitated Flavor Flav's career, his appearances were almost immediately accompanied by scathing criticism. In spite of the fact that Flav's over-the-top shenanigans remained much the same as they had during his rap days (the attire, catchphrases, etc.), the new televisual context in which he was now ensconced carried with it a history of problematic historical associations, stemming back to controversies over black representation in *The Birth of a Nation* (D. W. Griffith, 1915) and the television sitcom *Amos 'n' Andy* (CBS, 1951–1953; NBC, 1954–1966). Similar criticism surrounded the premier of *Flavor of Love*, a comedic version of the popular dating show *The Bachelor*, where a group of women competed to win Flav's affections. Though I have argued elsewhere that *Flavor of Love* is best understood as a satire of *The Bachelor* and white heteronormativity, many saw the show as just another example of a black man acting foolish for the pleasure of white audiences.[2] Now removed from the community-empowerment message of Public Enemy, Flav's performances were no longer seen as a helpful component of a larger message of uplift, but, rather, as a type of "negative" black image that harkened back to the cringeworthy buffoonery of early cinema and television.[3]

The issue, to put it plainly, was that Flavor Flav had become a negative representation. In other words, some perceived him to be perpetuating a stereotypical view of a black man, one that presumably helped to foster racist attitudes among television viewers. Indeed, much of the criticism of Flavor Flav's reality television performances charged him with "coonery," a term that combines the racist trope of the "coon" with the word "buf-

FIGURE I.1. Flavor Flav in *Flavor of Love.*

foonery." Comedian Chris Rock explicitly connected Flav's image to then-presidential candidate Barack Obama's political ambitions in his 2008 HBO comedy special, *Kill the Messenger*, suggesting that Flav's "modern day minstrelsy" (to quote one journalist) had the potential to harm Obama's chances of winning the election: "In order for black people to truly reach the Promised Land, Flavor Flav has to be shot. These are important times. We got a black man running for president. We don't need a nigger running around with a fucking clock around his neck and a Viking hat on his head."

Rock's statement evidenced a Du Boisian double consciousness, presuming that Flav's negative representation would be perceived by whites as indicative of all blacks, including Obama. Rock had conveyed a related sentiment years earlier in his *Bring the Pain* comedy special, in which he (now) famously stated, "I love black people, but I hate niggas." In *Bring the Pain*, Rock's "black people" versus "niggas" routine captured the politics of respectability that would later play out in his statements about Barack Obama and Flavor Flav: "There's black people, and there's niggas. And niggas have got to go. Every time [that] black people want to have a good time, ignorant-ass niggas fuck it up."

The logic of Rock's "black people" versus "niggas," or Obama versus Flav routines, relies on the assumption that those that perform blackness in a negative manner bear the responsibility when their positively performing counterparts have their rights and privileges taken away. Yet this reasoning overlooks the fact that neither positive black people nor negative "niggas" actually hold the structural power to confer or deny these privileges. The assumption that underlies Rock's routines, therefore, obscures the manner in which antiblack racism functions in ways both big and small, and it elides a broader consideration of structural oppression in favor of the logic that "one bad apple spoils the bunch." Lewis Gordon argues that this idea of the "racial representative" indicates a society that views blackness through the lenses of anonymity as well as overdetermination. Gordon writes, "We can stand as a society without responsibility for the blackness we exclude by way of the blackness we include, which we identify as blackness *in toto*."[4] Rock's punch line—that Flav must be sacrificed for the good of all black people—may have been a joke, but its implied violence suggests the genuine fears about the impact that negative representations have in the real world.

At the same time, however, Rock's joke about killing Flavor Flav reveals the slipperiness of the "negative" label, as well as the particularly thin barrier between categories of "positive" and "negative." Later in the set, Rock admonishes Flav, "Put a suit on, nigga," implying that Flav can indeed be made respectable (or at least enough to fool white people) via something as simple as changing his outward appearance. But if Flavor Flav can be made respectable by relinquishing the clock and donning a suit, does that not mean that Barack Obama might become a negative representation should he switch into a different racialized code of behavior? Flav's actions only became perceived as negative once he left the setting of Public Enemy and entered the already disreputable landscape of reality television, thus revealing that the categorization of his behavior, and hence his identity, depends on the context in which it circulates.

The comedian Katt Williams also took the 2008 presidential election as his inspiration in a routine for his special, *It's Pimpin' Pimpin'*. Whereas Rock chose to place the onus of Obama's election on Flavor Flav's shoulders, Williams shifts the burden onto those of the white voters. Williams begins by criticizing whites for failing to comprehend why Obama's campaign is so meaningful to black voters: "You selfish motherfuckers. White people, ain't y'all had all the goddamned presidents?" He then continues with a direct appeal, "White people, I don't think that you should vote for somebody just 'cause of their race, but I will say if you was ever going to vote for a nigga, if you was ever gon' vote for a nigga, this is the nigga to vote for. Right here. This is the one. Yes. Absolutely." By addressing whites instead of blacks, Williams correctly identifies the role of whites (and whiteness) in the discourse surrounding Obama's candidacy as well as in his election to office.

While Rock's routine unintentionally hints at the idea of Flav casting aside his negativity via a wardrobe change, Williams humorously, but accurately, observes the social construction of Obama's positivity. Obama's positivity is not a given, but, rather, a classification that arrives as the result of many socially legible factors such as his clean-cut appearance, his prestigious educational background, and his lack of any stereotypical markers of blackness. To this last point, Williams says, "He is nigga lite. This nigga been running for two years: he ain't had no baby mama come out the woodwork, this nigga don't owe nobody $200 for nothing, he ain't never had a pit-bull puppy, don't have an earring, never had a tattoo. Where the fuck did you get this nigga from, a cave in Salt Lake City some-goddamn-where?" Williams's joke points out the reality of Obama's popularity among white voters: namely, that it is predicated on a seeming exceptionalism to all things deemed too obviously "black."[5]

Humorous though the Williams routine may be, it hits on the reality about racial categorization that would hover over Obama's two terms as president. For all of Obama's intelligence, charisma, and thoughtfulness, his identity as a positive figure has never been stable or gone unchallenged. Instead, he has always performed a tenuous balancing act in the face of those who would read his unquestionably "black" moments as the tip of the iceberg for the negative blackness presumed to be hidden behind his respectable exterior.[6] For example, in 2009 when James Crowley, a white police officer in Cambridge, Massachusetts, arrested African American Harvard professor Henry Louis Gates Jr. for trying to enter his own home, Obama gave a press conference in which he plainly stated that racial profiling had probably played a role in the incident. However, after uproar by members of law enforcement as well as white civilians who viewed Obama's comments as "playing the race card," the president quickly retracted his statement and invited both Crowley and Gates to the White House to discuss the incident over beers. The famous "beer summit," as the meeting came to be called, showed just how delicate a position Obama found himself in as the first African American president. While his initial statement was a straightforward acknowledgment of the long, documented history of racial profiling by law enforcement and should have been uncontroversial, the very fact that Obama brought up race *at all* was enough to result in harsh criticism from some fronts. For, as Devon Carbado has noted, Obama had always been deliberate and strategic in the ways that he addressed or didn't address race.[7] The resulting beer summit, therefore, had less to do with reconciling tensions between Crowley and Gates or between the police and the black and brown victims of profiling, but, rather, had everything to do with Obama's identity as a positive, respectable black figure. As the beer summit at the White House demonstrates, however, this respectability often comes with the consequence of muteness. Or, to be more specific, the burden of respectability places limitations on the forms that certain types of discussions can take. Obama recalibrated his frank talk about race to avoid coming across (to some) as an angry, race-obsessed black man, going instead as the race-neutral mediator who could reconcile black and white.

Likewise, the respective Rock and Williams comedy routines demonstrate the contours of positivity and negativity when they serve as delivery methods for cultural critique.[8] Indeed, Chris Rock and Katt Williams themselves represent positive and negative poles. On a superficial level, the two comedians' positive and negative categorizations are most apparent in their use of language and in their respective professional backgrounds. Whereas Rock is judicious with his use of curse words and rarely discusses sex or drugs in his special (therefore adhering to a seeming code of respectability), Williams litters his statements with profanity of all types, most notably his liberal use of the n-word. And contextually, whereas Rock's identity is buffered by a respectability conferred by his time in media with a mixed audience—in popular television shows like *Saturday Night Live* and *In Living Color* and in Hollywood films—Williams's celebrity is largely confined to the black community. When he has appeared in films, like the 2007 Eddie Murphy vehicle *Norbit* (Brian Robbins), Williams has played characters indistinguishable from his onstage persona.

More broadly, Rock embodies a global cosmopolitanism with appeal to both black and nonblack audiences, while Williams more aesthetically and functionally invokes aspects from the history of black comedic traditions.[9] These differences first become evident in the two men's attire and styling in their specials. In *Messenger*, Rock alternates between three different outfits: an effortlessly stylish all-black suit; a more traditional black suit, white shirt, and black tie combination; and an all-leather ensemble. The variety of his wardrobe suggests that Rock would feel equally at ease on an urban street corner and on the Oscars red carpet.[10] Williams also wears a shirt and tie, but he completes his ensemble with baggy jeans and a jewel-encrusted belt buckle, incorporating aspects of urban street style and "bling culture" and negatively riffing on those sartorial symbols of middle-class profes-sionalism. Whereas Rock's hair is close-cropped, Williams sports his signa-ture straightened bob, a hairstyle that visually references 1970s drug dealer and pimp characters like the ones found in blaxploitation films like *Super Fly* and *The Mack*. The pimp reference is not accidental, as Williams titles his special *It's Pimpin' Pimpin'*, a marked contrast with Rock's *Kill the Mes-senger*, which broadcasts the truth-telling tone that Rock adopts as he talks about issues of social and political importance.[11]

The mise-en-scène and editing of the two specials, along with the come-dians' respective performative styles, likewise reflect different sensibilities. Rock's *Messenger* is a composite of his shows in Johannesburg, London, and New York, and this assemblage of footage evokes the comedian's widespread global appeal to a range of international audiences. The opening sequence, featuring grafs that list impressive statistics such as the names of the eight countries in which he has performed and the number of people who have attended his shows (554,781), conveys the wide reach of Rock's popular-ity. Rock confidently walks out onto the stage as a song, "Duffle Bag Boy" by the rap group Playaz Circle (feat. Lil Wayne), blasts over the speakers. Rock's body is presented in isolation—often in backlit silhouette—with cuts that alternate between his solitary figure and sweeping views of the audience. This device serves several purposes. First, it visually represents Rock as "Chris Rock the icon," rather than Chris Rock, the man performing comedy. Next, it creates a visual distinction between Rock and his audi-ence, separating the two into categories of performer and audience. This visual isolation reinforces the concept of Rock as exceptional as well as solitary: he stands apart from the audience both literally and figuratively.

Unlike Rock's cosmopolitanism, Williams might be said to possess "black common sense," insofar as his presentation of self and of his material draws more explicitly from a recognizable black cultural tradition rather than from a mainstream white sensibility.[12] The opening of Williams's *Pimpin'*, in con-trast to Rock's *Messenger*, connects the comedian to his audience as well as to a longer legacy of black comedians and their concert films. Williams's *Pimpin'* was shot during the Washington, DC, leg of his tour. Though it is the home of the United States government, DC is also colloquially known among its black residents as "Chocolate City" because of its rich history of black American history, culture, and activism.[13] *Pimpin'* opens with Williams

FIGURE 1.2. The opening of Chris Rock's comedy special *Kill the Messenger*.

FIGURE 1.3. Chris Rock onstage in *Kill the Messenger*.

visiting various black-owned and black-frequented establishments, such as the famous and historic Ben's Chili Bowl. These scenes do more than simply establish the setting for Williams's special, however. Rather, the anthropological opening is a conceit that many black comedians have employed to open their concert films in order to show their connection to the places and the people that inhabit them, especially in those locales with a particularly rich black cultural history.

This motif of community continues in the editing of the shots where Williams takes the stage. Whereas Rock appears in solitary profile, shots of Williams entering the stage are framed to show both the comedian and the audience at the same time. Like Rock, Williams enters to a rap song, "Int'l Players Anthem (I Choose You)" by UGK (featuring Outkast), but he takes several seconds to dance to the beat before launching into his routine. This seemingly inconsequential moment establishes the sheer joy that Williams takes in sharing this experience alongside the audience members. At one point, he lifts his arms as if he is conducting an orchestra or a choir, again reiterating the communal nature of his performative relationship to the audience.[14] Shots of the audience in *Pimpin'* are meant to show Williams's *connection* to the audience in contrast to Rock's isolation. Whereas the sweeping shots of the audience in *Messenger* highlight the sheer number of people in the concert venues—thus again confirming Rock's immense global popularity—the shots of the *Pimpin'* audience build on the earlier "anthropological" tone of the film to convey Williams's connection and membership with the audience members, stand-ins for the black community writ large.

At first glance, it is easy to be misled by the stylistic choices of the two comedians and assume that Rock's avowedly political stance (as indicated in the title of the special) automatically signifies that his material offers more insightful critique than that of Williams, but we should not presume that Williams's liberal use of curse words and his aesthetic similarity to blaxploitation characters disqualify his comedy from offering pointed analysis of matters of identity and politics. The form that Williams's critique takes, markedly different from that of Rock's, privileges a black insider knowledge between Williams and his predominantly black audience, one that is highlighted visually by Williams's aesthetic references to black popular culture (in his hairstyle and clothes), his use of black vernacular, and the subject matter that he takes on. As in the above joke about Obama being "nigga lite," Williams cites examples that would be instantly recognizable to black audiences—the pit-bull puppy and owing someone $200, most obviously—not just those stereotypes

FIGURE I.4. Katt Williams with Washington, DC, locals in *It's Pimpin' Pimpin'*.

FIGURE I.5. Katt Williams onstage in *It's Pimpin' Pimpin'*.

about blackness that have circulated in mainstream popular culture. And his repeated use of the word "nigga" to refer to the president—used in this context to imply camaraderie—brings Obama into the fold of black community rather than isolating him as the exception to it.[15]

Even more interesting than Williams's bringing Obama into the fold with his use of the n-word, however, is Williams's reference to Flavor Flav in the same special. Williams tells an anecdote about the time that he hosted the televised Comedy Central roast of Flav, and how he was angered at the unapologetically racist tone of the jokes directed at the rapper-turned–reality television star. Yet unlike Rock, whose comedy places the responsibility of racist perception primarily on Flav's shoulders, Williams directs his ire at the Comedy Central writers and producers: "I saw the William Shatner roast and the Pamela Anderson roast and it wasn't all about them being white. But on Flavor Flav's shit, every other word was 'Flav is a crispity, crackly, crunchity coon. He's a black sizzly, crunchity, crackly coon. Flav is a big black crispy, crackly, crunchity coon . . . all through the fucking script." By shifting the attention away from Flav's performance of negativity and onto the industrial factors that govern his performance, Williams brings issues of labor to the forefront, an emphasis that he reinforces when he explicitly addresses the economic motivation underpinning both his and Flav's acquiescence: "And the whole goddamned show I was mad, but I was mad at me that I was still fucking doing it the way I felt, but they had already told me how much they was gonna pay me, and, I had already spent it in my head, so I was in a fucked-up position."[16] Yet, rather than simply suggest that black performers are helpless victims caught up in the industrial and economic chokeholds of the media industry, Williams closes the routine by suggesting that there can, in fact, be a certain degree of agency in one's seeming adherence to stereotypes and other troublesome forms of representation. As Williams puts it, "If them motherfuckers was going to call you a crispity, crackly, crunchity coon *anyway*, you might as well get them motherfuckers for everything. Everything? Everything."

We may be tempted to read Williams's final statement as a nihilistic acceptance of racist perceptions of blackness. Yet what he is getting at, I believe, is the possibility of using the trope of negativity in ways that demonstrate self-awareness, agency, and even subversion. If one were to eschew the politics of respectability altogether and disregard the notion that media representations directly support or challenge racism, where would that leave categories of positivity and negativity? And if we were to refocus our attention away from just issues of representation and onto industrial practices and matters of labor, what new questions might we begin to ask, and what possibilities might we reveal in the process?

Positive/Negative

As the examples of Flavor Flav, Barack Obama, Chris Rock, and Katt Williams demonstrate, the categories of positive and negative are modes that individuals perform, sometimes deliberately, but more often unconsciously, which resonate with larger discourses of identity, race, politics, and norms of behavior in our society. These modes possess markers that are culturally legible and carry with them connotations about their bearers as well as a host of other related associations. They are not static but, rather, shift across time. And if the categories themselves are not static, then their bearers' hold on them is even less stable.

Designations of positive versus negative with regard to representations of blackness and black people can be frustrating. Taken as straightforward descriptors, they are limiting categories that do not allow us to access the full, complex range of images that circulate in the media, nor do they allow for the possibility of nuanced engagement with these images by the people that consume them. Conventional uses of "positive" and "negative" support politics of respectability and close off possibilities for multilayered conceptions of and performances of identity. At their worst, to invoke these categories uncritically reinforces racist ideologies that use discourses of black exceptionalism to further marginalize black behaviors and people that deviate from white, middle-class, heterosexual norms.

As a fan of various types of media, including "ratchet" images, I often feel frustrated when I hear people say things like "we need more positive/ progressive representations of black people on television" or "that depiction does nothing to advance black people in society." While on the surface, such declarations lay claim to the need for social change and the power of media to achieve it, these types of statements are based on several problematic assumptions. These include the notion that media representations have a direct and straightforward impact on people's ideologies, that media images matter more than histories of institutional oppression, and that audiences always interpret images in predictable and knowable ways. These suppositions are rarely questioned in the public sphere, but, instead, are taken at face value as objective truth.

Even those of us who try to escape the positive/negative dichotomy inevitably end up replicating it in other ways, such as discourses of "quality," which simply recast "positivity" in different terms. Auteurist-focused analyses run the same risk, with primacy being given to black filmmakers working outside of the Hollywood system, the assumption being that black filmmakers unencumbered by Hollywood's history of racism will inevitably produce the "right" kinds of images. And even when we explicitly state our desire to talk about representation in a way that eschews the positive/negative categories, as Melissa Harris-Perry did in her reality TV roundtable discussion in a July 2013 broadcast of *The Melissa Harris-Perry Show*, it seems hard to, even temporarily, leave aside the matter of whether these images *do* something to those who consume them.

The problem is that, try as we might, we cannot seem to shake the assumption that representations do the work by themselves. In other words, there is an unshakable belief that images do work outside of the histories and contexts in which they circulate. For instance, in 2015, Mattel released a limited-edition doll in the likeness of the African American director Ava DuVernay. The doll sold out in fifteen minutes, a sign of its immense desirability among DuVernay's fans. But what explains the excitement around the doll's release? A quick scan of tweets with the hashtag #AvaBarbie shows two presumptions about the doll: first, that the likeness of Ava DuVernay will encourage self-love among the little black girls who receive it, and, second, that owning a model of the director will inspire these girls to pursue a career in filmmaking. Yet the doll's only accessory is a director's chair. Unlike other professionally oriented dolls that Mattel produces, the Ava Barbie does not come with any accessories that would signal her career or allow her profession to function meaningfully in children's play.[17] It would be one thing, for instance, if the doll came with a camera and a clapboard, or if purchase of the doll provided access to an online app that allowed girls to create their own mini movies, something that the independent toy company GoldieBlox has in its lineup of toys targeted at young girls.[18] Instead, the Ava Barbie is simply a doll in DuVernay's likeness, and while it makes sense that fans of the director would want one as a collector's item, it is unclear exactly *how* the doll is supposed to inspire self-esteem or career ambition in young girls. It is as if the doll is assumed to magically achieve these goals simply by *being*, as if its actual function—how little girls will take it up and play with it—is irrelevant.

FIGURE 1.6. The Ava DuVernay Barbie doll by Mattel.

However, representations do not do the work by themselves, and, to take it a step further, they may not even do the work that we presume them to do. When we refer to media as either positive or negative, we imply that the images push perceptions of blackness in one of two directions: either forward or backward. But is that their only function? What about resistant reading? And irony? And pleasure? Where do those factor into the equation?

For those of us who disagree with this assessment of black images, the temptation is to find a way to get outside of the binary, to smash the positive/negative labels once and for all. This is valuable work, and I look forward to the day when these categories cease to govern our discussions of popular media. Yet we should not think that we have reached that point just yet. As I have already mentioned, the specter of these typifications lingers on in our analyses, whether or not we actually use the terms "positive" and "negative." And to be frank, I remain doubtful that, given the ongoing existence of structural and cultural racism, we will ever fully dismantle or escape the positive/negative binary, despite claims to the contrary. And if our strategy is simply to replace alleged negative images with positive ones, then we are merely adding more definitions of what it means to be black into circulation, without necessarily contesting the racist assumptions under which the negative ones were formed in the first place.[19] Though we may not always use such crude terms as "positive" or "negative" anymore, that does not mean that they do not hover over our work, in terms of which texts we privilege in our writing and which ones we do not. Moreover, if we eradicate the terms themselves, we risk losing the language to interrogate them and how they function, much like how operating in a climate of "color-muteness," to borrow Linda Williams's term, prevents us from naming racial oppression even as we continue to suffer its effects.[20]

While frustrations with the positive/negative binary have led many scholars invested in the study of black media to seek out ways to sidestep the binary altogether, I am reminded of Stuart Hall's warning that the power of cultural hegemony is that, while we may change the "dispositions and the configurations of cultural power," we do not necessarily escape them altogether.[21] At the same time, however, Hall likewise encourages us to avoid the overly cynical approach, the "zero sum game" as he puts it, that assumes that the structures of cultural hegemony effectively absorb and then stamp out any glimmers of significant change or diversity. We should take this part of Hall's statement seriously, in that it suggests that there is value in studying those texts previously deemed to be without value, damaging, or regressive.

Limiting though they may be, I advocate that we actually retain categories of positive and negative, not in a qualitative sense, but from the standpoint of strategic essentialism (as theorized by Gayatri Spivak). I am interested in using the categories to analyze how they come to be, but with the understanding that they are not connected to the intrinsic value that the texts possess. To use an analogy, I propose that we think of these designations categorically, similar to geographic neighborhoods. For, like the categories of positive and negative, neighborhoods are also delineated by artificial and often arbitrary boundaries, formed by specific sets of social and political developments, and defined by both those who willingly choose to inhabit them and those who are relegated there.

In the end, I am suggesting that it is not necessary to eradicate these categories as much as to deconstruct them: understand how they develop, where they are applied, how, and when. And further, by using these terms strategically, as critical race scholars have already done with strategic essentialism, we gain much in the way of developing a lens of analysis and language with which to understand and talk about what these texts are actually doing. Therefore, taking up Herman Gray's call to analytically shift discussions of identity and media "from signification and representation to resonance and experience," I propose that we actually embrace the designation of "negative" that has long been assigned to certain types of images. To activate the dictionary definition of "negative" as "expressing or containing negation or denial" reveals the ways that disreputable images such as those found in reality television, for instance, disrupt hegemonic norms regarding race, class, gender, and sexuality.[22] My understanding of these texts as *negative* is closely related to Kristen Warner's repurposing of the term "ratchet" to describe reality television shows such as *Basketball Wives* and *Love & Hip Hop*. In her analysis, the term encompasses the excessiveness and hypervisibility of the shows' depictions, their performative nature, their engagement with identity politics, and finally, their quality of being understood only through mediation. I embrace the term "negative" because of its historical use in defining certain types of black texts and because it implies a direct, tangential relationship to "positive" representations. If the current postracial, color-blind moment truly is a moment of color-muteness, then perhaps the negative image functions as the repository for those identities, experiences, and feelings that have been discarded by respectable media.

Negativity

This book focuses on the productive use of negativity as a paradigm for the analysis of black popular culture. The concept of negativity attends to the racially specific nature of the production, consumption, and circulation of black texts, while simultaneously emphasizing the mutually constituting nature of the positive and negative labels that these texts come to bear. Rather than view black texts as discrete objects of study (even when placed within larger contexts such as industry practices, circulation of stereotypes, genre specificity, etc.), the concept of negativity postulates that meaning in certain types of disreputable texts is primarily construed via their relations to other texts that occupy privileged positions as far as cultural capital, critical regard, and scholarly discourse. It should come as little surprise, then, that the dynamic relationship between positive and negative texts mirrors the fluid and mutually constituting nature of racial categories, as I have already hinted at in my discussion of Chris Rock, Katt Williams, and their respective understandings of how Barack Obama and Flavor Flav function within racially charged media environments. To highlight this dynamic, *Double Negative* uses examples that address issues of racial identity explicitly. If negativity, then, like race, is less an essential part of one's identity and more a social construction, what does this tell us about the categories of "positive" and "negative" as they pertain to blackness?

Negativity as Concept

This book offers two, interrelated definitions of a "negative" text. The first type of negative text is a qualitative one that is defined by its distance from normative, white hegemonic standards of quality. Flavor Flav's television show *The Flavor of Love*, because it showcased "unladylike" women of color competing for a nontraditionally desirable bachelor, is a good example of this form of negativity.[23] The second definition of a negative text is a formal category that functions as an inversion of another media text. In this second sense of the term, the film or television show in question may not be thought of as stereotypical or demeaning, but has simply been erased from critical discourse because its salient formal and ideological components are not recognized as bearing significant meaning. This is the case with a film like Eddie Murphy's *Coming to America* (John Landis, 1988). Though it does not indulge in the kinds of stereotypes that characterize *Flavor of Love*, its comedic genre and white director may have led to its dismissal as frivolous "entertainment," in contrast with more serious dramatic fare like *Do the Right Thing*, which the African American director Spike Lee released just a year later.

The concept of negativity derives first from the idea of a photonegative. In fact, my approach in this book is based heavily on the metaphor of a photographic negative, in which a positive image is considered normal (or, in the case of the media, normative) and a negative is the complete inversion of that image. I argue that these negative images engage in explorations of identity in a manner that is inversely proportional to contemplations of identity in respectable media texts.[24] Just as a negative is necessary for the production of a photograph, this book argues that the negative image is a necessary component for the production of the "positive" images that circulate throughout popular culture and scholarship. In other words, returning to my initial example, without Flavor Flav (and other negative representations of black masculinity), there could be no Barack Obama, to the extent that Obama's racial performance of black respectability is legible only because it contrasts with an equally recognizable trope of disreputable black masculinity.

The metaphor of a photonegative helps to elucidate the way that negativity functions in respect to black media texts. Yet this dynamic is not exclusive to black representation. Other discussions of alternative reading strategies, such as camp, for instance, likewise rely on an understanding of the relation between dominant and contested meanings. What further delineates negativity, then, is that it highlights the specifically racialized nature of these dynamics. To explicate, I incorporate two other metaphors—the linguistic and mathematical negatives. Linguistically, in nonwhite dialects, negatives often contradict standard rules of language. Indeed, the use of negatives, particularly a double negative, is a telltale sign of African American Vernacular English (AAVE), a variety of American English that is often misheard as simply "incorrect" or "broken" English. As Stefan Martin and Walt Wolfram note, "One of the most noticed characteristics of AAVE and many other varieties of English is the optional use of *negative concord*, also referred to as *multiple negation* and *pleonastic negation*."[25] By contrast, African Americans who speak standard American English—"proper" English, as many commonly refer to it—may sometimes be accused of "talking white," highlighting the racialized nature of language usage. Similarly, in media representation, texts determined to be "positive" are more likely to be those that bear resemblance to "proper" (e.g., white) films and television shows as far as the scenarios, characters, and behaviors that they portray, while "negative" texts are identifiable as such via their distance from those standards. And, finally, in mathematics, a negative integer has the power of rendering a positive integer negative when the two are multiplied. By extension, negative media representations are often accused of "setting blacks back" (sometimes all the way back to slavery), suggesting, even if hyperbolically, that a single negative image is powerful enough to undo decades and centuries of social and political gains.

As a framework, negativity helps to elucidate how tastes, politics, and modes of performance develop and change, and it reveals the ways that time forms our perceptions. Take, for instance, blackface minstrelsy in theater and early film, a type of black image that most people would undoubtedly decry as racist and regressive. While the practice has always faced strong criticism, some African American performers, such as the famed stage comedian Bert Williams, regularly appeared in blackface, finding that the makeup created a separation between his performative and real selves and allowed him to try on various comic personae.[26] As Louis Chude-Sokei argues, Williams's "blackface masquerade was as much a means of negotiating relationships between and among diaspora blacks in Harlem as it was an attempt to erase the intentionally projected racist fiction of the 'stage Negro' (or 'darky') from within the conventions of popular performance, from behind a mask produced and maintained by competitive projections and denials of black subjectivity."[27] Once blackface fell out of favor completely with modern society, however, those writing about Williams have revised the history of his performance, suggesting that Williams put on blackface against his will or because of the dearth of professional opportunities provided to him as a black man.[28] There is little evidence to support these revisionist claims; thus, these accounts reveal more about the changed perceptions of blackface than they do anything about Williams's actual sentiments. Shifting our attention to the contemporary moment, the example of Williams and blackface serves as an important caution against dismissing the complexity of alleged negative images and against ignoring the reasons behind why we do so.

What the idea of negativity offers, then, is a mode of analysis for *seeing* the work that these texts are doing in the first place. For, rather than cut off the analysis at the first sign of a stereotype or politically regressive construct, negativity seeks to move the discussion past this first level of scrutiny and on to the question of what meanings these texts hold relative to the culture that produces both them and their positive complements. For, as Pierre Bourdieu reminds us, these matters of taste, or, in my case, the matters of taste as they relate to the construction of negative texts, are given value in direct relation to socioeconomic and educational status and, by extension, racial status, too. Our ability to "read" or decipher a text, therefore, is based on our possession of the proper codes and language of appreciation or interpretation. As Bourdieu puts it, "The 'eye' is a product of history reproduced by education."[29] How, then, are we to "see" the meaning created in and by negative texts, when society—whether mainstream white culture or black respectability culture—has repeatedly obfuscated or dismissed it? Indeed, how are we supposed to see that which is constantly in danger of disappearing from the sphere of critical discourse? To complicate matters even further, how might we see the work that negative texts are doing in service of race, gender, sexuality, and class, when, as Matthew

Tinkcom argues about camp, the work is disguised as something else, such as stereotypes? How do we recuperate the work that these images do when they are packaged as objects that we would rather not see at all?[30]

To borrow again from Bourdieu, I am interested in providing a framework, a language, that would allow us to shift from "the 'primary stratum of the meaning we can grasp on the basis of our ordinary experience' to the 'stratum of secondary meanings,' i.e., the 'level of the meaning of what is signified.'"[31] Unlike Bourdieu, however, I am asserting a "bottom-up" approach to culture, whereby I focus my attention on developing an "eye" that would allow us to (1) understand the relationship between positivity and negativity, (2) comprehend the shifting nature of these categories, and (3) better read negative representations. To this end, "signification" takes on a dual meaning in this project, capturing both Bourdieu's basic semiotic definition and the racially and culturally specific "signifyin(g)" that Henry Louis Gates Jr. offers to describe a "meta discourse," expressed in black vernacular language, that allows for a criticism of aspects of white hegemonic structures outside the controlling gaze of whites, while also encouraging an intertextual dialogue that privileges the recognition and theorization of black cultural texts.[32] Riffing on Gates, I offer that when negative texts signify on white hegemonic as well as black hegemonic norms, they do so in a mode that is markedly different from their positive counterparts, one that is often embedded with troublesome performances and politics that obscure the more subversive work in which they are engaged. It is in these spaces, I contend, that *Love & Hip Hop* (VH1, 2011–) offers a glimpse of queer sexuality that is not often visible in white LGBT or black civil rights movements. Or we might note the ways that *The Associate* (Donald Petrie, 1996) troubles normative aesthetics of whiteness in cinema, a task that we do not expect from Hollywood films, particularly those heralded by white directors.

The Intervention

I want to be clear that I do not view positive images as inherently conservative or negative images as essentially subversive. Negative images encompass a wide range of politics and values: some challenge hegemony while others reinforce it. Yet what I find intriguing are the possibilities for queer, feminist, and otherwise nonnormative subjectivities in these negative texts, and the degree to which they are present without requiring "reading against the grain." What I am suggesting, then, is not an abandonment of emphases on genre and medium, but, rather, a means to enrich understandings of how they are deployed in the service of interrogations of racial identity.

I argue that reclaiming these overlooked images from black popular culture and offering an alternative history of their meanings and possibilities also provides a strong intervention in present-day debates about proper black behavior and the role of popular culture in the current sociopolitical moment. Moreover, as the veritable gutter of black media, negative representations serve as the repository for all of the feelings that positive images cast aside. I address this idea in more detail in chapter 4, where I discuss the function of reality television through the lens of affect and Frantz Fanon's concept of a "collective catharsis."

This is particularly important in the current historical and political moment, where the politics of respectability—an adherence to white middle-class ideals as a means of racial uplift—continues to operate within popular black thought. Even within the younger generation of media consumers who have grown up with distinctly postmodern musings on race, gender, and sexuality, the lure of the "positive representation" continues to factor into how they perceive and engage with images and representations. As Brittney Cooper writes, "Hip Hop Generation Black folks still have a deep love affair with respectability politics, or this notion that obtaining/creating a traditional nuclear family makes us grown up, middle class, and 'fit' to participate in the larger body politic, American dream and all."[33] Cooper's statement points to a growing trend of black cultural producers from the hip hop generation espousing neoconservative values and articulating an ideological and generational split through an adherence to a postracial identity and a rejection of black activist politics. This certainly seemed to be what the musician Pharrell Williams was gesturing toward when he defined his idea of "the new black" as a self-conscious "mentality" that one can be limited by or can overcome.[34] To those versed in neoliberal discourses about individual responsibility and "bootstraps," Williams's "new black" statements might sound disturbingly familiar. And though I do not suggest that Williams is consciously parroting the implicitly racist statements of the political right, I find that his statements, with their effortless intersection with postracial takes on race (which posit that the election of the first African American president signals that racism is a thing of the past), operate on the same principles.

Fredrick C. Harris traces the politics of respectability back as far as the post-Reconstruction era, where African Americans saw hard-won rights quickly stripped away and new racist laws implemented to keep them in positions of social and political inferiority. Harris summarizes the history of respectability in the following passage, which I quote here at length:

> For more than half of the twentieth century, the concept of the "Talented Tenth" commanded black elites to "lift as we climb," or to prove to white America that blacks were worthy of full citizenship rights by getting the untalented nine-tenths to rid themselves of bad customs and habits. Today's politics of respectability, however, commands blacks left behind in post–civil rights America to "lift up thyself." Moreover, the ideology of respectability, like most other strategies for black progress articulated within the spaces where blacks discussed the best courses of action for black freedom, once lurked for the most part beneath the gaze of white America.[35]

Harris's emphasis on the "gaze of white America" is important, because it suggests that Du Boisian double consciousness, the feeling of seeing oneself through the eyes of others, animates much intraracial policing of black images. These politics of respectability extend to the realm of television representation, where battles between respectability on the one side and authenticity on the other have provided a backdrop for nearly every black show that has entered primetime. Perhaps one of the most salient features of negative texts is the relatively scant critical discourse surrounding them in spite of the thoughtful or even provocative questions that they raise about representation and identity. Interestingly, many of the negative texts that I examine are quite popular as far as their reverberations throughout popular culture, making the absence of scholarly discussion of these texts unfortunate. Negative texts are often absent from serious analytics of black media, and yet, like ghostly apparitions, they materialize in discussions about their positive counterparts. Take the Bravo network's reality television show, *The Real Housewives*, for example. References to the show magically appear in Shonda Rhimes's discussion of *Scandal* as a "guilty pleasure" (a term that she uses pejoratively) and in Barack Obama's imperative to America's young people that they need to work harder at school rather than sitting at home and "watching *The Real Housewives*."[36] In both cases, the subjects of Rhimes's and Obama's speeches were not *The Real Housewives*, but each used the unquestioned "trashiness" of the show as a point of comparison for the questions at hand: the quality of *Scandal* and the merits of hard work, respectively.

Contrary to the dismissive tone of Rhimes and Obama, I am invested in exploring the merits of these texts. However, I am not at all interested in salvaging them from the metaphorical gutter. Indeed, some of the texts that I examine in this book may not necessarily offer much in the way of aesthetic or political contributions, but they are still "great artifacts," to quote Jeffrey Sconce, because of the ways that they crystallize particular debates around black representation at a given moment.[37] For instance, I would be hard pressed to argue that the often-sexist and misogynistic comedy *Strictly Business* (Kevin Hooks, 1991) rivals the emotional complexity or aesthetic beauty of John Singleton's *Boyz n the Hood* (1991), but, as *Business* captures certain anxieties around masculinity, racial identity, and professional success—anxieties that were reflected in numerous magazines and newspapers at the time—an analysis of the film offers insight into the media's representation of these anxieties, something that is not the project of Singleton's *Boyz*.

Relation between Positive and Negative Texts

Indeed, the mutually constitutive nature of positive and negative texts is part of a longer history of debates over representation in the media, debates that typically come down to issues of cultural authenticity, power, and media effects. Extending this positive/negative framework beyond media and into the realm of culture more broadly, many of the texts canonized in the study of black popular culture have also had a symbiotic "other." Throughout history, these comparative pairings concern themselves with matters of cultural authenticity, politics, and audience. For example, I am thinking here of how Richard Wright criticized Zora Neale Hurston's *Their Eyes Were Watching God*, accusing her of essentially "selling out" before the term was popular: "Miss Hurston *voluntarily* continues in her novel the tradition which was *forced* upon the Negro in the theater, that is, the minstrel technique that makes the 'white folks' laugh."[38] Hurston, however, was not interested in Wright's politics or in his criticism of her work. As she wrote to a friend, "I tried to be natural and not pander to the folks who expect a clown and a villain in every Negro. Neither did I want to pander to those 'race' people among us who see nothing but perfection in all of us."[39]

Shifting gears to film, we might also consider how Melvin Van Peebles's independent 1971 film *Sweet Sweetback's Baadasssss Song* is often compared (partly by the filmmaker himself) to the big-budget MGM blaxploitation classic *Shaft*, of the same year, with Van Peebles claiming cultural authenticity in contrast to the Hollywood studio's mainstream offering.[40] Or, more recently, filmmaker Tyler Perry referenced the Hurston and Wright debate in reference to his own fight with Spike Lee, who referred to Perry's work as "coonery and buffoonery" that harkened back to *Amos 'n' Andy*. In defense of his film and TV work, Perry argued that he was offering his black audiences characters and story lines taken from his own experiences in black communities, citing cultural authenticity as his defense against Lee's accusations.[41]

Finally, similar dynamics have operated in the world of network television. For example, while the National Association for the Advancement of Colored People (NAACP) petitioned to have *Amos 'n' Andy* (CBS, 1951–1953) taken off the air because they claimed that it represented African Americans negatively, African American viewers constituted part of the show's avid fan base.[42] The NAACP also took issue with ABC's *Beulah*, which starred a variety of black actresses playing the mammy-like titular character who works as a domestic in the home of a white family.[43] By contrast, Diahann Carroll's beautiful, sophisticated nurse in NBC's *Julia* (1968–1971) could not have been more different from the *Beulah* trope, leading *Ebony* magazine to cite the show as "another step in TV's evolution."[44] *Julia* creator Hal Kanter's decision to keep the show lighthearted and avoid delving too deeply into topics of race or racism struck some viewers and critics as overly saccharine and unreal. Thus, when *Good Times* premiered on CBS in 1974, *Ebony* magazine opened its advance review by claiming that "television viewers who protested that *Julia* was not a true reflection of black life can't say the same about the new CBS-TV series *Good Times*. The show is a slice of ghetto life as thick and juicy as a slab of salt pork simmering in a pot of collard greens."[45] Yet the "realistic" portrayals of *Good Times* set the stage for Bill Cosby's "positive" intervention into the television landscape with the premiere of *The Cosby Show* in 1984. When buzz about *Cosby* began to hit the press shortly before its premiere, it was against the backdrop of previous black television families that Bill Cosby discussed his new show. As Herman Gray points out, *Cosby* "quite intentionally presented itself as a corrective to previous generations of television representations of black life."[46] From the outset, the black press (aided by Cosby's own statements about the show's politics of representation) framed the new sitcom in comparison to its predecessors: "When Bill Cosby returns to NBC-TV this fall as star of a new half-hour situation comedy series, he will headline the only prime time show on television with an all-Black cast. There will be no token Whites and there will be no Blacks rapping in rhyme and break dancing in rhythm. There will be no Black stereotypes in characters that have been associated with some previous sitcoms with Blacks cast as co-stars."[47] As this brief survey demonstrates, black images in popular culture have always been evaluated to a large extent in direct relation to those that came before them, and always in the context of whether the images improve the perception of African Americans in society, as well as the supposed authenticity of the characters and experiences that they depict.

With this context in mind, cultural texts that do not meet the standards of respectability at the given cultural moment have often been labeled negative and positioned as the polar opposite of respectable programming and respectable viewers. When the attorney and media figure Star Jones called for a boycott of *Basketball Wives* in 2012, she expressed this dichotomy by taking to Twitter and calling on a nouveau Talented Tenth: "I'm asking all my high profile, platform having conscientious sisters who STAND FOR SOMETHING to just say #ENOUGHISENOUGH & call folk out! Be mad. But think about what I said. WE ARE BETTER than that. You're either part of the problem or part of the solution."[48] The cultural activist Michaela Angela Davis noted that the goal of her Bury the Ratchet campaign was to "get the spotlight off the ratchetness and on the successful women in Atlanta."[49] The problem with Jones's and Davis's arguments, however, is that they reinforce the notion that one type of representation must come at the cost of the other. It is always an either/or proposition in thinking such as this, rather than allowing for a both/and scenario. Or, more radically, might it be possible for the "successful women in Atlanta" to *also* be ratchet?

The Work That Negative Texts Do

Negative spaces can exist as havens for topics deemed outside of the boundaries of respectable texts, particularly when those topics have to do with matters of identity. Joshua Gamson makes this point about tabloid talk shows, arguing that they serve as spaces for the representation of, and engagement with, sexual nonconformity as well as a site where the contradictions of American society and values are put on display, debated, and consumed by audiences.[50] Similarly, reality television functions as the metaphorical gutter for the rejects of respectable black media representation. Interestingly enough, these individuals, groups, and topics that I refer to here as rejects happen to intersect and overlap with the same individuals, groups, and topics that are typically marginalized by mainstream and black uplift narratives in society. For instance, the shows that I discuss in chapter 4 include explorations of the sexuality of queer black women, a group chronically (and perhaps purposefully) ignored in scripted media as well as in real-life politics in favor of white, middle-class men.[51] This was made painfully clear when *The Advocate* ran its December 16, 2008, cover story, which declared "Gay Is the New Black," ignoring the intersectional identity that queers of color have lived with and expressed for quite some time. Interestingly, however, the reality show *Love & Hip Hop* features several queer men and women of color who occupy prominent places in the cast and associated story lines.

In my close readings of certain negative texts—*Coming to America*, 1990s Hollywood sellout comedies, Halle Berry's star image, and "ratchet" reality television—I find a potpourri of complicated explorations and anxieties about sex, gender, and class. Many of these negative texts open up possibilities for nonnormative feelings, experiences, and allegiances that, I argue, are simply not possible in the image-policed spaces of positive texts. The messy and shifting construction of Halle Berry's changing racial identity, for instance, is a process that most often occurs invisibly and "naturally." Watching Berry's persona transform from a positive to a negative text over the span of a decade, then, provides a rare glimpse into the inner workings of that process.

Negativity in Relation to Trash

In both popular and scholarly spaces, "trash" has always conveyed the notion of the antirespectable, anticanonical text. I obviously draw from existing discussions around trash in the ways that I think through the politics of negativity. Joshua Gamson's and Laura Grindstaff's books on TV talk shows, Eric Schaeffer's work on exploitation films, and Jeffrey Sconce's writings on trash all resonate with my understanding of negativity.[52] For instance, I draw on Sconce's work on "sleaze" as a way of thinking through my concept of negativity, which he describes in the following way: "Often, sleaziness implies a circuit of inappropriate exchange involving suspect authorial intentions and/or displaced perversities in the audience."[53] Like Sconce's description of sleaze, which he explains is less a historical category and more "an ineffable quality" or a "feeling one has about a film," I argue that negativity is primarily known via the "evidence of felt intuition," to quote

Phillip Brian Harper, rather than by any alleged "objective" criteria, the language of which is intractably coded in dominant norms anyway.[54]

As a cousin of trash, negativity includes some of the same liberatory pleasures associated with it. Writing about film art and trash, Pauline Kael argues, "Perhaps the single most intense pleasure of movie going is this non-aesthetic one of escaping from the responsibilities of having the proper responses required of us in our official (school) culture."[55] It is easy to see, then, the pleasures that the negative text offers in place of its positive counterpart. Free from the politics of respectability—in fact, often constructed in antithesis to the politics of respectability—negative texts offer a respite from the all-too-real responsibilities of racial uplift and image management.

To be specific, what many commonly refer to as trash is actually a reference to mass or low culture. Mass/low culture exists conceptually in direct contrast to high culture, as Theodor Adorno, Walter Benjamin, Pierre Bourdieu, Raymond Williams, and others have theorized.[56] And while more contemporary scholars such as Jeffrey Sconce have productively argued that this divide is much fuzzier, with mass/low culture being embraced by ostensibly high art cultures such as avant-garde movements, these analyses do not fully account for the complications that race brings into discussions of taste and culture.[57] For, if this book aims to highlight the way that whiteness functions invisibly in media, it must also point out that whiteness occupies a similar default position in *scholarship* on the media. In other words, we should productively trouble these existing discussions of taste and culture by first acknowledging that whether we use adjectives such as high, low, mass, or trash in front of the word "culture," all of these descriptors are still referring to *white* culture, in that the producers, texts, and fan communities that constitute the foundations of this scholarship do not typically include people of color.[58] Therefore, though my analysis of negative texts borrows heavily from discourses on trash, it diverts from this body of literature in important ways. Unlike Eric Schaeffer's definition of classical exploitation films, for instance, the negative texts that I examine may be produced and distributed by Hollywood studios, can employ high production values, engage A- or B-list stars, and may continue to circulate in popular culture long after their initial release.

Hence, an analysis of black mass culture necessitates both a different framework and a different category than those mainstream cultural texts associated with "trash." This discussion of taste and race must take into account the historical debates over the politics of representation. Whether it is the NAACP-organized boycott of *Amos 'n' Andy*, the promotion of *The Cosby Show* by black news outlets in the mid-1980s, or the online petition that prevented the airing of rapper Shawty Lo's *All My Babies' Mamas* (Oxygen), the politics of black representation have always involved ongoing, frequently tense relationships among community groups, activists, cultural producers, and viewers.[59] And while conversations about taste in white culture have sometimes involved similar debates (the controversy over the MTV reality show *Jersey Shore* comes to mind), black images in film and television have been embroiled in political debates since the earliest days of film and television. Though seldom explicitly acknowledged, blackness has been an indelible component of media imagery since the birth of cinema, predating continuity editing, sound, and color, as scholars such as Jacqueline Stewart and Linda Williams have pointed out.[60] And where blackness has appeared onscreen—typically in racist and stereotypical ways—controversy and political action have followed. The accolades lavished on the narrative and technical superiority of D. W. Griffith's *The Birth of a Nation* (1915) by President Woodrow Wilson at the time of the film's release were quickly countered by the recently formed NAACP's picketing of the film across the nation, and the film prompted African American filmmakers such as Emmett J. Scott, Noble and George Johnson, and Oscar Micheaux to create their own films and film companies as correctives to Griffith's heinous misrepresentations.[61]

Agency

Though much of my discussion emphasizes the active ways in which negative representations push back against hegemonic norms, this project does not concern itself with agency in the more traditional senses of the term. Rather than focusing on African American–produced media, I am interested in the idea of "black" as it comes to be defined in the process of circulation throughout pop culture. Without this flexibility, black cult classics such as *Coming to America* would not be considered "black" films, thus causing us to miss a valuable opportunity to examine the ways that Eddie Murphy managed to transform a standard Hollywood offering into a uniquely and identifiably black text, in spite of the intentions and efforts of the film's white director. Stuart Hall addresses this messy definition of "black" in his important essay "What Is This 'Black' in Black Popular Culture?," which I quote here at length:

> It is this mark of difference *inside* forms of popular culture—which are by definition contradictory and which therefore appear as impure, threatened by incorporation or exclusion—that is carried by the signifier "black" in the term "black popular culture." It has come to signify the black community, where these traditions were kept, and whose struggles survive in the persistence of the black experience (the historical experiences of black people in the diaspora), of the black aesthetic (the distinctive cultural repertoires out of which popular representations were made), and of the black counternarratives we have struggled to voice.[62]

Hall's emphasis on the hybridity within popular culture, a system that is always in flux and constantly responding to its own elements, offers a more inclusive concept of black popular culture than a strict adherence to the race of the filmmaker or the film's political focus. For example, even though John Landis directed *Coming to America*, the film not only has become firmly associated with Murphy but also has turned into an iconic film of black popular culture.[63] In this way, *Coming to America* represents the cultural hybridity that Hall rightly notes is a feature of many texts of "black" popular culture. Directed by a white director, starring an African American superstar, distributed by a mainstream Hollywood studio (Paramount), and featuring a large number of well-known African American actors in supporting roles (James Earl Jones, Madge Sinclair, John Amos, Calvin Lockhart), the film shows "black popular culture" to be an interracial collaborative effort. Building on Hall's assertion that hybridity need not undermine the specific blackness of a cultural product, I attribute the film's cultural resonance within black communities to the "black" aspects of the film revealed in its cultural in-jokes and created through its constant recirculation through other black cultural texts. In other words, the film takes its place in the black cultural pantheon primarily in hindsight and via intertextuality, rather than through some initial adherence to an arbitrary and rigid definition of a "black film." Thus, I reject the idea that a black director is what makes a film "black," choosing instead to focus on the ways that the text's reverberations in black communities and spaces confer its blackness.

While I acknowledge that negative representations sometimes fall prey to the same limiting constructions of race as their positive counterparts, I believe that the power of the negative image rests in its ability to shift the dynamics in popular culture. We see negative texts actively influencing mainstream popular culture and pulling *it* into the gutter in certain ways, such as the influence of the reality show *Love & Hip Hop* on the current television darling *Empire*, a subject that I explore in the conclusion. And, unlike the Bakhtinian carnivalesque, these are not shifts that simply bubble up temporarily only to be ultimately reabsorbed by dominant culture and robbed of their subversiveness. Nor are these subcultures that exist as a sort of parallel, underground universe to that of mainstream culture. Rather, the reverberations of negative texts function as tremors that irrevocably weaken the foundation on which their positive counterparts are constructed. These are, in fact, performances that matter in spite of the fact that they have traditionally been understood as inconsequential as far as articulating ideas about black identity. To this end, I examine the ways that they privilege disreputable behavior, characters, genres, and media as the means to negotiate the dynamics of culture, race, and power.

I connect these aspects of negativity to a long-standing tradition of black cultural practices that date back to the era of slavery, and which are often found in the seemingly frivolous spaces of comedy, historically, and, more recently, in genres such as melodrama and reality television. Lawrence Levine has convincingly argued that black humor, in particular, is a coping mechanism "essential to black survival and the maintenance of group sanity and integrity" in the face of American racism as well as a strategic mode of delivery that allows African Americans to discuss topics considered too taboo to tackle directly.[64] As an inverted image of a positive, the negative image likewise stands in defiant juxtaposition against the tenuous mores of racial uplift that so-called positive images create. Thus, I am less interested in creating a category into which black media texts can be lumped together than I am in thinking through the ways that negativity-as-framework helps us see the work that these texts do on their own, as well as in their reverberations in larger black culture. Moreover, negativity reclaims black texts that may have been excluded from more traditional black film and television canons, and it emphasizes the significance of black audiences and intertextuality to confer meaning, rather than the limited purview of critics and scholars.

Negativity as Meta Discourse

Because negative texts are not often canonized in scholarship or cited on media critics' "best" lists, it is difficult to identify them. This marks yet another of the difficulties in analyzing negative images, as they are at risk of disappearing from critical discourse altogether if not preserved in some fashion of scholarly attention. *Double Negative* argues that we can recognize negative texts via their positive inversion, or by finding evidence of them at the secondary form or level, such as in the ways that they are taken up in other popular culture texts. Because negative texts, by definition, do not receive primary attention, this secondary recirculation is an important space for the preservation of negative texts' cultural meanings and legacies.

Take, for instance, *Coming to America*. Though the film fared well at the box office, it has not garnered much in the way of scholarly analysis. Yet the film is as close to a black cult classic as one can get, with references to the film's plot, characters, costumes, and music continuing to circulate throughout black popular culture even today. The problem, however, is that the secondary spaces in which this negative text functions are *themselves* negative spaces and thus do not serve as evidence of the film's validity, but, rather, as evidence of its location in the figurative gutter. For example, in *The Real Housewives of Atlanta* spinoff *Kandi's Wedding*, Kandi Burruss, a songwriter and *Housewives* cast member, designs her upcoming African-themed nuptials to her fiancé, Todd Tucker, based on *Coming to America*. Interestingly, Burruss modeled her own wedding style after the arranged bride that Murphy's character rejects in the film, not the woman whom he eventually falls in love with and marries. Burruss's choices speak to the scenes and imagery from the film that captured popular imagination, precisely those that were not mentioned in the newspaper and magazine reviews of the film at the time of its premiere. Burruss's engagement with the film, however, sheds light on how it functions as a negative text. Interestingly, the characters and plot elements that she chooses to incorporate into her wedding are not those from the film's fairly conventional Hollywood A-plot. Instead, the parts of the film that appear to be the most memorable are those that constitute the B-plot, which I will later argue are the specifically "black" and "negative" moments in the film. Burruss's use of these suggests that the real meaning of *Coming to America* is located in these moments, in the "negative" register that the trained critics of the time did not pick up on.

Categories of Negativity

Though I offer negativity as a broader concept for the study of certain types of black media texts, I also categorize different forms of negativity in order to better understand how negativity functions. Therefore, each chapter of this book examines a variation of negativity, using specific media texts as case studies. The case studies provide an explanation for how these texts become negative, the implications of that designation, and an exploration of what texts offer us as far as an understanding of how the media and racial identity intersect. Unsurprisingly, many of the negative texts that I identify and discuss in this book occupy multiple categories at once.

Formal Negativity

Formal negativity involves a text that becomes a "negative" because one or more of its formal qualities—aesthetics, mise-en-scène, narrative, and so on—can function as an inversion of those of typical positive texts. Although this type of negative text may not have a direct corollary in the positive realm, it gestures toward practices and genres either in mainstream media representation or in black media. Chapter 1 examines *Coming to America*. Though produced by a mainstream Hollywood studio, Paramount, the lighthearted romantic comedy has become a favorite among black audiences. While it lacks any explicitly political themes (and, in fact, contains many stereotypes of Africans and African Americans), I am interested in the way that the film reverses the standard formula for conventional romantic comedies by emphasizing its comedic B-plots rather than its main romantic story line. The film also contains, after the closing credits, a sly inversion of Al Jolson's famous blackface performance in *The Jazz Singer*.

Relational or Comparative Negativity

In relational or comparative negativity, the positive counterpart directly overshadows the negative text. For instance, another explanation for *Coming to America* becoming a negative text is because of its chronological location between Robert Townsend's independent satire of Hollywood's racism, *Hollywood Shuffle* (1987), and Spike Lee's brilliant portrayal of race relations in the critically acclaimed *Do the Right Thing*. *Shuffle* directly criticized the racial tokenism that Townsend saw Murphy embodying within Hollywood, while *Do the Right Thing* announced a bold synthesis of independent and Hollywood sensibilities and an unapologetic stance on racial representation. Chapter 2 focuses on a group of black comedies produced in the early to mid-1990s, which I refer to as the "sellout films." These include *Strictly Business* (Kevin Hooks, 1991), *Livin' Large* (Michael Schultz, 1991), *True Identity* (Charles Lane, 1991), and *The Associate* (Donald Petrie, 1996). In contrast to the so-called hood films, or the social realism films most often associated with the period (*Boyz n the Hood*, 1991; *South Central*, 1992; *Menace II Society*, 1993), I argue that these comedies form a countercanon and are concerned with addressing questions of assimilation and upward mobility. Situated historically amid changes to network programming and the resurgence of black-themed films in Hollywood, these films ask different questions about blackness than their counterparts, address different anxieties, and examine different social phenomena.

Circumstantial Negativity

In circumstantial negativity, a media text is categorized due to the issues and debates surrounding it, rather than because of a direct relation to its positive counterpart. As I have argued elsewhere, Eddie Murphy's star image as a "crossover" star impacted the way that people understood, and potentially misread, the politics of his films and television appearances.[65] In chapter 3, I examine the star text of Halle Berry, whose persona shifts from "black girl next door" to "the white man's whore" over a period of ten years, the turning point coming with her appearance in the television miniseries *Alex Haley's Queen*. I consider the ways that intertextuality and publicity materials around Berry's film and television roles shaped the way that her racial identity was presented to and read by the public. I discuss, for example, how black magazines consciously attempted to rewrite Berry's celebrity persona in order to make believable her role as a woman passing for white. Prior to *Queen*, Berry's film roles and celebrity persona marked her as unquestionably black. In the 1991 film *Strictly Business*, Berry had functioned as a symbol of authentic blackness in contrast to the film's "sellout" protagonist. This built on her existing characterization as an "around-the-way girl" in films such as *Jungle Fever* (1991) and *Boomerang* (1992). With Berry's casting in *Queen*, however, African American publications such as *Jet* and *Ebony* attempted to merge Berry with the character she played, despite Berry's own vehement objections.

Strategic Negativity

Chapter 4 examines media texts that make full use of their location in the metaphorical "gutter" of media that is negativity, taking advantage of their distance from the politics of respectability to explore topics that their positive counterparts do not typically address. Here I focus on the genre of reality television, and more specifically, on the shows that Kristen Warner has labeled "ratchet": *Basketball Wives*, *Love & Hip Hop*, and *The Real Housewives of Atlanta*. These are the shows that routinely serve as examples of negative representations, with the activist Michaela Angela Davis launching a campaign to get them taken off the air, *Grey's Anatomy's* and *Scandal's* executive producer, Shonda Rhimes, referring to them as "guilty pleasures," and President Barack Obama using them as examples of what responsible, hardworking young people should *not* spend their time watching. I argue that, as a genre, reality television escapes critical attention because of its negative status and because the genre itself masks the real labor of cast and crew as "reality." I then do close readings of some of the shows' more interesting moments in order to examine how they address issues such as black versus white motherhood, black queer sexuality, and female empowerment.

False Negatives

I conclude *Double Negative* with a discussion of the FOX network television drama *Empire*. The show's critical and popular success would seem to indicate a shift in taste cultures and the dismantling of respectability politics on network television. However, I argue that while *Empire* liberally borrows from key elements that comprise the melodramatic black-cast reality programs discussed in chapter 4, the show simply repackages positive representation under a different guise, creating what I refer to as a "false negative." Specifically, the conclusion examines how *Empire's* A-list cast, powerful network, and acclaimed executive producer effectively buffer the negative aspects of the show.

EDDIE MURPHY, *COMING TO AMERICA*, AND FORMAL NEGATIVITY

The guy on *Trading Places* was young and full of energy and curious and funny and fresh and great; the guy on *Coming to America* was the pig of the world—the most unpleasant, arrogant, bullshit entourage . . . just an asshole. —**JOHN LANDIS**, speaking about Eddie Murphy

My significance in film—and again I'm not going to be delusional—was that I'm the first black actor to take charge in a white world onscreen. That's why I became as popular as I became. —**EDDIE MURPHY**

There is a curious moment at the end of the Eddie Murphy star vehicle *Coming to America*. The film, a romantic comedy, centers on Murphy as Prince Akeem: an African prince who travels to New York to find his bride. Along the way, Akeem and his sidekick, Semmi, become friendly with a group of men who hang out at the downstairs barbershop. As the closing credits roll, revealing the names of the actors playing the various characters, the camera cuts to Saul, the elderly Jewish man who is one of the barbershop regulars. As one of the few white characters in the film, Saul's presence in the black barbershop space creates a visual and narrative contrast with the other men who form the barbershop's Greek chorus. Indeed, black barbershops themselves have a complicated history in regard to race relations and segregation in this country, making Saul's presence noticeable because of its historic significance, and yet also natural in the film's cinematic presentation of a racially and ethnically diverse neighborhood in Queens, New York.[1] Saul's whiteness serves an important narrative function as he becomes the "white" voice in the barbershop's discussions, such as in a recurring debate over the best boxer of all time: Saul either suggests a lone white boxer or else, in a stroke of immigrant solidarity, defends Cassius Clay's right to change his name to Muhammad Ali. Therefore, it comes as a shock when the credits reveal that Saul is played by none other than Murphy himself.

I remember sitting in the theater when the closing credits appeared and it was revealed that Murphy and Arsenio Hall had played not only the main characters but also several supporting ones as well. I was a child, and much of the performative ruse that might have been obvious to the adult members of the audience was pure movie magic for me. My mother had seen the film once already, and as the movie came to its conclusion and the credits began to roll, she leaned down and whispered with a smile, "Pay attention to who plays who." As the credits revealed the various roles that the two actors played, there was laughter throughout the packed movie theater and a bit of surprise, but most of the characters had been legible as Murphy and Hall even through the extensive makeup and wigs designed to disguise the two actors' natural features. But it was the revelation of Murphy as Saul that sent a palpable wave of shock through the audience, so convincing had been Murphy's racial masquerade.[2]

Beyond the fun of the ruse, Murphy's whiteface performance of the Jewish Saul in *Coming to America* also represents an inspired twist that signifies on the history of Jewish performers of blackface minstrelsy. In film, the Jewish performer Al Jolson played perhaps the most famous blackface character in *The Jazz Singer* (Alan Crosland, 1927). Murphy's Saul even begins the joke that he tells over the closing credits by saying, "Wait a minute, wait a minute!"—the first words spoken by Jolson in *The Jazz Singer*. Murphy's whitefaced Saul not only acknowledges one aspect of racial representation on the screen but also subverts it by reversing the formula. If Jolson emphatically concluded his statement in *The Jazz Singer* by telling us "You ain't seen nothing yet!" then Murphy's reveal at the end of *Coming*

FIGURE 1.1. Eddie Murphy as Saul in *Coming to America*.

to America informs us that we have not, in fact, truly "seen" him at all up until this moment.

As a play on Jewish blackface, Murphy's portrayal of Saul in *Coming to America* represents a formal inversion, or, more specifically, a type of formal negation, of Hollywood's conventional strategies of representation. Murphy reverses the race and the politics of the Jewish performer in blackface at the level of makeup and performance. Murphy-as-Saul, however, is just one example of the many ways that *Coming to America*, primarily through Murphy's influence, takes a standard Hollywood formula, one that was designed to appeal to all audiences, and reforms it into a culturally black film—a film that continues to have particular resonance with black viewers. It is this "flipping of the script" (to borrow a phrase from black vernacular) that constitutes what I am referring to as "formal negativity," or the inversion of standard modes of mainstream Hollywood and network television storytelling practices at the levels of plot, performance, and production.

In addition to reversing the existing traditional logics of black and Jewish cinematic performance, *Coming to America* also contains other interesting reversals of standard Hollywood conventions. For example, the film inverts the usual romantic comedy formula of A-plot and B-plot. Typically, the A- and B-plots are clearly delineated not only narratively but also by casting. In other words, the stars of the romantic comedy inhabit the A-plot, with supporting characters occupying the B-plot, often for comic relief. For instance, in the Murphy vehicle *Boomerang*, Murphy occupies the romantic A-plot, but comedic relief is provided through supporting characters played by actors such as Tisha Campbell, David Alan Grier, Eartha Kitt, and Martin Lawrence. This distinction is blurry in *Coming to America*, however, as Murphy and Hall play characters in both plotlines. In doing so, the film's structure is a callback to Murphy's stint on *Saturday Night Live* (SNL), where he played several different characters. Further, Murphy's immense and unmistakable influence on the film runs contrary to auteurist theories that would place John Landis, the director, as the main creative force behind the film. Not simply a challenge to director-centric theories in film studies, this reimagining of Murphy as the visionary behind the film rather than Landis likewise complicates our understanding of how we define a film as "black." Is it possible for a white director to make a "black" film, where "black" is understood not just by the race of the cast but also by its cast, themes, politics, and popularity with black audiences? *Coming to America* would suggest so and, therefore, troubles the commonly held assumption that Hollywood-produced films are only capable of promoting films ideologically aligned with whiteness. As I have argued elsewhere, "Hollywood films can and do offer thoughtful explorations of race and racism, even though their methods of doing so may be more fraught than those of independent films."[3] Finally, Murphy himself, as arguably the biggest movie star of the 1980s with success primarily in white-cast films, exemplifies formal negativity as he constantly works within the very structures that Hollywood typically uses to ensure white privilege and black marginalization in order to ultimately subvert them and destabilize whiteness in his film and television projects.

I am not interested in strict ideas of intentionality: it is entirely possible that Murphy may not have been *trying* to be overtly political with his performance as Saul. Yet a focus solely on intentionality misses the mark in this case. Even if Murphy's goal was simply to show off his mimicry skills, his performance still reminds viewers of the role that Jewish performers have played in black/white race relations since the days of theatrical minstrelsy; it also functions as the voice of the white everyman, offering viewpoints against which the black characters can then push.[4] And, supporting characters in *Coming to America* reinforce this black-oriented worldview. Reverend Brown, drawn from Hall's personal experiences, draws a connection to the tradition of the black church, or perhaps more specifically, deftly articulates some of the recognizable (to black audiences) eccentricities of the black church. And Clarence and the other barbers tap into an iconic component of black neighborhoods, perfectly capturing the ways that the black barbershop functions as an important site of black camaraderie and critical discussion.

Murphy the Matinee Idol

Coming to America would eventually go on to gross $128 million domestically and $160 million internationally, making it one of the most financially successful black-cast films in history. So why has there not been more critical discussion of it? As I argued in the introduction, *Coming to America* has suffered from the unfortunate timing of being wedged between the more critically appreciated films *Hollywood Shuffle* (Robert Townsend, 1987) and *Do the Right Thing* (Spike Lee, 1989) as far as discussions of 1980s black film are concerned. However, there is a less precise, but perhaps just as likely answer to this question, which is that *Coming to America*'s success *as* a Hollywood product has characterized it as *less black* than these other two films. In other words, it is the film's very success that makes us skeptical, as if confirming that only a color-blind, universal, not really *black* black film can do well on the global market. It is as if *Coming to America* is automatically precluded from the type of serious consideration that we might give to one of its contemporaries (like *Hollywood Shuffle* or *Do the Right Thing*) because it is a comedy that came out of a Hollywood studio, was helmed by a white director, and starred the biggest crossover actor of the 1980s. Landis's own statements about the film only seem to corroborate this interpretation: "What was nice was that it was a big hit, all over the world, and no one ever thought of it as a black movie."[5] In many regards, this skepticism of the Landis-directed, "color-blind," black-cast film is rightly deserved. As a large and powerful studio, Paramount could hire a strong comedic director and provide him with the budget to create a glossy, grand film with rich sets, costumes, and a lush score. The fact that Murphy, the film's centerpiece, was arguably one of the nation's (if not the world's) biggest stars at the time may not have guaranteed box-office gold, but it was certainly a good predictor of it.

This skepticism about Hollywood is based on the knowledge that Hollywood's formula has, undoubtedly, constantly worked to disenfranchise

African Americans and lock them into stereotypical tropes since the emergence of cinema. In spite of Murphy's incredible success in the 1980s, many of his roles, especially when he played comedic sidekicks to white leads (such as in his star-making turns in *48 Hrs.* and *Trading Places*), tiptoed too closely to the kinds of buffoonish stereotypes that many African Americans were eager to leave behind. It is accurate, therefore, to suspect that Hollywood "success" has often translated into "hegemonic" and "stereotypical" when it comes to black representations, particularly comedic representations, as Hollywood has traditionally relegated black characters to roles meant to serve as comedic relief. It is no wonder then, that those critics and scholars who are all too familiar with how Hollywood operates would rightfully regard *Coming to America*'s triumph at the box office with skepticism.

All that being said, however, *Coming to America* is far from being a typical Hollywood product. As a joint venture between Paramount and Murphy's then newly formed production company, Murphy enjoyed an unprecedented amount of control over the film.[6] This, coupled with Murphy's reputation as an international celebrity, ensured that the film reflected his sensibilities to the same extent as, if not more than, those of the director and the executives at Paramount.

First and foremost, Murphy himself challenges the idea that one must be independent and outside of Hollywood in order to offer a black-centered perspective. Though he may have found success within the Hollywood industry, and often supported its ideological constructs in his own projects and performances, this does not fully account for his politics or how his work reflects them. I want to push back, therefore, against an implicit assumption that mainstream success and black common sense (as discussed in the introduction) are fundamentally incongruous. It is Murphy's consistent quality of mainstream acceptability, I would argue, that has led many scholars to overlook the sociopolitical significance of Murphy's work (going back to SNL) and to interpret his film and television performances as inherently apolitical.[7] That claim is based less on Murphy's actual performances and more on the presumed incompatibility between social critique and crossover success. For example, J. Fred MacDonald dismisses Murphy's success on SNL by noting that the comedian "scored well in two minstrel favorites."[8] The use of the word "minstrel" is telling, because it references not only the form of Murphy's performances on SNL (in the tradition of minstrelsy and vaudeville) but also the type of humor that Murphy is presumed

FIGURE 1.2. Eddie Murphy and Dan Aykroyd in *Trading Places*.

FIGURE 1.3. Eddie Murphy and Nick Nolte in *48 Hrs*.

to be performing: stereotypical and designed for a white audience. Donald Bogle acknowledges Murphy's direct address of race and racism in his film roles, but he similarly dismisses the possibility of any real politics behind it: "Murphy's movies paid lip service to racism (perhaps even exploited it) but took no stands at all."[9]

Such statements conflate Murphy's film and television work, his success in the 1980s, and his personal life, resulting in critiques that are rarely about Murphy's individual roles, but more about the idea of Murphy himself. In the 1980s, Murphy represented a brand of black comedian that seemed ready-made for crossover popularity. He got his start not in local black establishments but in suburban comedy clubs, and his ascension to superstardom would be signaled by his tenure on a predominantly white-cast sketch-comedy show, *Saturday Night Live*. The context of the time period is key to understanding why Eddie Murphy, and the *type* of comedian he symbolized, would be so successful on both television and film. His appeal as a "crossover" star—one who could attract both black and white audiences—had everything to do with his casting in big-budget action films and successful comedies alongside already-established white stars such as Nick Nolte and Dan Aykroyd. Murphy's early film career took a predictable course for "token" black performers in predominantly white films and television shows: he provided the urban edge to contrast with the white characters, playing the comedic relief to his white costars. His entry into pop culture superstardom also followed a predictable and well-trod path, one that plenty of African American stars before him had similarly taken. For example, while not comedians, actors like Lena Horne and Sidney Poitier rose to prominence in the days of classic Hollywood primarily via their appearances as the sole black figures in otherwise white films. This was not, of course, by any choice on their part, but because Hollywood created space for African American performers in only these tokenized ways. Though Murphy arrived on the scene decades later, Hollywood's logic for including blackness had changed little, so it is not surprising that Murphy's career took a similar trajectory. That Murphy functioned according to Hollywood's racist strategies for black representation is without question. Yet I contest the easy assumption that Murphy's function as a crossover, tokenized black star automatically signifies "sellout" politics.[10] True, Murphy, especially early in his career, played the comedic relief to white characters and often tiptoed on the line of buffoonish stereotype. And it is this aspect that many scholars and critics have focused on when discussing Murphy's larger politics and performances. Bambi Haggins argues that Murphy's "apolitical" invocation of black culture and identity in his comedy is indicative of an "I got mine" philosophy that was part of an overall 1980s emphasis on individuality.[11] Nelson George contends that Murphy's meteoric rise, alongside Ronald Reagan's election to the presidency, fully indicates the "schizophrenic nature of the American experience in the 80s."[12] Describing the factors behind Murphy's appeal, he writes, "Because of his youth, his background, and the fact that he has only a passing connection to the old-school black comedy circuit, Murphy's views of what is funny and how to articulate that sense of humor differ from those of black comedy stars of the '70s. He isn't angry or intensely political or overly socially conscious."[13] And even when Murphy signed an exclusive deal with Paramount for his production company to develop film and television projects for the studio, establishing a rare degree of control for a young African American actor, naysayers still accused Murphy of selling out: the director Spike Lee criticized Murphy for only owning 50 percent of Eddie Murphy Productions, with his white managers splitting the remaining percentage between them.[14]

Each of these critiques of Murphy is important for understanding the larger social and industrial factors that informed the nature of Murphy's film and television work, and also his stardom. I disagree, however, with the assumption that Murphy sacrificed political relevance when he crossed over into mainstream film and television in the conservative 1980s. Instead, I suggest that Murphy's performances walked a fine line between marginalized black "insider" humor and mainstream white comedy. True, Murphy's humor differs from that of Bill Cosby and Richard Pryor. Both of those comics addressed race directly either in their performances or in interviews, even if their perspectives and modes of address in doing so were radically different. Murphy, on the other hand, often steered clear of such a straightforward discussion of racial issues. True enough, this tightwire act of Murphy's occasionally slipped into buffoonery, but at other times he injected black viewpoints into predominantly white media texts. On the surface, Murphy's performances appeared to be tailored to appeal to mainstream white audiences. Many of his characters and sketches, however, contained aspects of subversive black humor that spoke to black audiences and black perspectives. Take, for example, Murphy's *White Like Me* short film on SNL, in which Murphy goes undercover as a white man to expose racism in America. On the one hand, Murphy's comedic presentation of white privilege (cocktail parties on the public bus and unlimited cash from banks) is so over the top that all kinds of viewers, regardless of race, would be able to find humor in it. On the other hand, Murphy's public verification of white privilege resonates in a particular way with black viewers, who likely see *White Like Me*'s scenarios as slight exaggerations, but not too far removed from reality.

Murphy's work is particularly important in the context of black representation in the media during the 1980s. The era was characterized by an emphasis on carefully coded rhetoric aimed at downplaying the continued significance of racism. On the political front, the arrival of Reaganism and the New Right ushered in a wave of conservatism that permeated social and political discourses. As Jimmie L. Reeves and Richard Campbell note, conservatives exploited existing antiwelfare and anti–affirmative action sentiments and employed rhetoric about black immorality, most notably in the form of the black "welfare queen" and the "war on drugs," "to gain popular support for economic policies that favored the rich."[15] Furthermore, a new emphasis on political correctness that often took the form of a seemingly neutral, color-blind rhetoric made frank discussions of race all the more difficult. According to Reeves and Campbell, "By denying the existence of institutionalized racism, attributing black failure to lack of initiative or impoverished values, and adulating black stars as proof that racial barriers to success had evaporated, Reaganism simultaneously tapped into historically deep undercurrents of racism in American culture and absolved whites of any implication in that history."[16]

Herman Gray contends that the mainstream media was complicit in this politically problematic shift in language: "We witnessed the formation and institutionalization of discourses, articulated by Reagan and engineered by his sophisticated spin doctors, that moved quietly but steadily from 'African Americans' to 'welfare,' from 'equal opportunity' to 'preferential treatment,' from 'racism/discrimination' to 'reverse discrimination,' from 'tax recipients and social entitlements' to 'taxpayers and civic responsibility,' from 'morality' to 'immorality,' and from 'shared public responsibility' to 'private charitable giving.'" Through its immediacy and pervasiveness, television quietly framed these shifts, announcing the news daily in softer, shorter, more visually dramatic, and conceptually simpler bites.[17]

Part of the oversight of Murphy's contributions may have had to do with his emergence as a crossover star in this era, as these discourses impacted not just the political and social arenas of the time but also popular black entertainment. Television programs like *The Cosby Show*, with its representation of the upwardly mobile African American Huxtable family, unwittingly aided the shift from explicitly racist rhetoric to more subtle, racially coded discourse. As Sut Jhally and Justin Lewis argue in their study of *Cosby*'s reception, "The Huxtables proved that black people can succeed; yet in doing so they also prove the inferiority of black people in general (who have, in comparison with whites, failed)."[18] On an ideological level, therefore, *The Cosby Show* presented blackness as separate from African Americans, a state of being that one could "transcend" if one so desired.[19] This rhetoric not only failed to recognize the continuation of racial inequalities in the 1980s but also promoted a mythical image of American political progress while covering up the fissures that continued to exist. These fissures actually grew wider as Reagan's government cut social welfare programs and reversed the gains accomplished by his liberal predecessors.

The conditions that facilitated Murphy's rise to fame were emblematic of a larger transformation occurring in film and television at the time, one that placed the emphasis on "crossover" and the appeal of black performers and black cultural products to nonblack audiences and consumers. On the radio and in record stores, the term "urban" became the preferred way to refer to music by African American artists because it signified blackness in a vague sense but avoided an explicit mention of race.[20] This, in turn, meant that record companies raced to discover new artists and redefine existing ones to fit in with this new "crossover" world. Whitney Houston's marketing as a pop diva, for example, rather than as a soulful R&B songstress, demonstrated this new trend. Michael Jackson also represented the crossroads between past and future as the artist who straddled the line between the traditional black music world of Motown (the last of the great Motown artists) and the new era of MTV.

Given this broader context, it is easy to dismiss Murphy's early performances as simply reinforcing the conservative ideologies and representational strategies that Reeves, Campbell, Gray, Jhally, and Lewis sketch out. In fact, in both his television and film appearances, Murphy exploited his tokenism and its resulting tensions. Murphy grounded his comedy in aspects of his black identity, with the visual markers of blackness often serving as significant components of the jokes. His SNL Gumby character, for example, drew its humor from the amusing contradiction between Murphy's own youthful, hip blackness and the green cartoon character's white, Jewish voice and borscht belt humor. Likewise, his "Mister Robinson's Neighborhood" sketch played on the contradiction of the beloved

FIGURE 1.4. Eddie Murphy in *Trading Places*.

children's show set in an urban ghetto. However, the logic of mainstream appeal dictated that his blackness be used in the service of making white audiences laugh while not alienating them, and therefore his performances could sometimes descend into racial clichés and stereotypes. For instance, Murphy's clownish antics in the opening scenes of *Trading Places* veered dangerously close to the kind of buffoonery that Robert Townsend would later criticize in his film *Hollywood Shuffle*.

Yet much of the criticism against Murphy's television and movie roles seems to come—at least in part—from a tendency to conflate the actor's biography with his intentions and, hence, the political efficacy of the characters that he plays. Writers like Watkins, Bogle, George, and others all make a point to note Murphy's upbringing in integrated neighborhoods and comedy settings, often contrasting him with the oft-told tale of Richard Pryor's childhood in a brothel. This reliance on biography confers a kind of black cultural authenticity on Pryor while denying it to Murphy. The fact that Murphy began his career on the predominantly white SNL, and that his first major movie roles were targeted to white audiences, become "evidence" of the ineffectiveness of his performances. George writes, "Unlike Richard Pryor and Bill Cosby, the men he would succeed as the nation's most celebrated funny man, Murphy is a product of the post-soul world—television, movies, and a relatively color-blind world define his life experiences. Like his white SNL peers, Murphy's point of reference is pop culture, not a world of pimps and prostitutes, or an inner-city 'hood."[21]

Similarly, when the director John Landis emphasizes Murphy's middle-class background, it is to undermine Murphy's claims to black cultural authenticity: "Eddie never had to struggle; he grew up in an integrated, middle class neighborhood, started doing stand-up comedy in New York when he was seventeen, by the time he was eighteen he was on *Saturday Night Live*, and by the time he was nineteen he had been in *48 Hrs.* and *Trading Places*."[22] This comment by Landis perfectly captures the way that much of the criticism of Murphy's work falls back on a perception of blackness that equates hardship (which Landis phrases as "struggle") with cultural authenticity, dangerously reasserting a kind of essentialized blackness that locks black performers into limited categories and denies the variety and fluidity of cultural blackness itself.

If we read deeper into Landis's comments (made in response to interviewer Steve Weintraub's acknowledgment of Murphy's meteoric rise to stardom at a young age), we see that what the director is actually criticizing is Murphy's success, as if his achievements in the world of film and television were somehow character flaws. While this may have more to do with Landis's own personal bitterness with Murphy's seemingly easy ascension to superstardom—Landis began his film career at eighteen as a mailroom clerk at 20th Century Fox—the negative spin that he places on Murphy's accomplishment draws on broader historical discourses of the "uppity Negro" that have historically treated African American success with suspicion while also condemning African American desire for success as a character flaw rather than the virtue that it is for whites.[23] Such discourse is dangerous precisely because it reinforces essentialized notions of blackness that treat success as antithetical to cultural legitimacy (a topic that I explore in more detail in chapter 2 with my discussion of the "sellout films" of the 1990s). In addition, to find fault with Murphy's lack of a "struggle" obscures the hardships that Murphy experienced as a black actor in Hollywood, which may not have met the criteria for the "hard knocks" upbringing that some writers and Landis associate with the term, but which undoubtedly proved difficult for Murphy as he tried to find his footing first as a performer and then later as a director and producer in a landscape that may have supported *him*, but certainly was not any more open to blackness writ large.

This insistence on personal experience oversimplifies the hybridity and complexity of black popular culture and the experiences of black people in general. Such covert assertions of "authenticity" for Pryor because of his brothel background ignore the impact that nonblack culture (and non-black comedians) clearly had on the way that he (along with numerous other black comedians) crafted his act. Nelson George and others continue this trend in their discussion of Murphy. At best, these analyses of performers' backgrounds ignore the multivalent aspects of these comedians' influences. At worst, they reinforce the notion that a black comedian's performative identity and essential nature are one and the same.

And yet Murphy's skillful navigation of comedy, racial identity, and audiences is itself part of a longer tradition of black comedy. While some scholars and critics have questioned the sociopolitical significance of these black representations designed for crossover appeal (particularly given that so many occurred within the confines of lighthearted comedic fare in both film and television), others argue that humor has a long history as a tool of social criticism and catharsis among black communities.[24] For instance, Mel Watkins notes that black comedic traditions have included "two disparate strains of humor: the often distorted *outside* presentation in mainstream media (initially by non-African Americans) and the authentic *inside* development of humor in black communities (from slave shanties and street corners to cabarets) as well as in folklore and black literature, films, and race records."[25] In other words, there is a distinction between the type of comedy that blacks performed primarily for white audiences (e.g., minstrel shows) and the type performed by blacks for black audiences (e.g., race films). While the former entertained white audiences with stereotypes, the latter offered social commentary and criticism.

Of course, the line between these two forms of humor was not always clearly drawn, and seemingly straightforward black performance tropes might include subtle barbs aimed at whites.[26] Within black communities, comedy—particularly in the forms of parody and satire—has historically functioned as a tool for African Americans to criticize mainstream institutions and practices while operating *within* mainstream institutions and practices, a way of pointing out issues and problems while avoiding detection. Thus, black performances such as Murphy's, rather than being apolitical, were often polysemic texts that could be read one way by white audiences while possessing an entirely different meaning for black ones. Such is the case with Murphy's assemblage of characters in *Coming to America*, who provide comic relief throughout the film for white audiences but tap into deeper aspects of black culture for black ones.

Murphy's identity, then, as a comedic "crossover" star did not minimize the subversive elements of black humor or black critique embedded in his work. By contrast, because his early performances on SNL, 48 Hrs., and Trading Places were tailored to please both black and nonblack audiences, he created sketches, characters, and performances that seamlessly combined social critique and mainstream appeal. And, of course, Murphy certainly was not the first black performer to bring black forms of humor to mainstream film and television. Flip Wilson's popular eponymous variety show included a variety of characters from black experience, such as his preacher, Reverend Leroy. And Richard Pryor's popularity in the 1970s (including his short-lived The Richard Pryor Show) brought black comedy into the mainstream as well.

Moreover, the assessment of Murphy as apolitical does not reflect Murphy's own understanding of both his function in Hollywood and his role as a black man within it. As he himself opined about the politics of his comedy, "The thing people have to understand is that I'm aware of the power that I have as a film maker, as an actor and politically. But people seem to think that I'm operating without an agenda. But I have an agenda. I am also aware that change is something that has to happen gradually. Change is something that has to be done . . . quietly. It's not about going in there and rocking the fucking boat. You can rock the boat, or you can sail smoothly to your next destination."[27] While some may have felt that Murphy's words were simply paying lip service to the criticisms that he was receiving, his statement demonstrates an acute awareness of his position within the industry, one that he would repeat throughout his career and demonstrate in a number of ways, from his development of black-centered projects to the casting of his films.

If nothing else, Murphy demonstrated that he had a very perceptive understanding of his own role and function in Hollywood. For instance, in 1990, Murphy discussed his desire to make a film about black revolutionary leader Malcolm X: "I wouldn't star in that story, because it would detract from the seriousness of the piece. People would be sitting around the first hour of it, just trying to buy me."[28] In addition to his realistic take on his image in Hollywood, Murphy also understood and acknowledged his own token status in the industry. True, these acknowledgments were often bound up with self-aggrandizement (in the "I got mine" mentality that

Haggins points out), which is perhaps why many critics have tended to cite his attitude as individualistic rather than political. Still, Murphy always spoke of his career from the perspective of a marginalized figure working from within the Hollywood system. When Murphy states, "I don't think I'm an actor. I'm a matinee idol," he does not mean that he is *above* regular actors. Instead, he understands that what sells in Hollywood is his image, his celebrity, rather than his actual talent. Murphy demonstrates a similar awareness in his comments about Hollywood's relationship to Spike Lee and other black directors: "Without me, I don't think the studios would have put out a movie like *Hollywood Shuffle*, or backed *I'm Gonna Git You Sucka*, or bought *She's Gotta Have It*. Five years ago in Hollywood, all the studios were thinking, 'We gotta get us a nigger. We gotta get one.' It was like a situation comedy. This is why it's weird when a guy like Spike Lee attacks me. He don't realize that he's around because of the 'Let's get us one, too' attitude."[29] Granted, Murphy does not give Robert Townsend, Keenen Ivory Wayans, or Spike Lee the credit that they deserve for making truly remarkable films, or the possibility that Hollywood recognized them based on their own merits. Yet Murphy's "We gotta get us one" theory rings true in terms of Hollywood's approach to blackness, where, as Monica Ndounou has argued, studios seek constant reassurance of the viability of black marketability before tentatively backing black films, and, even then, they demonstrate an illogical reluctance to "take a chance" on them.[30]

One of the problems with misunderstanding Murphy's ethos is that it can lead us to overlook those truly remarkable moments when Murphy *does* reveal his explicitly political side. For instance, post–*Coming to America*, Murphy would use his clout in the industry to employ African American actors in black-cast and mixed-race films. As Ndounou notes, "Murphy and his films exemplify the paradox of black box-office success, as the majority of his projects began to feature fewer roles for other black actors. However, in order to reverse this trend, Murphy produced seven theatrical releases, six of which are films with predominantly black casts."[31] This is an example of Murphy's work behind the scenes and his navigation of the politics of the industry. Yet another example, and one that I want to explore in detail, demonstrates the way that Murphy's performance style itself offers political critique within the guise of an easy affability. He employed this strategy in his speech at the sixtieth Academy Awards in 1988, a noncomedic, "straight" setting. Tasked with presenting the award for Best Picture,

Murphy began with a little light comedic banter and then ad-libbed the following:

> At first when they came to me and said that they wanted me to pres-
> ent the award for Best Picture—my management came and told me
> that they had picked me—and my first reaction was to say, "No, I
> ain't going." And my manager said [high-pitched, nasally voice], "But
> why?" I have a white manager; that's how he talks [high-pitched, na-
> sally voice]: "But why?" I said I'm not going because they haven't
> recognized black people in the motion pictures. And he said, "What
> are you talking about? Black people win Oscars." I said, well, black
> actors and actresses have won Oscars throughout sixty years. I think
> Hattie McDaniel won the first one, then Sydney Poitier won one, and
> Lou Gossett won one. And I'll probably never win an Oscar for saying
> this, but hey—what the hey: I got to say it. Actually I might not be
> in any trouble because the way it's been going it's about every twenty
> years we've been getting one, so we ain't due until about 2004. By
> that time, this will all have blown over. I said that I wasn't going and
> my manager said, "You just have to go, you can't snub the Academy."
> So I came down here to give the award. I said, "But I just feel that we
> have to be recognized as a people. I just want to let you know [that]
> I'm going to give this award, but black people will not ride the ca-
> boose of society and we will not bring up the rear anymore and I want
> you to recognize us. He said, "Well, fine, it's done." I said, "Now when
> do I have to be there?" He says, "Well, you don't have to get there
> until about nine or ten because it's the last award of the evening."

At that point, Murphy read the nominees.

Murphy's Academy Awards speech was classic Murphy. By narrating the story as a conversation between himself and his manager (using his skills of mimicry to imitate the manager's "white" voice), Murphy created a degree of narrative distance between himself and his critique, thus slyly avoiding a direct confrontation with his audience. This indirect approach calls to mind a statement that he would later make about addressing racial subject matter with white audiences: "I'm not there to chastise my audience."[32] Though this was keeping in line with Murphy's reputation for not being an in-your-face kind of comedian with regard to race, it was also a slick package—a Trojan horse—for the content of his speech: a direct attack on

FIGURE 1.5. Eddie Murphy at the sixtieth Academy Awards.

the Academy's racial politics. And Murphy's reputation as the world's big-gest celebrity, and the type of "safe" black crossover star that the conserva-tive Academy loved to elevate, was precisely what gave him the platform to make his speech in the first place.

Reflecting on this moment two years later, Murphy recalls his thought process leading up to it, one that reveals a man hyper aware of the Academy audience and the tone that he needed to take to address its members: "War-ren Beatty told me it was the wrong time, and I'm thinking, Well, when *do* you accuse the Academy of being racist and be heard—unless you're doing the nominees for the best picture? They're listening right there. Where am I gonna say it? In *Ebony*? They don't read *Ebony*."[33]

Murphy's hard-hitting comments seem a world away from the stereo-typical antics that he demonstrated in some of his predominantly white films, yet this is at the crux of Murphy's identities as both performer and producer. In the long span of his career, Murphy has displayed a compli-cated relationship with Hollywood. He has played a sizable amount of comedic, token, and sidekick roles in predominantly white films such as *48 Hrs.* (Walter Hill, 1982), *Trading Places* (John Landis, 1983), *Beverly Hills*

Cop (Martin Brest, 1984), *Bowfinger* (Frank Oz, 1999), and *Shrek* (Andrew Adamson and Vicky Jenson, 2001). Yet, on the other hand, Murphy has just as often played the lead in films comprising majority-black casts, including *Harlem Nights* (Eddie Murphy, 1989), *Boomerang* (Reginald Hudlin, 1992), *Vampire in Brooklyn* (Wes Craven, 1995), *The Nutty Professor* (Tom Shadyac, 1996), *Life* (Tom Demme, 1999), and *Norbit* (Brian Robbins, 2007). And Murphy has starred or costarred in multiracially cast films like *The Distinguished Gentleman* (Jonathan Lynn, 1992) and *Tower Heist* (Brett Ratner, 2011), and played supporting roles in black-cast films such as *Dreamgirls* (Bill Condon, 2006). Because he functions in widely differing ways, depending on the film, the cast, and the director, it is tempting to analyze Murphy's work—*Coming to America* in this instance—based on the sole constant across his films: Murphy himself. This is why, I believe, it is so easy to fall back on his biography as a kind of shorthand in place of critical analysis. Yet Murphy—in both his real-life role as star and producer and in his broader function as "matinee idol"—is as much a dense and complicated text as are the equally complicated media texts that he creates.

Coming to America: Murphy vs. Landis

As I already mentioned, Murphy's performance of Saul in *Coming to America* represents an inspired take on the tradition of Jewish comedians in blackface, one that comes together as a result of Rick Baker's gifted makeup skills, but predominantly from Murphy's extraordinary talent for mimicry. Yet Landis initially proposed the idea, and Landis took credit for Murphy as Saul. According to him, he was so disgusted after learning about black-faced Jewish performers such as Al Jolson that he decided to turn the tables on the tradition and place the black Murphy in whiteface.[34] Interestingly, in Landis's account of how the character came to be, he diminishes Murphy's role in Saul's creation, claiming that Murphy was hesitant—even nervous—about pulling off the character:

> At the time of *Coming to America*, I had read this article, that I was really offended by, about Jewish comics in blackface—Eddie Cantor and Al Jolson and stuff. I thought it was really ignorant, so I just said, "Eddie, I'm gonna have you play an old Jew." And he said, "What?" He didn't believe me, and I said, "Rick Baker can make you

an old Jew." So, we got him in the test makeup, and the test makeup totally convinced Eddie. He had the accent down, Deborah [Nadoolman Landis] made him a hump for his coat, and he went around to the Paramount offices flirting with secretaries. He realized, "I can do it." He was so funny. And what we discovered was that the makeup freed him.[35]

Landis's version of events presents the director as the driving force behind Murphy's inspired portrayal of Saul, giving full credit to Landis with a nod to the makeup artist, Rick Baker, for Murphy's transformation. And while Baker's contribution deserves accolades, it is curious and suspicious that Landis's lone reference to Murphy's incredible talents for imitation only gets a passing mention: "He had the accent down." Moreover, Landis's story suggests that Murphy lacked the inner confidence in his abilities to pull off the character until Landis (with the help of Baker) convinced him otherwise. Yet anyone familiar with Murphy's work would know that Murphy never shied away from an opportunity to show off his skills of mimicry. Many of Murphy's most iconic SNL performances were his imitations: James Brown, Stevie Wonder, and, most relevant to his eventual portrayal of Saul, his Jewish take on the children's character Gumby. And Murphy had already played a white man in the SNL short film *White Like Me*. What Murphy did with his portrayal of Saul, therefore, was a riff on the Jewish blackface tradition as well as a platform for him to showcase his immense talent. And while Landis might try to obscure the latter by emphasizing Saul as *his* creation, it is impossible to deny that it was Murphy's comedic genius that turned Saul from a cultural reference point to a living, breathing, and incredibly memorable character.

The question over who deserves the credit for Murphy's Saul is emblematic of a larger dynamic at work in *Coming to America:* the matter of authorship in black texts with white directors. Conventional thinking would say that it is the political view of the director that most greatly affects a film, yet *Coming to America*, and specifically the contributions of Eddie Murphy as both producer and star, complicates this notion. Though most discussions of film authorship emphasize the primacy of the director, this frame of analysis becomes quite complicated in the case of *Coming to America*, as it is just as much, if not more so, influenced by Eddie Murphy as by John Landis. As star and head of the production company responsible for bringing the film to Paramount, Murphy wielded a large amount of influence

FIGURE 1.6. Eddie Murphy as Stevie Wonder.

that quite often superseded that of Landis. Therefore, it should not come as a surprise that the most memorable jokes and scenarios in the film are those that Murphy and Hall improvised, which were rooted in the specificity of their own black cultural experiences.

This is not to say that Landis was a passive bystander in the making of the film by any means. In fact, Landis had a very specific vision for *Coming to America*. In contrast to Murphy's invocation of black comedic styles and traditions, Landis was quite invested in making a "color-blind" romantic comedy to rival the classic films of that genre, like *It Happened One Night* (Frank Capra, 1934), *His Girl Friday* (Howard Hawks, 1940), and, more specifically, the "royal in disguise" twist on the genre found in films such as *Roman Holiday* (William Wyler, 1953).[36] And, indeed, *Coming to America*'s A-plot adheres to that classic Hollywood formula, something that certain film critics picked up on immediately. While the film critic Gene Siskel, for instance, mentioned Murphy's various incarnations in the film, he reserved his highest praise for Murphy's more restrained performance as a romantic lead, arguing, "For the first time, he doesn't seem nervous about filling every second with a wisecrack." In fact, Siskel's cohost, Roger Ebert, felt that Landis had executed the formula a little *too* well: he criticized the film for being too much of a standard romantic comedy and deemed

FIGURE 1.7. Eddie Murphy as Gumby.

FIGURE 1.8. Eddie Murphy in *White Like Me*.

the plot "old fashioned," "hackneyed," and "recycled."[37] In other words, if anything, *Coming to America* was a failure, in Ebert's assessment, because of Landis's over-adherence to the conventions of the genre.

In contrast to Landis's color-blind romantic comedy, Murphy very much understood his film as a *black* film, with insider humor, characters, and references that, while still humorous to nonblack audiences, were more fully legible to those familiar with black communities and culture. As he stated in an interview with the Biography channel, "I'd hear people say 'the most successful black film of all time' and they would say . . . *Waiting to Exhale* or one of those movies and I'd be like *Coming to America!*"[38] Though his statement seems inconsequential at first glance, it confirms that Murphy did, in fact, view the film as a black film, unlike Landis, who touted the film's nonblackness during its filming and continues to do so today.

If mainstream critics missed the blackness of the film, it may have been because many of the distinctively black elements of *Coming to America* are found in either the "throwaway" moments of the film or concentrated in the B-plot that centers around the Queens residents. These aspects of the film adhere more to Murphy's sketch-comedy background and aspects of black comic traditions, in stark contrast to the mainstream romantic comedy A-plot spearheaded by Landis. As Siskel and Ebert did, other critics quickly noted this bifurcation between Landis's "classic" film and Murphy's black comedy, even if they registered this disconnect in terms of confusion rather than the product of two distinct concepts for the film. Vincent Canby of the *New York Times* criticized the film's failure to meet the requirements of the romantic comedy genre, writing, "It is a romantic comedy, though nobody except the star seems aware of the fact."[39] Bambi Haggins notes that, "as the romantic center of the film, Akeem is imminently likable but not a memorable, comic character."[40] Yet this genre "confusion" provides us with evidence of the film's polysemic nature, suggesting that we look back at the production of *Coming to America* and more closely at the film itself.

Murphy's crucial influence on *Coming to America* is easy to ignore if one uses a conventional auteurist lens to analyze the film. In other words, as is standard in much of film studies, credit for the film's vision typically goes to the director. It does not really matter if one readily associates Landis with the likes of canonical auteurs like Jean-Luc Godard, Howard Hawks, or Alfred Hitchcock, or even with more contemporary directors with distinctive film styles like John Hughes, Spike Lee, or Quentin Tarantino. The larger point is that, in spite of the significant scholarship done in areas such as reception studies, the overwhelming tendency is still to prioritize the film's director and credit him or her with the bulk of the important choices that make up a film's nature and its politics, especially the casting and the performances of the actors. Yet what becomes clear when examining accounts about the production of *Coming to America*, the disparate reviews that the film garnered, and the film itself, is that it was never, at any point, a straightforward presentation of Landis's vision. On the contrary, Murphy was at the helm of *Coming to America* from the beginning, throwing his celebrity weight around at nearly every level of the production, from the film's original concept to the casting and, according to Murphy, even down to Landis's own hiring. While Landis and other key members of the production (including Paramount executives) certainly wielded influence over the film's elements, Murphy was absolutely the force behind some of the more distinctive aspects of *Coming to America*, including key aspects of the casting and, certainly, the memorable performances.

In addition to the critics' reviews of *Coming to America*, Landis's and Murphy's respective descriptions of the film (found in numerous interviews and articles) suggest that while the two men were physically present on the same set, they were working on two entirely different films. For Landis, *Coming to America* was a "once upon a time" type of "comedy fable" (as evidenced by the language of the film's trailer): a "classic" tale that, while centered on black people, did not derive its meaning from their blackness. What resulted then, in the production of the film, was two headstrong and stubborn men battling over the nature of what kind of film *Coming to America* would be, with the result being that they each created two different films within the same package.

Murphy and Landis clashed from the beginning of production. And while both men have wildly different accounts of the source of the conflict, the fundamental issue seems to come down to power and control, with both men jockeying over who would rule the set, and, more broadly, who would be identified as the visionary behind the film.[41] As the director, Landis theoretically had control over all aspects of the film in front of the camera: the cast and their performances, the set design, makeup, musical score, and final editing of the film. This meant that, again in theory, Landis should have been responsible for the narrative arc of the film, the extent to which characters' performances played into stereotypical archetypes, and where the audience's attention would be directed upon viewing the film. In most scenarios, the director's vision for the film and for the performances would serve as the guide for the film's star, no matter how famous that star might be. Clearly, this is the expectation that Landis had when he signed on to direct Murphy in *Coming to America*, yet Murphy's superstardom, force of will, and growing power behind the scenes would directly challenge this way of doing things.

Part of Landis's expectation was the direct result of his work with Murphy on the 1983 film *Trading Places*. Murphy had been young and still in the midst of transitioning from television and SNL to the world of big-budget Hollywood features. *Trading Places* was only Murphy's second feature, and while his name was certainly a draw, he had not yet achieved the kind of stardom that would allow him to carry an entire film on his own. Yet, by the time that Landis signed on to direct *Coming to America*, Murphy was no longer the newcomer trying to find his way in the industry. Instead, Murphy wore multiple hats during filming. He was the star and the developer of the film's concept, and, though he was not credited as a producer, his production company brought the project to Paramount. As the film's star, Murphy was one of the biggest box-office draws in the world, with a string of hit movies to his credit. As I already mentioned, Murphy possessed the rare ability to bring in both black and white audiences, inviting each to share in the laughter of his antics while managing to avoid alienating either. An immensely talented comic who also exuded warmth and likability, Murphy made white audiences feel hipper without aggressively challenging their ideologies or privileges; with black audiences, he created a sensation of insiders sharing a private joke. Murphy was, in sum, a 1980s Hollywood studio's dream come true—box-office gold—and any director or studio at the time would have bent over backward to work with the young star.

But beyond his brilliance in front of the camera, Murphy had begun to develop a keen business sense and an appreciation of his own value in Hollywood in the years since he first arrived on SNL and on the set of *48 Hrs.*, his first film. In 1983, while still a cast member on SNL, Murphy signed an exclusive $15 million, five-picture deal with Paramount. The *New York Times* reported that, in addition to Murphy's starring in a string of films for the studio, his recently formed Eddie Murphy Productions, a partnership between Murphy and his managers Robert Wachs and Richard Tienken, would also develop projects for Paramount.[42] This deal would ultimately be responsible for *The Golden Child* (Michael Ritchie, 1986), *Beverly Hills Cop II* (Tony Scott, 1987), and Murphy's standup comedy film *Eddie Murphy: Raw*

(Robert Townsend, 1987). Then, in 1987, the *New York Times* reported that Murphy had signed another five-picture deal with Paramount, for more money, with *Coming to America* scheduled as the first film produced under the renewed deal. In the article, Murphy expressed his hopes to use the deal to expand his role in film beyond that of an actor, citing Woody Allen as an inspiration as someone who wore multiple filmmaking hats.[43] Murphy was only twenty-six years old and in a position of immense power at a major Hollywood studio. At the same time, he was fully aware that his youth and blackness rendered him a perpetual outsider in the industry, regardless of how popular he was or how much money his image might bring to the studio. Three years after signing the deal and two years after the release of *Coming to America*, Murphy reflected back on his position at the time of signing this deal. Speaking to a journalist about his reaction upon hearing from Landis that Paramount executives were "afraid" of Murphy (Landis's way of expressing the fact that studio execs were deferring to Murphy's wishes), Murphy declared, "Well, good! Because there's no way they're gonna respect me. They can't respect me. I was twenty-six years old. Imagine me in the office of a fifty-year old guy in a suit. Naturally, he'd look at me, a kid, talking about 'I want to do it *this* way,' and he'd say, 'Yeah right. Sure, sure.' Then on top of that, I'm this black man making demands. He'd look down his nose at me. So if I don't have his respect, at least let him have some fear. Let me have something."[44]

Thus, the Eddie Murphy that walked onto the set of *Coming to America* bore little resemblance to the Murphy that Landis had first met on *Trading Places*. Landis registered the difference: "The guy on *Trading Places* was young and full of energy and curious and funny and fresh and great; the guy on *Coming to America* was the pig of the world—the most unpleasant, arrogant, bullshit entourage . . . just an asshole," and "We had a good working relationship, but our personal relationship changed because he just felt that he was a superstar and that everyone had to kiss his ass. He was a jerk. But great—in fact, one of the greatest performances he's ever given. The character he plays in *Coming to America*, Hakeem [sic], is *so opposite* of what Eddie really was: a gentleman, charming and elegant, as opposed to this jerk-off."[45]

Landis's words are, once again, telling, not because they offer an unbiased account of Murphy's behavior, but because they get at Landis's perception of Murphy once Murphy had risen to superstardom and begun to take greater control over the projects in which he appeared. Perhaps Murphy did "feel like he was a superstar" at the time of filming, but then again, wasn't he? And moreover, as the force responsible for bringing the film to fruition in the first place, why shouldn't Murphy have expected or even demanded a certain level of deference from those working on the film? Would such an attitude have been notable coming from a white producer and superstar?

Furthermore, Murphy may have had yet another reason to feel that *Coming to America* was his film rather than Landis's. The journalist David Rensin claims that Murphy had the option to direct *Coming to America* himself. Certainly, the terms of his deal with Paramount made such a possibility plausible, yet the studio hired Landis to helm the film instead. Murphy takes credit for the decision to place Landis in the director's chair rather than step into the role himself. According to Murphy, he was the one who proposed to Paramount that Landis be hired to direct the film out of a sense of loyalty to the director, whose own career and reputation had taken a hit after a controversial accident on the set of his 1983 *Twilight Zone* movie, which caused the deaths of three actors (including two children): "I went to Paramount and said I wanted to use Landis. But they had reservations: His career was fucked up. But I said, 'I'm gonna use Landis.' . . . I made Paramount hire him."[46] Murphy claims to have also intervened when Paramount initially balked at Landis's salary demands, ensuring that the director received the salary that he wanted.

Yet, once on the set, Landis seemed intent on showing Murphy, as well as everyone around him, that he had Murphy firmly under control. In Murphy's retelling of events, Landis made several attempts to undermine Murphy, both directly and in front of the cast and crew. For instance, he warned the actress Shari Headley to avoid fraternizing with Murphy (allegedly out of fear that Murphy would try to sleep with her). He told stories about working with Michael Jackson on the set of *Thriller*, using that as a warning to Murphy for how he dealt with black megastars: "One of his favorite things was to tell me, 'When I worked with Michael Jackson, everyone was afraid of Michael, but I'm the only one who would tell Michael, "Fuck you." And I'm not afraid to tell you, "Fuck you."'"[47] The tensions on *Coming to America* finally reached a climax when Landis confronted two writers from Murphy's production company who were visiting the set and accused Murphy, in front of the writers and the entire *Coming to America* cast and crew, of cheating the men out of money. According to Murphy, "I playfully grabbed him around the throat, put my arm around him and I said to

Fruity, one of my guys, 'What happens when people put my business in the street?' And Fruit said, 'They get fucked up.' I was kind of half joking. Landis reached down to grab my balls, like he also thought it was a joke—and I cut his wind off. He fell down, his face turned red, his eyes watered up like a bitch and he ran off the set. Fuckin' punk."[48]

Even while acknowledging that Murphy's account of the events may not be totally objective or accurate, placing his and Landis's versions of things in conversation with each other forms a composite picture of the tensions on the set, which were exacerbated by power, control, and also race. It certainly cannot be a coincidence that Landis used his experience with the other black crossover superstar of the 1980s—Michael Jackson—as a cautionary tale to Murphy. *People* magazine reported that Deborah Nadoolman Landis, the costume designer for the film and Landis's wife, had allegedly made racist comments directed at Murphy and the friends who accompanied him to the set (with rumors of yet another resulting physical altercation between Murphy and Landis).[49] And Landis "jokingly" threatening castration seems highly symbolic of the central conflict between the two men: Landis's desire to emasculate Murphy, to put the brash young actor "in his place." We must also understand this action within the context of Murphy's assertion that he was indeed the boss on the set, in stark contrast to Landis's desire to adopt a more conventional director-as-boss model. For not only was Murphy arguably the most powerful player in regard to *Coming to America*, he also *knew* that he was. It is this aspect of Murphy's persona—his understanding of his own value to the studio and in the global marketplace and his unapologetic embrace of it—that is reflected in Landis's comments about Murphy's "arrogant" attitude.

Murphy's account of the filming of *Coming to America* and of the public perception of him indicate a man who was all too aware of the interconnected racial and power dynamics at play on the set and in Hollywood. As he told *People* magazine around the time of the film's release, "As much as we like to think we're liberals, society has this underlying bed of racism. It's like this thing I keep hearing about my 'entourage.' If Michael J. Fox walks into a restaurant with his friends, it's Michael J. Fox and his guests. When Eddie Murphy walks into a room with his friends, it's like, 'Oh, my, it's Eddie Murphy—and his entourage.'"[50] Though he does not name names, it is clear that Murphy's comments were, at least in part, a direct reference to the recent events with Landis on the set of *Coming to America*, but they also reference a larger issue with the way that society understands the "uppity" black man. Even if Murphy did travel frequently with an entourage (photographs and accounts reveal that this "entourage" was mainly family members and close childhood friends), what exactly was so egregious about that? It is as if Landis, critics, and society as a whole expected Murphy to act less like a star who enjoyed the fruits of his success and more like someone who should simply have been *grateful* to be working in the first place. Yet this was not, nor had it ever been, Murphy's attitude about the hard-won gains of his career, not even when he was a nineteen-year-old newcomer on SNL. As Murphy told *Rolling Stone* magazine in 2011, "My significance in film—and again I'm not going to be delusional—was that I'm the first black actor to take charge in a white world onscreen. That's why I became as popular as I became."[51] I would argue, however, that Murphy took charge offscreen as well, and while Hollywood had sufficiently evolved to (somewhat) embrace the former, it was simply not ready for the latter.

Coming to America's Shadows

The conflict between Murphy and Landis signified more than simply a clash in two men's personalities. Instead, their inability to see eye to eye indicated a larger ideological mismatch. For, as I already mentioned, whereas Landis saw the film as a "color-blind" romantic comedy, Murphy clearly envisioned it as a black cultural text. For instance, Landis's comment that *Coming to America* did well internationally and "no one ever thought of it as a black movie" reflects his own limited perceptions about the supposed incongruity between blackness and marketability, and it also demonstrates the industry's overall belief about the inability of black films to sell in the global market, an erroneous perception that Monica Ndounou argues is an unfounded myth.[52] In other words, in Landis's understanding, blackness was antithetical to the film's universality and, hence, success.

At the same time, however, Landis's insistence on the film's "universality"—really, code for whiteness—reveals just how very black the film was. We might, then, interpret Landis's statements about the film's color-blindness not just as his limited perception of the film but also as his (and the studio's) attempt to rein in or apologize for the unquestionably black spin that the film was taking, largely through Murphy's influence and the performances by both Murphy and Hall. Take, for instance, the ongoing comedic reference to the Jheri curl hairstyle that runs through the film, best captured by the sight gag in the film where Soul Glo heir Daryl's family

FIGURE 1.9. Ad for "Soul Glo" in *Coming to America*.

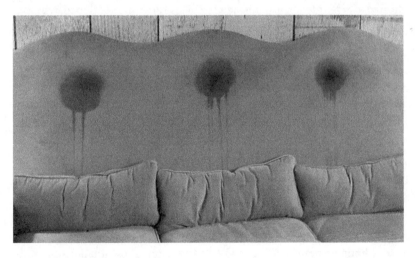

FIGURE 1.10. The Jheri curl sight gag in *Coming to America*.

members get up from the couch where they are sitting, only to leave grease stains on the fabric where their heads were positioned. The joke is funny to anyone who is able to see the connection between their hairstyles and the sofa stain, but it would have been particularly amusing to those who were familiar with the immense popularity of the Jheri curl hairstyle during the 1980s.[53] The cultural specificity of the gag runs contrary to Landis's repeated emphasis that *Coming to America* be a comedy rather than a *black* comedy. In a 2011 interview, for example, a *New York Times* writer, Mekado Murphy, asked Landis whether production executives objected to the Jheri curl jokes. Landis replied, "I remember the studio saying people won't get Jheri curl jokes. I said, you know, if it's funny, it's funny. It's not that it's funny because you're black. It's funny because it's funny."[54] It is clear that when the studio raised questions about whether "people" would understand the jokes, they meant that they worried that white people would not understand a joke about a hairstyle rooted in black culture. Thus, even though Landis's response is meant to highlight the racial universality of the film's humor, his admission of the studio's anxieties confirms that the film was indeed trafficking in a kind of black cultural specificity, one that made Paramount executives nervous.

As I already mentioned, the brash and sometimes belligerent nature of Murphy's performance in *Coming to America* demonstrates the fundamental pleasure in all of Murphy's 1980s films: the incorporation of black humor into conventionally mainstream settings and genres. In Murphy's films, despite their larger adherence to generic conventions, the actor infuses each role with characteristically black elements of humor. In *48 Hrs.*, while he does not answer the racist sentiments of Nick Nolte's character with anger (a fact pointed out by Ed Guerrero), he uses rapid-fire smack talk to disarm the hateful comments. In her review of the film for the *New York Times*, Janet Maslin suggests that the film creates these scenarios just to highlight the way that Murphy's character will navigate them. Referring to a scene in which the character finds himself in a redneck bar, she writes, "If you don't think Mr. Murphy can talk his way out of this, then you'll just have to watch him and see how it's done."[55]

Maslin's comment suggests that part of the enjoyment in *48 Hrs.* comes primarily from Murphy's performance rather than from the narrative construction of the film (which, as I mentioned, collapses into stereotypes). Murphy's body of work, therefore, might warrant another type of critical interpretation if viewed from this perspective. This is most evident in *Coming to America.* Critical reception of the film is founded on a faulty premise: critics and scholars alike incorrectly read the film as a romantic comedy, when it would be better understood more along the lines of a variety show: a connection of humorous vignettes that highlight black perspectives on everyday life. When the film is viewed as a romantic comedy, the critique that it falls short of posing any relevant questions about blackness is a valid one. Yet, when viewed as a collection of black-oriented sketches, *Coming to America* is a different film altogether.[56]

This genre "confusion" and the discrepancy between Landis's efforts toward universality versus Murphy's focus on blackness play out in the formal elements of the film, most notably in the distinction between the A- and B-plots. In some ways, this narrative slipperiness of *Coming to America* connects to a longer history of Hollywood films featuring comedians that subvert the classical plot in order to highlight or privilege the comedic performances. Henry Jenkins, for example, uses the term "anarchistic comedy" to describe how the films of the Marx Brothers disrupt classical film style as well as social order.[57] Like Jenkins, who sees the Marx Brothers' films as representing the interplay between ethnic vaudevillian traditions and the classical, white Hollywood narrative form, I see *Coming to America* and much of Murphy's body of work as having a foot in two worlds: black vernacular humor and standard Hollywood modes of black representation.

In this regard, *Coming to America* is the perfect film for the Hollywood strategies of the 1980s, which sought crossover hits that would appeal to both black and white audiences. The film is a sly integration of insider black humor wrapped within the guise of a mainstream cultural product designed to appease nonblack audiences—a series of black comedic vignettes connected by a formulaic romantic narrative. Though scholars such as Bogle have asserted this possibility regarding individual performances of African Americans within films, they do not expand this concept to the level of genre and how the film critiques generic conventions. What might be gained, for instance, in viewing *Coming to America* as a story of a colorful group of characters in a black Queens, New York, neighborhood who interact in various ways with a visiting African prince? Bruce Babington and Peter William Evans argue for this type of interpretative flexibility in their analysis of the Hollywood musical, arguing, "The point is that it is there, in the song and dance, that the most intense meanings are registered. If you look for them primarily in the elliptical non-musical narrative, thinking of the numbers as pure spectacle (which they clearly cannot be since they employ referential signs), you will be disappointed."[58] If we stretch this logic to apply to *Coming to America*, it is possible to see what is missed when evaluating the film straightforwardly along the lines of its ostensible genre and the primary plot of the African prince in search of his bride. But if we choose to see that story line as the glue that ties together the various vignettes, then the entire thrust of the film is repositioned and the instances of black humor and commentary come to the forefront.

Coming to America is a film made memorable by its cast of supporting characters. Strike up a conversation with any fan of *Coming to America*, and before you know it, you will find yourself engaged in a listing of the film's most memorable lines of dialogue and scenes, such as the singer Randy Watson (also performed by Murphy) shouting "Sexual Chocolate!" to an unresponsive crowd, or the barbers Morris and Clarence verbally jousting about Cassius Clay's right to change his name to Muhammad Ali. Without a doubt, the film's memorable dialogue, scenarios, and characters aid in its continuous reverberations throughout black popular culture up to the present day. Interestingly, as I already mentioned, many of the film's most cited moments derive from the supporting characters and one-off scenes rather than from the main characters and the A-plot about Akeem's search for a wife. Moreover, it is important to note that characters like Clarence, Morris, Randy Watson, and Reverend Brown do not follow the typical Hollywood formula in terms of their function within the film's narrative. Their actions do not relate to, or significantly advance, the film's main story line. And though they sometimes appear in scenes with Akeem and Semmi, their appearances are typically stand-alone affairs.

Take, for example, the scene where Akeem and Semmi attend the Black Awareness Rally in search of better-quality women than what they have so far encountered in their visits to New York City nightclubs. The setup for the scene begins in the barbershop, where Clarence (played by Murphy) tells Akeem (Murphy) that there will be nice women at the rally. From there, the film cuts to the interior of the Black Awareness Rally, where we see the bombastic Reverend Brown (played by Hall) addressing the attendees. Reverend Brown then introduces Randy Watson (Murphy), and Watson introduces his band, Sexual Chocolate. After an earnest and yet utterly mediocre (at best) performance that results in a smattering of lukewarm applause, Watson concludes in dramatic fashion by dropping his microphone and exiting the stage. Easily one of the most memorable scenes in *Coming to America*, the majority of the Black Awareness Rally scene bears no relevance to the main plot, except perhaps as a build-up to the moment when Akeem's eventual bride, Lisa, takes the stage after Watson to plead for donations. I would argue that Lisa's part in the scene is clearly overshadowed by Hall's and Murphy's performances, making them the stars of this particular segment.

As this example hopefully makes clear, *Coming to America*'s supporting characters and seemingly extraneous vignettes form a secondary focus throughout the film. As I mentioned earlier, we might even view the film as a series of sketches (similar to Murphy's work on SNL) loosely connected to the A-plot of Akeem's search for love. In fact, the virtuoso performances by Murphy and Hall as the supporting characters create this interpretative possibility, as they tend to outshine everything and everyone else whenever they appear. This matters because, unlike the film's A-plot and characters, which Landis praised for their "universality" (meant to convey their appeal to white viewers), the memorable supporting characters and scenarios are squarely grounded in black culture.

In this way, *Coming to America* follows Murphy's tried-and-true formula, a "universal" main plot that would appeal to white viewers with culturally specific vignettes legible to black viewers. I have already argued that Murphy's success as a performer (first on SNL and then as an actor) and his dismissal by critics are the result of his ability to blend fare aimed at pleasing white audiences with culturally specific material legible to black ones. Likewise, *Coming to America* employs a similar formula. In an era where the modus operandi for Hollywood was "crossover" (contrary to the niche products of the blaxploitation craze of the 1970s or the explosion of black films that would arrive in the early 1990s), *Coming to America*'s composition satisfied the industry's desire for films that could appeal to white and black audiences simultaneously.

By way of analogy, Sut Jhally and Justin Lewis have argued that *The Cosby Show*, that other exemplar of black-cast crossover success, employed a representational strategy of foregrounding universal themes while relegating black culture to the background. Thus, black viewers might see black art on the Huxtables' walls, posters of black musical artists in the children's rooms, or Heathcliff wearing sweatshirts emblazoned with the logos of historically black colleges and universities, but viewers could choose to be "color-blind" to these markers of cultural blackness. Yet, as the filmmaker and scholar Kevin Jerome Everson suggests about artwork, often the background of a painting is more interesting than the foreground.[59] And

FIGURE 1.11. Akeem and Lisa in *Coming to America*.

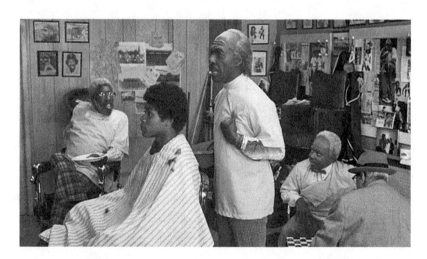

FIGURE 1.12. The barbershop characters in *Coming to America*.

as black viewership of *Cosby* demonstrates, black viewers often chose to concentrate their attention on the black background while white viewers missed these cultural cues altogether.

Likewise, this phenomenon occurs in *Coming to America*. This interplay between the film's universal and black aspects—the foreground and background—extends to its casting and structure. The film itself is a black-cast version of a recognizable, standard Hollywood romantic-comedy formula. The "disguised royalty falls in love with a commoner" plot is similar to that of classic studio-era films of the 1940s and 1950s. In his comments about making *Coming to America*, Landis referred to the film as "the first big Hollywood picture where the color of the principals' skins had nothing to do with the plot." Though Landis acknowledged that the film contains black cultural humor, he emphasized that the film was a "Hollywood fairy tale," the implication being that *Coming to America* was definitely not a "black" film (in his estimation). Deborah Nadoolman Landis reiterated this perspective when she describes the film as "color-blind." Notably, both Landis and Nadoolman Landis reference the film's commercial success on a global and international level, implicitly suggesting that it was the film's avoidance of overtly "black" material that led to its high box-office returns.

These comments are troubling, but not surprising, and they reinforce the intentional "universality," "color-blindness," or plain old whiteness of the film's A-plot. And yet it is the film's casting that complicates, and ultimately subverts, Landis's assertions about the film's racial politics. The division between A-plot and B-plot is blurred, I would argue, precisely because Murphy plays both the "universal" Akeem and the culturally black supporting characters. In other words, had superstar Murphy only played Akeem, with lesser-known actors playing Clarence and Randy Watson, for instance, the A-plot would clearly take a dominant position as far as the narrative. However, Murphy occupies both the main and the supporting narratives; furthermore, Murphy's comedic talents for improvisation and impersonation—things that his fans would seek out due to his history on SNL and in previous films—are highlighted in the vignettes rather than in the main story line.

In fact, Richard Schickel inadvertently hints at this possibility in his *Time* review of the film. He writes, "Murphy is seen—more accurately unseen—as a half-senile barber, a trashed rock singer and, most remarkably, a crotchety old Jewish gentleman." This concept of Murphy as "unseen," as he slips in and out of various characters and embodies their varied individual and racial subjectivities, is the radical move in the film. Furthermore, the notion of the invisibility and malleability of the black performer echoes Mel Watkins's description of black humor as the "shadowy comic vision that satirizes and humanizes America's main body."[60]

In *Coming to America*, it is Murphy's embodiment of these various subjectivities that makes the film such a racially polysemic text. Murphy is a straightforward romantic lead (Prince Akeem), an ethnic white man who serves as the catalyst for discussions of race (Saul), and a menagerie of characters who provide glimpses of black American culture (the barbershop, the Jheri curl phenomenon, black church performers). It is easy to focus too closely on the novelty of his performances while losing sight that these characters are *vehicles* for Murphy. Even when Murphy physically disappears into white skin as the character Saul, the racial charade still functions as a tool for Murphy to make black-inflected cultural criticisms. Indeed, Murphy-as-Saul provides a good extended example of how the young actor blended his performance and politics and straddled the line between acceptable Hollywood fare and a more biting, black-inflected form of criticism.[61]

Placing an ethnic face on white identity (as opposed to the generic white "everyman" that Murphy played in the SNL short film *White Like Me*), Saul is Jewish, elderly, and clearly comfortable interacting and arguing with his black friends in the barbershop.[62] His ethnic identity, or what I call "off-whiteness," complicates Hollywood's typical depiction of whiteness, suggesting a spectrum of racial and ethnic identities that do not neatly align along a simple black/white binary. In fact, one could argue that Saul's seeming naturalness in the black barbershop is partly due to his own marginalization from dominant whiteness due to his Jewish identity, and the setting of the barbershop references long-standing community relationships between Jews and African Americans.

Yet Saul is also a straw man for a racial debate that one might argue can only take place so freely within the fictitious world that *Coming to America* represents. In some ways, Saul's presence as the resident white character in the barbershop's free-speech zone allows the film to give a brief glimpse into the world of black and white social dynamics such as in the following exchange:

CLARENCE: You must be out of your goddamned mind! Joe Louis is the greatest boxer that ever lived. (I'll be with you boys in a minute.) He was badder than Cassius Clay, he was badder than Sugar Ray, he's badder than . . . who's that, you know, the new boy? Mike Tyson—look like a bulldog. He's badder than him, too! He'd-a whipped Mike Tyson's ass. He'd whip all they asses.

SAUL: What about Rocky Marciano?

CLARENCE: Oh, there they go! There they go! Every time I start talkin' about boxing, a white man got to pull Rocky Marciano out they ass. That's they one. That's they one. "Rocky Marciano. Rocky Marciano." Let me tell you something once and for all: Rocky Marciano was good, but compared to Joe Louis? Rocky Marciano ain't shit.

SAUL: He beat Joe Louis's ass.

In the scene, Saul's seemingly innocent query about Rocky Marciano provides the basis for another of Murphy's avatars to attack just one example of a cultural "me-tooism" that might be funny within the realm of a discussion about boxing, but that was also taking place in the real world, particularly in the 1980s when a growing number of whites were co-opting victimhood status and making claims of reverse discrimination in issues such as affirmative action in education and employment.[63]

Saul also becomes a vehicle to establish Murphy's place in the canon of comedy greats. Rather than setting up the character as an explicit political statement about whiteness, the aged and humorous Saul serves as a showcase for Murphy's own comic persona and impersonation skills. This is most evident in the closing credits, which I describe at the opening of this chapter but want to provide more detail for now. African drums play as the closing credits roll. The sequence includes most of the multiple characters played by Eddie Murphy and Arsenio Hall. After nearly all of the actors have been shown, the character of Saul appears on the screen, and after a brief delay, Eddie Murphy's name is shown below the image. The delay between the image and the name serves as a reveal to the audience, who are meant to be surprised by Murphy's seamless portrayal and the realization that the believable Jewish character was actually a black man. Even the *New York Times* did not dare give away the surprise in its review of the film. Of Murphy's portrayal of Saul, Vincent Canby would only vaguely reference it as "so off-the-wall and so disguised that one can only be sure who has been playing whom by watching the closing credits."[64] As the credits sequence comes to a close, Saul exclaims, "Wait a minute, wait a minute. Stop right there!" The music halts, and Saul takes the spotlight and begins the following joke:

> A man goes into a restaurant, and he sits down, he's having a bowl of soup and he says to the waiter, "Waiter, come taste the soup." Waiter says, "Is something wrong with the soup?"
>
> He says, "Taste the soup."
>
> He says, "Is there something wrong with the soup? Is the soup too hot?"
>
> He says, "Will you taste the soup?"
>
> "What's wrong, is the soup too cold?"
>
> "Will you just taste the soup?!"
>
> "All right, I'll taste the soup. Where's the spoon?"
>
> "Aha."

The reveal and the joke serve as a showcase for Murphy's comedic talents but also assert his place in the long tradition of famous Jewish comedians. By telling a joke first popularized by Jack Benny, Murphy establishes himself as the successor to that brand of Jewish comedy. Later, he would show off his ability to speak Yiddish (or at least fake it) in *The Distinguished Gentleman*, and he would eventually go on to remake Jerry Lewis's classic *The Nutty Professor*.

Reverberations

These various components of Murphy's performance as Saul suggest the complexity of Murphy's comedic work—the layers that constitute his appeal to white audiences (and white-owned film studios) as well as to black ones. Furthermore, beyond the textual elements of *Coming to America* that confer its "black" status, the movie's postproduction circulation also confirms that Murphy's efforts to create a black film outside of our traditional understanding of one were successful. To conclude this chapter, I want to take a look at the film's afterlife, or its cultural reverberations, to explore how it has become firmly entrenched as a canonical piece of black popular culture. For, as a film whose more interesting facets have been overlooked because they exist primarily in the "negative" space of the film (due to Landis's framing, the film's A-plot, and the fact that it is a product of a major studio), it is only fitting that we explore how these elements have "developed" in the years since the film's release.

Interestingly, in spite of Landis's oft-repeated assessment of the film as a universal, color-blind tale with appeal to "everyone," Paramount clearly did not share the same opinion. As Siskel and Ebert revealed during a conversation with Oprah Winfrey on her television show in May 1988, Paramount executives were so nervous about how the film would perform after an unenthusiastic press screening in New York that they quickly withdrew all advanced screeners, thus preventing critics from having an opportunity to view the film before its release. Such a move was unprecedented for a film of such scale from a major studio.[65] According to Siskel and Ebert, this move by Paramount demonstrated the studio's lack of faith in its product, itself rather shocking given the presumed wide appeal of the film's classical Hollywood plot and the popularity of its star. Siskel went a step further in his analysis of this decision by the studio, contextualizing it as an act based on a lack of faith, but also a case of, in sum, condemning the film to a lackluster performance at the box office: "I am offended by a film company that has so little regard for its own product that it won't show it. . . . I think that they damn it by not showing it."[66] Ebert teased out the larger implications of this move for the success of the film, noting that reviews, even if favorable, would now appear days after its release rather than on opening day, thus failing to generate the appropriate buzz needed to bring people into theaters. In other words, Paramount's choice to pull screeners for fear of the film's poor performance might very likely create a self-fulfilling prophecy.

It makes no sense that Paramount would make such a rash decision, given the product that they had on their hands, unless, of course, it was the film's unapologetic cultural blackness that gave them pause. For it is totally illogical that Paramount—after investing so much money in the film's production—would panic and pull all of its screeners and thus potentially undermine the film's success in the face of the results of a single prerelease screening. Even though the film had a well-known director, a big budget, glossy Hollywood production values, a classical plot, and a celebrity star, still these things did not bolster the studio's confidence in its product. Yet this move makes sense if we recall Paramount's uneasiness around Coming to America's Jheri curl jokes and assume that the studio, despite Landis's pronouncements of color-blindness, was very aware of and concerned about the blackness of the film. This matters when we place this into the context that Ndounou provides about the industry "logic" of black films: "In an industry that uses racial markers to categorize and evaluate its products, films with predominantly black casts are often labeled 'urban' and, as a result, tend to fall outside the wide-release category. Regardless of genre, these films are perceived as niche films with limited market appeal. Such perceptions affect film conception, investment decisions, production, marketing, and distribution."[67] Could this have been the reason that Paramount pulled the screeners of *Coming to America*? It seems not only plausible but also likely. In spite of the fact that the film contained all of the ingredients necessary to generate box office success, its recognizable blackness was simply too much for the studio, blinding them to the gem in their possession. As Siskel put it, "Frequently, the film companies don't know what they have."

Of course, the world recognized what Paramount had, and *Coming to America* would go on to earn $128 million domestically and $160 million internationally. But perhaps more significantly, the film continues to circulate throughout black popular culture decades after its release. The reverberations of *Coming to America*'s vignettes throughout black popular culture suggest that, indeed, viewers found the black "background" of the film far more interesting than the white, universal foreground. As I mentioned in the introduction, Kandi Burruss, a songwriter and *Real Housewives of Atlanta* cast member, designed her wedding (captured in the Bravo *Housewives* spinoff, *Kandi's Wedding*) around a *Coming to America* theme: specifically, Akeem's lavish engagement ceremony to his prearranged bride, Imani, whom he subsequently abandons in order to go to New York in search of his true love. As I previously stated, it is Akeem's *failed* engagement at the beginning of the film rather than the fairy-tale wedding at the end—the culmination of the romantic A-plot that guides the film—that Burruss found memorable, iconic, and legible to her guests. Burruss's wedding included lions, a choreographed African dance number, a lace and nude-illusion gown, and a man singing "She's Your Queen to Be"—all elements featured in the Landis film. And, in one episode of the show, Burruss's mother expands on the comparison between the wedding and the *Coming to America* engagement when she quotes Imani's oft-repeated line "whatever you like" as a derisive commentary on Burruss's apparent subservience to her fiancé. Burruss's choice speaks to the scenes and imagery from the film that captured the popular imagination, precisely those that would not have been mentioned in the mainstream newspaper and magazine reviews of the film at the time of its premiere.

References to *Coming to America*'s black elements continue to appear in a wide range of places throughout popular culture. Like Burruss, the

FIGURE 1.13. Akeem and Imani in *Coming to America*.

FIGURE 1.14. Imani, the jilted fiancée.

FIGURE 1.15. Kandi Burruss on her wedding day.

rapper Snoop Dogg chose the film's engagement scene as the theme for his son's eighteenth birthday party. Questlove, from the band the Roots, named his side project the Randy Watson Experience. The black-owned hair-care company Oyin Handmade sells a leave-in conditioner called "Juices and Berries," a nod to a line in *Coming to America* where Akeem informs Clarence the barber that he uses no chemicals in his hair, "only juices and berries." And, in his final White House Correspondents' Dinner in 2016, President Barack Obama ended his remarks by saying "Obama out!" and then dropped the microphone, a nod to Randy Watson. In fact, these "supporting" characters are so well known that when I presented a version of this chapter at an academic conference, rather than play a clip of Eddie Murphy as Randy Watson, I simply mentioned the character's name, pointed to a black person in the audience, and waited with confidence for him to help me make my point about the film's resonance, which he did, by shouting "Sexual Chocolate!"

The afterlife of these characters and scenes from *Coming to America*'s B-plot reveals that, indeed, Murphy's impact on the film is its enduring legacy and that viewers recognize and appreciate the cultural specificity of the supporting characters and their associated vignettes. In contrast to the lead characters of Akeem and Lisa, it is the supporting personalities that have continued to stand out in the almost thirty years since the film's release. Characters such as Reverend Brown, Clarence, and Morris are

FIGURE 1.16. Eddie Murphy as Randy Watson, dropping the microphone.

FIGURE 1.17. President Barack Obama's "drop the mic" moment at the 2016 White House Correspondents' Dinner.

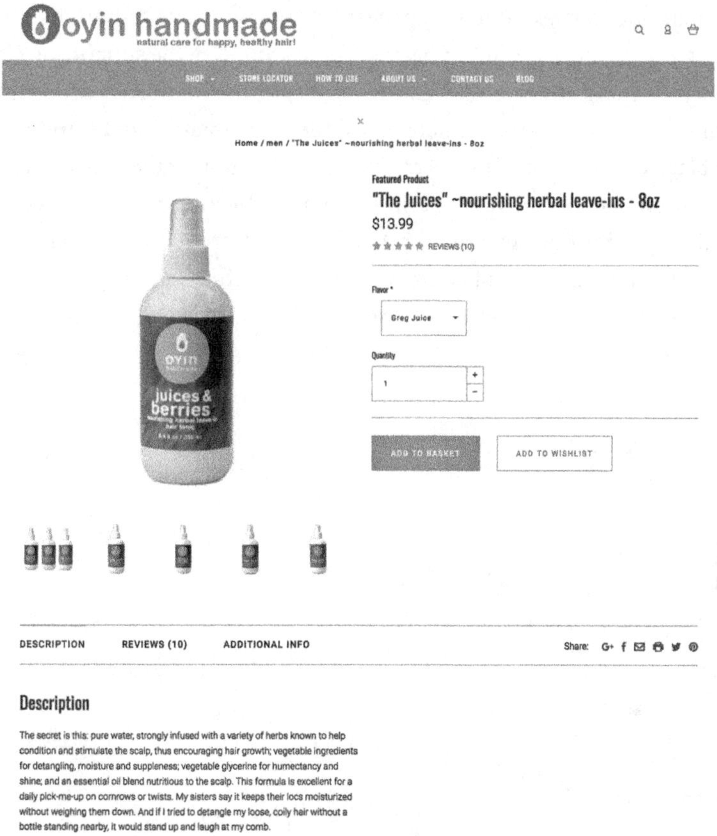

FIGURE 1.18. Oyin Handmade's "Juices and Berries" hair product.

rooted in black cultural institutions: the black church and the barbershop, respectively. Indeed, the banter between Clarence and Morris—consisting of a good-natured blend of bluster, teasing, and debate—would be familiar to those audience members who regularly frequent black barbershops. And the juxtaposition of Reverend Brown's scriptural references against his overt sexual and popular culture references would be both recognizable and comical to those acquainted with that particular type of black preacher.[68]

In hindsight, it is easy to see why *Coming to America* has been overlooked and dismissed for so long. All of its main features—the studio that produced it, the man who directed it, the industrial and social factors that created its star—suggest that the film would be a standard-issue Hollywood product, one that exploited blackness in order to garner white laughter. Yet, by examining the film's "negative" side—found in the supporting characters, the film's afterlife, and Eddie Murphy's interventions behind and in front of the camera—we are able to see the film's identity and significance as a black cultural text. This recalibration of the film's importance matters, not just for the sake of appreciating *Coming to America*, but because of the implications for our analysis of other films that productively trouble categorical understandings of genre, politics, and authorship.

RELATIONAL NEGATIVITY
The Sellout Films of the 1990s

This is the truth. This is what's real.
—Theatrical poster for *Menace II Society*

A comedy about makin' it!
—Theatrical poster for *Livin' Large*

Reimagining Success

Negative texts cannot be defined according to a static set of criteria. In the last chapter, I noted that the lack of critical attention surrounding *Coming to America* may be the result of its chronological location between two important black films: *Hollywood Shuffle* and *Do the Right Thing. Coming to America* was a big-budget Hollywood film, with a mixture of comedy, romance, and drama, starring one of the world's biggest celebrities of the time. In other words, there is little in the film that would seem to qualify it as a negative representation, at least in the ways that films that trade in demeaning stereotypes are often labeled. And yet *Coming to America* forms an inversion to the two films between which it is wedged, perhaps for these very reasons. Unlike *Hollywood Shuffle*, which was an independently produced satire of Hollywood's racism, *Coming to America* was, at least on the surface, white director John Landis's unreflexive vision of Africa and black America. In contrast to *Do the Right Thing*, which begins with a comedic tone only to shift into drama and tragedy in the film's second half, *Coming to America* employed one of Hollywood's most recognizable genres, the romantic comedy, to tell the story of Prince Akeem in America. Though, as I argued in the last chapter, Murphy's influence and performance complicate such a straightforward reading, it is easy to see why, at least on paper, *Coming to America* was perceived to be little more than Hollywood's latest attempt to import a little blackness into otherwise standard fare. Compared with the decidedly more racially ambitious work of *Hollywood Shuffle's* and *Do the Right Thing's* emerging black directors, Robert Townsend and Spike Lee, respectively, there is little question as to which films caught critics' and scholars' attention.

Similarly, the group of films that I take up in this chapter, what I call the "sellout films" of the 1990s, are, in many ways, similar to *Coming to America*. For the most part, these films—*Strictly Business* (Kevin Hooks, 1991), *Livin' Large* (Michael Schultz, 1991), *True Identity* (Charles Lane, 1991), and *The Associate* (Donald Petrie, 1996), among others—are comedies either produced by or distributed by Hollywood studios. While many of the films do have black directors at the helm, the films themselves are black versions of more conventional Hollywood fare, with predictable characters, situations, and outcomes. Most significantly, these films were part of the same boom in black film production that also led to films such as *Boyz n the Hood* (John Singleton, 1991), *South Central* (Steve Anderson, 1992), and *Menace II Society* (the Hughes Brothers, 1993). That second grouping of films, the so-called hood films, dominates both popular and scholarly imaginations whenever discussions of black film in the 1990s arise. Overshadowed by these gripping dramas, whose plots seemed ripped out of contemporary news headlines, the "sellout films" have received scant attention, in spite of the many titles in this category.

In this chapter, I examine the ways that a particular set of comedic films focusing on narratives of black success in the white corporate world form a countercanon to the more popularly written-about social realism films of the same time period. Some of these films place a 1990s, hip hop consciousness spin on the trend of "uplift films" from the 1980s, where professional success and material wealth signify having "made it" in a white world. For instance, in *Strictly Business*, a "white-acting" black man lands a career-changing deal once he accepts his blackness and begins to act accordingly. Films such as this one emphasize the necessity of embracing one's cultural identity rather than assimilating completely, even if their plotlines ultimately seem to embrace the same institutional structures and ideologies that marginalize nonwhite identities in the first place. At the same time, however, many of these films revise and even criticize the narratives of uplift and success that had been popular in black-cast films in the 1980s by focusing more closely on the personal costs of "selling out."

The messages of these films are often contradictory in their politics. At times they promote a culturally progressive vision of racial identity; at other times, they fall back on convenient assimilationist discourses that promote "balancing" one's blackness with the more widely acceptable forms of whiteness demanded by corporate settings. And nearly all of these films use some form of sexism, colorism, homophobia, or classism to define the boundaries of black and white identities. Finally, as comedies, these films, which I group together under the loose title "sellout films," fall in line with a larger trajectory of Hollywood's representation of blacks predominantly in humorous scenarios rather than in serious ones.

For these reasons, the sellout films are rarely discussed in either popular or scholarly accounts of 1990s black film. Rather, discussion of this time period has been dominated by *Boyz n the Hood* and *Menace II Society*, among others. Ed Guerrero, however, reminds us that early 1990s films featured a diverse range of topics and story lines. Indeed, there were numerous comedies produced during this same time that tackled all sorts of issues related to black experiences, of which the sellout films, focusing on the tension between professional success and personal identity, were a subset. Unlike their hood film counterparts, which center on coming-of-age narratives that take place in urban ghettos, the sellout films focus on adults undergoing identity crises as a result of their professional ambitions. While the hood films tackle the very literal life-and-death decisions that young black men face, the sellout films address the emotional, social, and psychological nuances of "succeeding" in a white world. Given recent scholarship on subjects such as "working" one's race, racial microaggressions, and the link between everyday racism and health, these films provide a glimpse at how filmmakers negotiated these same issues in the midst of national debates about affirmative action.[1] Further, while many of these films employ aspects of realism in ways similar to their hood counterparts, they are more readily identifiable by their utilization of humor, irreverence, and even surrealism. By employing these different representational strategies, the sellout films suggest that realism and drama are not the only (or necessarily the best) modes for exploring the complicated experiences of black life.

The 1990s and the Proliferation of Black Film

Numerous industrial and technological changes contributed to the boom in black media production during this time period. Hollywood studios shifted away from the "one-size-fits-all" approach that had characterized the promotion of the "crossover film" of the 1980s and began producing movies designed to appeal to specific markets. An expansion of cable channels saturated the airwaves with a variety of diverse programming. Major networks developed television shows to capture urban sensibilities and urban viewers. The proliferation and affordability of vcrs increased people's ability to manage their time and watch (and rewatch) films and television shows at home.

Like the blaxploitation boom of the 1970s, an economic downturn in the 1990s was also the catalyst behind the explosion in production of black-oriented films. Guerrero notes that the high profits enjoyed by Hollywood in the late 1980s, particularly 1989, led Hollywood studios to invest in the increased production of costly films. This investment, however, quickly turned into a financial burden when the war in the Persian Gulf resulted in decreased consumer spending, especially on entertainment. Facing another financial crisis not unlike the one experienced after the fall of the studio system in the late 1960s, Hollywood turned its attention to black-themed films in order to draw in their reliable standby: black audiences.[2] Shifting away from the promotion of blockbuster crossover films aimed at attracting the largest possible viewing public, they now began to target multiple niche markets with a diversity of products. This shift increased the opportunities for African American filmmakers and for black-oriented films. Hip hop, as a musical genre as well as an aesthetic sensibility, had successfully transitioned from an inner-city art form into a global commodity culture.[3] Furthermore, the crack epidemic that began in the 1980s, the 1992 Los Angeles riots, and rising tensions within urban areas created a heightened and fetishized fascination with the black underclass and ghettos that the mainstream news media exploited to its full advantage. These factors spurred the explosion of gritty, urban-centered popular films that focused on the lives of black youth, such as *Boyz n the Hood* and *Menace II Society* (as I have already mentioned), *Straight Out of Brooklyn* (Matty Rich, 1991), *Juice* (Ernest Dickerson, 1992), and *Clockers* (Spike Lee, 1998).

Hollywood not only actively pursued films with black casts and black themes, but also provided support to black filmmakers. Directors such as Spike Lee and Robert Townsend had fought to bring black images and experiences to the screen in the previous decade. Now, filmmakers like the Hughes Brothers and Mario Van Peebles (*New Jack City*, 1991) took full advantage of the opportunities created by their predecessors.

Though the hood film was just one type of black popular film prominent in the 1990s, this genre showed the large impact of black social concerns and cultural forms on popular media. As hip hop gained more traction in the mainstream, its influence on film became evident during this time period. Employing what Donald Bogle calls a "hip hop/rap aesthetic and sensibility," many films prominently featured rap artists in their casts, such as Ice Cube as Doughboy in *Boyz n the Hood* and Ice T as undercover cop Scotty Appleton in *New Jack City*.[4] Black music like rap and R&B added cultural relevance and youth culture appeal to the images in the form of well-publicized film soundtracks. For instance, well-known rap groups such as Naughty by Nature and Cypress Hill appear on the soundtrack for the film *Juice*. This was similar to the phenomenon that had occurred in the blaxploitation era, with movie scores provided by artists like Isaac Hayes for *Shaft* and Curtis Mayfield for *Super Fly*. In addition, the focus on the grittiness of ghetto life—Ricky's tragic death in *Boyz n the Hood* or African American/Korean tensions in *Menace II Society*—gave these films a "ripped from the headlines" quality that blurred the line between fiction and reality. Finally, the chilling crackhouses in *Jungle Fever* (Spike Lee, 1991) and *New Jack City* showed the devastating impact that the American ethos of capitalism and materialism had on inner-city communities.

The year 1991, in particular, was a watershed moment for the release of black-themed films on the big screen. According to Guerrero, that year alone saw "the release of twelve films directed by African Americans, along with over twenty other productions that starred or had significant roles for black actors."[5] Of these, the hood films—exemplified by Singleton's *Boyz*, Van Peebles's *New Jack City*, and the Hughes Brothers' *Menace*—are what many individuals and scholars associate with this period of production.

FIGURE 2.1. A scene from *Boyz n the Hood.*

Writing about the same time period, Kevin Harris observes that this period of production was also indelibly characterized by certain overlapping traits, one of which was an emphasis on realism.[6] This emphasis is clearly on display in films like *Boyz* and others, which employ contemporaneous discourses about black youth, violence, and South Central Los Angeles as crucial plot and setting elements.

This wave of black programming coincided with new conceptions of racial identity that began taking root at the same time. In stark contrast to previous eras, an emphasis on multiculturalism swept through popular culture, with racial diversity suddenly carrying valuable cachet and marketing potential. As Herman Gray notes, television programs such as *The Cosby Show* had forged new territory in the 1980s by appropriating familiar genres such as the family sitcom in the service of black perspectives and stories. At the same time, however, *Cosby* located its blackness in its upper-middle-class familial settings, with little consideration of the institutional or structural practices that shape the contours of blackness. Thus, even though the show presented blackness, it did not delve into the significance of blackness for its characters and their lives. As Gray points out, "The show seemed unwilling to critique and engage various aspects of black diversity that it visually represented."[7] As the Reagan era came to a close, however, the sheer proliferation of black media would usher in an unprecedented degree of diversity both among and within black films and television shows.

The emergence of this new diversity of black representation meant that, for perhaps the first time in history, plots and narratives were able to go beyond the mere fact of blackness onscreen and into a consideration of the complex meanings and ongoing process of being black. While the hood films address coming-of-age issues in inner-city environments, the sellout films that I explore focus on blackness in decidedly different settings: the middle-class and upper-middle-class environs of corporate America. The juxtaposition of these two settings and their accompanying characters and narratives highlights the diversity that, I argue, characterized black media of the 1990s and set it apart from the media of previous decades. These various settings and styles marked a productive development in the representation of black images onscreen, as it began to hint at the complexity—sometimes dramatic and sometimes comedic—of black lives and experiences.

The Rejection of Realism

By the 1990s, black iconography had become a regular feature of mainstream culture. Further, the mere visual appearance of blackness onscreen was no longer an adequate marker of the blackness of the media text itself (similar to Gray's argument about *The Cosby Show*). Therefore, films needed more than just black bodies to articulate their cultural affinity. For instance, the hood films sought recourse to specific themes well known within black discussions of representation: authenticity and realism to delineate "real" black culture from a more commercialized version of it. This emphasis on authenticity and realism is no doubt the main reason why this subgenre has come to represent the entirety of 1990s black film production in the popular imaginary, in spite of evidence to the contrary. As Wahneema Lubiano notes in her essay "But Compared to What?," the shortage of diverse black images throughout cinematic history has, understandably, resulted in a celebration of those representations, perceiving them as telling the "real" story of black experience. But, as Lubiano reminds us, categories of what is "authentic" or "real" are not ideologically neutral, but, instead, correspond to hegemonic definitions of "truth" with respect to race, gender, class, and sexuality.

Narratively speaking, Lubiano's words serve as a reminder that realism is not, nor should it be valued as, the sole way to interrogate nonhegemonic conceptions of identity. She writes, "Deployed as a narrative form dependent upon recognition of reality, realism suggests disclosure of the truth (and then closure of the representation); realism invites readers/audience to accept what is offered as a slice of life because the narrative contains elements of 'fact.' Realism, then, temporarily allows chaos in an otherwise conventional or recognizable world, but at the end the narrative moves toward closure, the establishment of truth and order."[8] Thus, though we may be tempted to view the hood films' realism as the "true" representation of blackness, we must remember, as Lubiano urges, that this semblance of authenticity was, first and foremost, constructed via a series of aesthetic and narrative decisions by individual filmmakers and studios. For example, while *Boyz* may have touched a nerve with audiences, critics, and scholars because of its unflinching portrayal of the fragility of black male adolescence in South Central Los Angeles, the filmmaker's decision to push women to the margins of the film's story was a choice that reflected the filmmaker's perspective rather than any objectively "authentic" blackness.

As I have already mentioned, the sellout films largely eschew narrative realism, often asking audiences to suspend their disbelief at some of the plots' twists and turns in order to engage with the larger issues that the films raise. These films also explicitly represent the process of cultural transformation, often presenting it as strategic and self-aware performance. In *Strictly Business*, Waymon must learn new codes of blackness in order to succeed in his personal and professional lives. In *Livin' Large*, Dexter sees a sellout version of himself appearing in his television set, a self-conscious nod to the power of the media in constructing black images. Miles in *True Identity* and Laurel in *The Associate* both become white as part of a ruse, assisted by friends who are makeup artists. Keeping Lubiano's argument in mind, I am interested in examining the ways that these films, with their avoidance of matters of realism, function differently from their hood counterparts. In other words, what aspects of the black experience is comedy able to elucidate that drama cannot? And, assuming that the sellout films use comedy to sort through the messy territory of black success, how might an in-depth analysis of these films change our understandings of the importance of a genre (comedy) assumed to be "just entertainment" and little else?

Strictly Business: The Quintessential Sellout Film

On the surface, the hood films embodied by *Boyz* and the sellout films that I take up in this chapter have little in common besides the fact that each genre features all-black casts. Yet the genres are connected in both industrial and thematic ways. Monica Ndounou argues that "the most eco-nomically successful genres that feature original screenplays are hip-hop gangsta films and comedies," thus making these two categories of films the ones most likely to be produced, distributed, and exhibited by Hollywood.[9] Of this latter category, *Strictly Business* is a good example of a typical 1990s black comedy in that its premise focuses on the cultural and professional identity crisis of its main character. It is the story of Waymon Tinsdale III (Joseph C. Phillips), a successful New York real estate broker with little con-nection to black culture. Waymon develops a tentative friendship with Bobby (Tommy Davidson), a mailroom clerk, and the two strike a deal: if Bobby can help Waymon meet Natalie (Halle Berry), the girl of his dreams, Waymon will set Bobby on the path out of the mailroom and toward becoming a real estate broker. Along the way, Waymon learns valuable lessons about the importance of community solidarity and the limits of stereotyping.

Based on this quick description, *Strictly Business* and similar films seem a world away from the gangs, violence, and coming-of-age plots that animate films like *Boyz* and *Menace*. However, I would argue that the sellout films narratively take up where the uplift portions of the hood films leave off. For example, at the end of *Boyz*, the epigraph just before the closing credits states that protagonist Tre goes on to attend Morehouse College in Atlanta, and his girlfriend Brandi enrolls at Spelman College. Let us imagine that Tre and Brandi graduate, develop successful careers, marry, and have a son. Determined to leave the violence of South Central behind them and pro-vide a different life for their child, Tre and Brandi move to the suburbs and raise their son, Waymon, in a predominantly white setting. Upon growing up, Waymon then goes on to become a successful commercial real estate broker in New York. However, even though Waymon possesses financial and educational privilege, he is lacking in his cultural knowledge of and connection with other African Americans. This is where the plot of *Strictly Business* picks up. In this way, we might view the sellout films as the inevi-table narrative progression of the hood films' story lines. Further, while the two types of films are in some ways quite different, they both empha-size negotiations of identity within a social context, asking what it means to be black when various forces pull an individual in different directions.

I use *Strictly Business* as the seminal example of the countercanon sellout films because it contains all of the key elements that I identify in the genre: "selling out" as the main theme, explicit consideration of whiteness and its implications for African Americans, tension between personal identity and professional success, and a plot resolution that ultimately rewards cultural blackness. Though other films (including the hood films, black-cast films from other periods, and white-cast films throughout history) may contain one or more of these characteristics, the sellout film genre contains all of them, albeit in different forms.

Strictly Business, like the other films in the genre, revolves around the basic conceit of "selling out," or the notion that a person has compromised their personal integrity for some kind of material gain. In this film and in others, the narrative tension derives from the lead characters' decision to cast aside their blackness in order to obtain professional success. For the most part, *Strictly Business* illustrates this via a fairly simplistic assessment of racial identity. The film sets up a clear contrast between sellout executive Waymon and authentically black mailroom clerk Bobby. The film lays this out in an early scene. After Bobby interrogates Waymon about his lack of effort to advocate for Bobby's entry into an important professional training program, the two have the following exchange:

BOBBY: That's bogus. Why you illin' like that?

WAYMON: Now see? That is what I am talking about. "Illing"? What kind of word is that? And look at the way you're dressed.

BOBBY: I work in the mailroom, man. What am I supposed to wear, an Armani suit?

WAYMON: No, but you don't have to speak and dress so . . . so . . . how do I put this?

BOBBY: Black?

WAYMON: Well, yes: black.

BOBBY: You know what, G? You are straight up whiter than the whitest white man. I thought there was a little bit of black under that tired blue suit you got on. But I see what time it is now. Thanks for nothing, Mr. Tinsdale.

Throughout the film, Waymon stumbles over his lack of cultural awareness, he does not understand black slang, and his wardrobe is limited to a sea of boring gray and blue suits. The film makes it clear that these aspects of his assimilated racial identity are ultimately detrimental to his personal and professional well-being. Problematically, however, the film understands

FIGURE 2.2. Waymon and Bobby in *Strictly Business*.

"selling out" in terms of not only racial identity but also masculinity. At its worst moments, *Strictly Business* reproduces the sexism and capitalism that are part of the same hegemonic structure by which individuals like Bobby and Waymon are themselves oppressed. This is most obvious in the character of Waymon's girlfriend, Diedre. Played by fair-skinned actress Anne-Marie Johnson, Diedre is a cartoon villain whom the film simultaneously connects to fears of selling out as well as of emasculation. Diedre's first appearance in the story (by phone) comes immediately following Bobby's speech where he questions Waymon's cultural authenticity, thereby linking her character to the larger issue of Waymon's sellout identity. Throughout the film, Diedre's "aggressiveness" is demonstrated through her physical strength (she beats Waymon at squash), her dominance and selfishness in the bedroom, and her unabashed decision to choose a man with her head rather than with her heart. Further, the film repeatedly emphasizes her lack of sexiness (in contrast to Berry's Natalie) by making her skinniness the butt of a series of jokes by Bobby, such as her ability to "hula hoop with a Cheerio." The emphasis on Diedre's thin, "unwomanly" body is reminiscent of the final scene in the film *Working Girl* (Mike Nichols, 1988), a white-cast film that centers on issues of identity and professional ambition, where the villain Katherine is insulted with a reference to her "bony ass." In both *Strictly Business* and *Working Girl*, these female villains serve as foils to their "appropriately" feminine counterparts. Suzanne Leonard has argued that popular films of the 1980s tend to provide emotional rewards for female characters who acquiesce to conventional gender norms, while "the fates are typically not so rosy for the women coded as sexually and economically ambitious."[10] Similarly, *Strictly Business* demonizes Diedre for challenging norms of what constitutes attractive gendered behavior and appearance, while praising Natalie for adhering to them.

Film critics did not miss this less-than-progressive narrative. Armond White argues that the film promotes the chauvinistic pursuit of women and material goods, while simultaneously reducing black culture "to its most craven aspects rather than its most honest or humane."[11] White is correct in his assessment that the film does not truly explore the facets of blackness, choosing instead to offer the most obvious—and I would add, cinematic—markers of blackness in the form of style and bodily performance. For example, Waymon's cultural transformation into a "homie" is illustrated via a shopping montage, similar to Vivian's famous shopping scene in the film *Pretty Woman* (Garry Marshall, 1990). And the film introduces Natalie through the use of slow motion and a tilt-up—pausing at her cleavage—highlighting her sexual desirability in clear cinematic language. Such devices are standard Hollywood fare, of course. However, the seamless joining of these conventions with the film's definition of blackness only serves to underscore White's critique.

While all of this is undeniably true, films are complex texts. Though the criticism of *Strictly Business*'s blatant sexism is merited, other elements of the film warrant closer inspection and analysis. In other words, we need not take an "all-or-nothing" approach when examining this film or others like it. Therefore, I am interested in pivoting and focusing on the ways that the film defines racial identity, both as cultural construct and as a system of varying degrees of access to privilege. Further, I am interested in how the film's conventions—the same ones that led to its stereotypical depiction of blackness—offer a critique of whiteness as both representational and a narrative device. Because, while I agree with White that the film presents black culture as little more than wearing flashy clothing and using slang, I would argue that the film's presentation of whiteness, though less obvious, is the more nuanced and intriguing contribution.

Maybe White did not attend to *Strictly Business*'s depiction of whiteness in his critique because he felt that it mattered little in comparison to the film's shortcomings. Perhaps, however, it is symptomatic both of the way that whiteness operates invisibly in film as well as real life and of the still-

FIGURE 2.3. Diedre in *Strictly Business*.

FIGURE 2.4. Natalie in *Strictly Business*.

touchy subject of blacks who "act white." Therefore, to properly analyze how the film constructs Waymon's "acting white" beyond the obvious clothing and speech-pattern devices, we must turn our attention first to the actual white characters in *Strictly Business*. In particular, I am interested in the ways that the three main white characters articulate different forms of white privilege and "white" behavior. Taken together, these characters provide important context for Waymon's personal and professional struggles.

The three significant white characters in *Strictly Business* are Mr. Drake, Waymon's boss; David, Waymon's colleague and competitor; and Gary, David's protégé and Bobby's former mailroom coworker. Each bears a different relationship to whiteness. As boss of the company and the resident patriarch, Mr. Drake holds the power to make or break Waymon's career. The film characterizes him as kind, fair, and authoritative, similar to other such patriarchal tropes found in films like *Working Girl*, thus reinforcing the notion that, for minority characters in these types of films, success is only possible when conferred or validated by a white, heterosexual man.[12] The viewer first sees Waymon's colleague David, the most significant white character in the film, when he and Waymon enter the office building together: the similarity between the men's attire and actions (they both approach the receptionist for their mail and messages) constructs them as professional equals and eventual rivals. After the receptionist gives a chilly response to David, we learn that he has had a previous sexual encounter with the woman but subsequently dumped her. The film will recall this incident later in the plot. Finally, there is Gary, a young man who worked with Bobby in the mailroom but who gets promoted into the training program once David decides to sponsor him (the same training program to which Bobby sought entry). Though in many ways these characters are standard fare for a workplace-centered comedy, their presence within a predominantly black cast complements the various types of racial performance taking place throughout the film.

Less obvious are the ways that the film uses David and Gary as examples of the pitfalls of "acting white," which carry important implications and warnings for the black characters. Though Waymon is under the impression that David is his friend, the film has him ignore several clues to the true nature of David's character. In one scene, David and another white coworker disparage Harlem and then jokingly question whether Waymon has ever visited the neighborhood or, in fact, grew up there. The "jokes" are actually racial microaggressions, defined by critical race scholars and psychologists as "brief and commonplace daily verbal, behavioral, or environmental indignities, whether intentional or unintentional, that communicate hostile, derogatory, or negative racial slights and insults toward people of color."[13] Interestingly, Bobby is the first to identify David as a racist, though Waymon is quick to jump to David's defense. The film thus suggests that Waymon cannot recognize, or "see," racism, and this links Waymon to notions of "color-blindness" that attempt to pass off a willful denial of race as an example of racial progressiveness. Waymon is indeed "acting white" by pretending as if his own color and the subtle racism of his coworkers do not exist.

The film reinforces this concept of acting white toward the end of the film, when Waymon and Natalie break up. After having finally romantically connected, Natalie visits Waymon at the office. Distracted by a business deal that has just fallen apart (which Waymon mistakenly believes Bobby to be responsible for), Waymon treats Natalie in a dismissive manner, prompting her to storm out of the office and resulting in a very public confrontation between the couple at Waymon's place of business. The scene functions as a callback to David's interaction with the receptionist at the beginning of the film, thus suggesting that Waymon's callous treatment of a woman that he has just slept with is also a form of "acting white."

David's protégé and Bobby's friend, Gary O'Hara, offers a slightly different version of whiteness in the film. Ethnic and working class, Gary is the white version of Bobby. These factors place him in a particularly interesting subject position, as his whiteness is the lone asset that he has at his disposal. Unlike Mr. Drake and David, Gary does not benefit from financial or educational privilege, and he does not hold any power within the company. Thus, although he is white, he also occupies a marginalized identity at work, like Bobby and Waymon. And, like Bobby and Waymon, Gary seeks professional advancement as a means to better his life. Thus, even though he is friends with Bobby and is an honest person, he acquiesces to David's plan. Though he appears to benefit from his whiteness via his connection with David, we later learn that he is a pawn in David's schemes. In the end, Gary's confession leads to the revelation that David is an unscrupulous businessman as well as a racist. By choosing to turn on David and realign himself with Bobby, Gary rejects his most obvious means of advancement—his connection to David. Thus, I would argue that Gary essentially rejects at least a

FIGURE 2.5. David and Gary in *Strictly Business*.

portion of his whiteness. His refusal to "act white" and cover up for David is about his rejection of his own white privilege and his subsequent solidarity with his black friend.

Placed within this context, what it means for Waymon to "act white" is about more than just his clothes and speech—it is about the fact that whiteness itself is presented as undesirable in the film. Hal Hinson, a *Washington Post* film critic, noted this theme yet bristled at its implications. Observing that the film aimed many of its comedic barbs at Waymon's lack of blackness, Hinson writes, "By the movie's standards, there's nothing worse than this. And, it is not just a question of a black man acting white; it's being white period that's bad."[14] Hinson continues with this scathing assessment of the film and its director: "While denouncing prejudice, Hooks bottles his own brand of reverse racism and sexism."[15]

It is worth unpacking Hinson's claim of "reverse racism" because it exposes both the typical invisibility of whiteness and the angry reaction that occurs when whiteness is "outed." Dwight McBride argues that the language of reverse discrimination is an attempt by whites and the political right to reclaim what they perceive as "special privileges" enjoyed by minorities. He writes, "Victim status has become sacred turf in the battle for 'special privileges' that, conservatives have argued, blacks and other people of color used for their own gain."[16] At best, Hinson's statement about the director Kevin Hooks's "reverse racism" ignores the antiblack social reality in which the characters in *Strictly Business* find themselves and in which the film was made.[17] At worst, such a pronouncement places the burden of negotiating racial identity on the shoulders of the black characters and director, thereby missing one of the film's truths—namely, that the system of racial oppression necessitates a rejection of whiteness in favor of cultural solidarity and cooperation.

This last point largely went unnoticed by the critics, but it is perhaps the film's most powerful, albeit subtle, statement. Though Waymon does indeed learn to "act black" by the end of the film, his final professional triumph comes by way of a group of black businessmen who save his real estate deal. When the film first introduces the Halloran brothers, we see them sitting in a Harlem bar speaking with Natalie. Waymon assumes them to be involved in illegal activity, due to his own stereotypes about the neighborhood and other African Americans. Interestingly, however, the film trusts that the audience shares Waymon's misperception, as the final plot twist relies on the reveal of the Halloran brothers as the owners of the Harlem Savings and Loan Bank. The Halloran brothers serve as the film's exemplars of the "right" way to be black: they speak in black vernacular, maintain ties to the community, but are also incredibly professionally successful. Their success comes from their investment in the community, literally and figuratively. The reveal at the end highlights the correct path for Waymon as well as connects to Bobby's earlier speech to Waymon (and the audience) about the perils of snap judgments. Ultimately, this plot resolution rewards cultural blackness, which places the charge of reverse racism in a clearer context. In the end, it is not being white that the film criticizes, but accepting the ideology that "acting white" is—in its behavioral and structural forms—preferable to "acting black."

Livin' Large: Media as Threat to Blackness

While *Strictly Business* deals with the aspects of "selling out," the 1991 film *Livin' Large* makes this cautionary tale a literal one. The movie follows an aspiring news reporter, Dexter Jackson (Terrence "T. C." Carson), as he confronts the pressures to conform to the cultural and behavioral standards that are presented to him. As Dexter grows more successful, he makes a series of compromises that win him increased professional success but at the loss of his loved ones, his community, and his own black identity.

Livin' Large presents Dexter's increasing whiteness, or his "loss of soul," as a media-specific illness. Throughout the film, though Dexter's transformation is evidenced in a number of ways, the most striking illustration is when Dexter witnesses his televised image turn white before his very eyes. Each instance occurs after Dexter has committed a particularly heinous crime against his community or his own sense of self. The first instance comes after Dexter charges a popular local soul food restaurant with damaging the health of its patrons by serving fatty, fried foods. Sitting at home in his new apartment (which is painted white and contains all-white furniture), Dexter watches his image on the television and then is startled to see that the image has a narrower nose, thinner lips, and straight hair. The instances progress: when Dexter exposes a local car thief who is also black, his television image develops lighter skin and blue eyes. By the end of the film, when Dexter agrees to marry his white coworker in order to boost ratings and solidify his on-air popularity, he watches in horror as his completely whitewashed image—keen-featured, blue-eyed, white-skinned, and blonde—stares back at him from the television. Though the film is comedic, these surreal scenes border on horror, calling to mind, in particular, William Crain's blaxploitation horror film *Dr. Black and Mr. Hyde* (1976), where a mild-mannered black doctor accidentally transforms himself into a white-skinned, monstrous version of himself. Though it is not clear whether *Livin' Large*'s African American director, Michael Schultz, was familiar with the 1976 film, the film's straddling of generic boundaries suggests one of the significant ways in which the sellout films break from the constraints of realism in the interest of telling their stories.

By limiting the whiteface to Dexter's televised image, *Livin' Large* presents the media as the means by which African Americans' identities can be erased or made more aesthetically and culturally "mainstream." Furthermore, by making Dexter both image and spectator, the film taps into discourses about the damaging psychological impact that "negative" black representations might have on African Americans' perceptions of themselves. The film presents the media-viewer relationship as symbiotic and mutually affective: Dexter's betrayals cause his image to become whiter, which in turn has an unsettling impact on the real Dexter watching the image. In the first instance where his image has straighter hair but is still brown-skinned, Dexter wears tan pants and a colorful patterned shirt. The next time he wears a suit. When his image is finally completely and unmis-

FIGURE 2.6. Dexter regards his whitened media image in *Livin' Large*.

takably white, Dexter appears dressed in an all-white tuxedo (in prepara-
tion for his wedding).

This warning against the destructive power of the media continues to
gain momentum through the use of the whiteface image. Toward the end
of the film, the image ceases to be a mere reflection of Dexter and takes
on a life of its own, teasing Dexter, giving him orders, and finally insulting
him by referring to him as a "stupid ass nigger" when Dexter refuses to
marry his white co-anchor. Impervious to Dexter's attempts to turn off the
television, the image only disappears when Dexter unquestionably states
his commitment to being black and violently breaks the television set. This
explicit connection between whiteness and the media suggests a criticism
not only of upward mobility but also of the so-called progress that would
seem to be signaled by an increase in the number of black images on television, a focus on quantity rather than quality. Schultz began his career in the
1970s with notable films such as *Cooley High* (1975) and *Car Wash* (1976),
and he thus had lived through the blaxploitation boom of the era followed
by the relative scarcity of black-cast films in the 1980s. It is not surprising,

FIGURE 2.7. Dexter as a news anchor.

then, that *Livin' Large* presents a cynical perspective on the possibilities of media representation or, specifically, what happens when African Americans lose control of their representations.

The anxiety over losing control that the film portrays echoes Mark Anthony Neal's concern about "the void of both community and history for the post-soul generation" and the production of "a generation of consumers for which the iconography of blackness is consumed in lieu of personal relations, real experience, and historical knowledge."[18] The fear evidenced in *Livin' Large* is that Dexter's black image will turn into little more than a marketable commodity for the news media, one that is quite literally devoid of any blackness. Even Dexter's final image as a newscaster—blazer, kente-cloth vest, a hairstyle that is neater and more controlled than before—suggests that his ultimate success is based on a newly refined and commodified version of his black self. However, although Dexter does succeed with a "new and improved" blackness, the film's final message is that there is a place for Dexter's blackness in a professional setting because he *creates*, rather than *finds*, a version of racial identity that works for him.

The whiteface in the film visually represents Dexter's struggle to carve out a black identity that will be both personally satisfying and professionally acceptable. In the end, Dexter's true success is not that he becomes a popular newscaster, but that he does so without sacrificing his racial subjectivity.

True Identity: Race as Strategic Performance

Like *Livin' Large*, *True Identity* takes up the issue of representations of African Americans in the media, also featuring the transformation from white to black. In contrast to *Livin' Large*, however, *True Identity* uses race switching not as a warning against "selling out," but as a strategy for survival in a racist world. The actor/comedian Lenny Henry plays Miles Pope, a struggling actor who must disguise himself as a white man in order to escape a hit put out on him by the Mafia. The plot weaves the story of Miles's survival with his efforts to become a successful actor, playing the types of parts he deems worthwhile. In this way, *True Identity* sets itself up as a commentary both on the relationship between African Americans and the entertainment industry and on the strategies employed by African Americans to "survive" in a hostile society.

Miles's performance of different types of whiteness suggests the ways in which white identity is itself an unstable construct that is defined against other forms of racial and ethnic identity. Many examples of whiteface in the media present a very specific type of whiteness that fails to acknowledge the range of diversity of white identities, lapsing into what the scholar Bambi Haggins refers to as "a cartoon version of whiteness" that lacks resemblance to actual white people.[19] *True Identity*, however, plays with the concept of the varieties of whiteness. Though Miles's physical appearance while in his white disguise remains constant, he shifts his performance to signify different types of whiteness, depending on the situation in which he finds himself. When Mafia hitmen arrive to kill Miles, he portrays a WASP-y, yuppie form of whiteness. Later, when the same hitmen mistake Miles for one of their own, Miles changes his demeanor to perform a version of stereotypically Italian speech and demeanor, even taking on the persona of the actual Sicilian hitman whom Miles accidentally killed in self-defense.[20] In addition, the white characters themselves perform a type of whiteface. Frank Langella plays Leland Carver, an Italian American Mafia boss who adopts a WASP persona to hide *his* "true identity" from the authorities and rival mobsters. In this way, the film displays the many ways in which white identity is constantly in a process of destabilization and reconstitution.

Valerie Smith argues that *True Identity* is a film that is all about the performance of identities, within and across boundaries of race, gender, and class. Citing the examples I just mentioned, Smith contends that the film shows the ways in which passing occurs in spaces outside the black/white binary. By understanding the film as illustrating the concept of "passing," Smith argues that *True Identity* differs from other passing films (such as Douglas Sirk's 1959 melodrama *Imitation of Life*) in part because it presents *all* identities, not just blacks passing as white, as performances. She writes, "Miles's performance as pimp, Othello, Darryl Brown (James Brown's fictional brother), Frank La Motta, indeed, even Lenny Henry's performance as Miles Pope himself, points to a range of black (and indeed white) types and indicates the extent to which racial identity is shaped by issues of class, region, and nation."[21] The film thus highlights the more nuanced types of passing that typically escape conventional nonwhiteface narratives. Lenny Henry is himself passing as American (he is British), Miles passes as other types of black characters, and even ethnic white characters are revealed to be passing for WASPS.

The film links Miles's literal survival to his success in the world of acting, as evidenced by the various identities that he must believably take on in order to stay alive. This supports an assessment of *True Identity* as a truly *postsoul, postblack* film, in which all forms of identity are essentially performative acts. In addition, I contend that in *True Identity*, the sojourn into white subjectivity is one of necessity in a society structured to ensure African Americans' failure. Therefore, I want to nuance Smith's assessment of the film: Miles Pope does not treat whiteness as just another performance; it is, quite literally, the role *for* his life. His initial and immediate disgust at his whiteface disguise ("I don't want to be white!") indicates that he views the physical transformation from black to white as something other than just theatrical performance and more as the type of performance that constructs one's identity, in the way that Judith Butler and others have argued so convincingly about gender and sexual identity.

By showing the process of Miles's transformation, *True Identity* makes the point that all identity, but particularly white identity, must be created, reinforced, and properly performed in order to be successful. The scenes that show Miles applying his whiteface makeup lay the foundation for all of the other scenes that depict Miles and the "real" white characters applying the other markers of whiteness: language, behavior, mannerisms, and so on. If the whiteface makeup is simply a veneer, then so are these other indicators of white identity.

Unlike *Strictly Business* and *Livin' Large*, which portray whiteness as incompatible with black subjectivity, *True Identity*'s very literal representation of "acting white" treats it as a vehicle for black solidarity and black empowerment. In one scene, for instance, a whitefaced Miles hails a cab for another black man on the street who is unable to get one to stop. Another scene connects Miles not only to a larger black community but also to a larger history of whiteface representation. Miles is on the run from the mobsters and hops into a cab to make a quick getaway; the actor/director Melvin Van Peebles has a cameo as the cab driver. With Miles applying his whiteface makeup in the backseat, Van Peebles begins a lecture about how white people need to remember their heritage, a coy and knowing reference to his own satirical whiteface film, *Watermelon Man* (1970).[22] He continues that there is only one way for a black man to make it in the white man's world, and the camera cuts to Miles, now fully made up in his whiteface disguise.

This wry bit of humor punctuates the idea that acting white is a strategy that African Americans can use to navigate a racially hostile world. *True Identity* offers a nuanced view of how individuals perform identities in the media as well as in social situations, but it also retains a sense that such performances must always maintain a responsibility to the greater black community. Whether it is Miles's use of his temporary white body to assist a fellow brother on the street, or his desire to play well-respected parts such as Othello instead of pimps and hustlers, the film argues that identity performance is not simply "play."[23] Instead, it is a strategy for survival.

The Associate and Intersectionality

The sellout films that I have discussed up to this point challenge rigid standards of blackness, particularly in their attempts to deal with an upwardly mobile black middle class. However, these critiques of certain models of blackness often run the risk of resurrecting other, equally troubling, images of black identity and behavior, a tension that Mark Anthony Neal views as emblematic of the postsoul aesthetic. Most often, these films rely on gender tropes to anchor the narratives and characters, even as they actively challenge racial stereotypes. In *Livin' Large*, for example, Dexter demonstrates

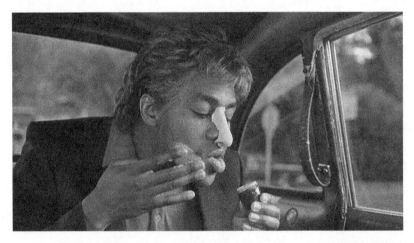

FIGURE 2.8. Miles applies his makeup in *True Identity*.

FIGURE 2.9. Cameo by Melvin Van Peebles in *True Identity*.

stereotypical displays of sexist behavior toward his white female coworker to signal his return to the "right" kind of black manhood. And *Strictly Business* problematically equates female ambition with whiteness and emasculation on the one hand, and hypersexuality with racial authenticity and sexual desirability on the other. Thus, even though these films work to critique certain models of assimilation, they often fall back on misogynistic concepts of gender (though this is certainly not limited to the sellout films). I would argue, however, that these flaws are consistent with the ambivalence that Neal describes in the postsoul aesthetic, the "meta-identities" that incorporate both modern and "premodern concepts of blackness."[24] In fact, a particular strength of the sellout films is the way that they illustrate this ambivalence by virtue of their engagement with whiteness and whiteface.

The Associate explores the consequences of the very same strategy when employed by black women. The film's depiction of the obstacles facing Whoopi Goldberg's character, Laurel, as well as the harsh critical responses to the film demonstrate the struggles of trying to speak to issues of racism and sexism simultaneously. The film illustrates, in a literal and figurative fashion, the ways in which a society that privileges whiteness and maleness renders black women invisible. Significantly, the critical reviews of the film fall prey to the same sexist and racist attitudes that the film tries so hard to elucidate. Like Hinson's review of *Strictly Business* where he charged the film with reverse racism, these reviews of *The Associate* show the challenges of representing black women's intersectionality in popular media.

In *The Associate*, Goldberg plays Laurel Ayres, a Wall Street investment broker who is passed up for a well-deserved promotion in favor of the mediocre, white male colleague that she trained. Frustrated with a system that ignores her hard work and talent, Laurel leaves her successful firm in order to start her own business. She quickly discovers, however, that the white men who refused to promote her are standard types within the financial world, and she is unable to find anyone even willing to take a meeting with her. In a moment of desperation and quick thinking, Laurel invents an imaginary business partner named Robert Cutty. White, male, and older, Cutty lands Laurel meetings, acclaim, expensive cigars, and sexually available women. When she can no longer make excuses for why Cutty never appears in person, Laurel dons whiteface drag and manages to deceive even the most curious and prodding individuals. Laurel's creation quickly spirals out of her control, however, and she discovers that her colleagues would rather deal with a nonexistent white man than with a very real black woman. She attempts to "kill" her creation but finds herself framed for his murder. In the end, Laurel finds a way to destroy her creation once and for all and establish a very successful business on her own, taking another marginalized woman (an older, white secretary) as her new, real partner.

The Associate takes the invisibility of black women as its theme, and it quite explicitly argues that this invisibility is the result of an active process that renders white masculinity as the norm at the expense of women such as Laurel. Her very existence cannot be recognized until an unseen, white male partner validates it. The film is heavy-handed with this message: clients call and ask to speak with Robert Cutty, actually refusing to speak with Laurel and being very vocal about their desire to deal with a white man rather than a black woman. In one notable scene, a white billionaire tells Laurel that when he hears the word "firm," he expects to see two men. Individuals only engage her in order to get closer to the mysteriously absent Robert Cutty, and clients regularly fail to notice Laurel in the room: they are quite literally "color-blind." The film demonstrates how a white man who exists only in people's imaginations still has the power to erase the existence of a flesh-and-blood black woman. Of course, the film makes it clear that Laurel was already quite invisible well before she invented her partner, and that her invisibility is the direct result of the numerous white men who form the good old boys' club of Wall Street, with the fictitious Robert Cutty being the one who puts the final nail in her coffin.

In addition to its bold sermon about the position of black women in the workplace in relation to white men, the film supports this message in its structure. Unlike films such as *White Chicks* (Keenen Ivory Wayans, 2004), *The Associate* avoids showing Goldberg in her whiteface drag as Cutty through most of the movie. Laurel's first appearance as Cutty comes in the second half of the film, and her total time in drag and whiteface is fairly brief. In spite of the sensational spectacle of Whoopi Goldberg playing a white man, the film refuses to provide a physical manifestation of Laurel's partner for the majority of the story, allowing Laurel to take center stage and become visible, if not to her colleagues, then to the film's viewers.[25] If Cutty is the figure that continually erases Laurel's identity, then the film rejects a narrative device that might condemn Goldberg's black female body to the same fate.

The film also uses a clear distinction between white male space and female space to emphasize Laurel's inability to break the glass ceiling. When

FIGURE 2.10. Whoopi Goldberg as Laurel in *The Associate*.

she goes to an exclusive social club in order to meet with a prospective client, she quickly learns that women are not allowed beyond the lobby. In another scene, Laurel sends a celebrity golfer to take her place at a golf-course business meeting. What these scenes demonstrate is Laurel's inability to penetrate white male spaces. Though she eventually finds ways around this, the fact remains that Laurel is both literally and figuratively barred from the settings and situations where deals are brokered and decisions are made.

Despite the explicitness of the narrative, critics in the popular press managed to overlook this purposeful representational strategy and then, in their criticism of *The Associate*, reinforced the same structure that the film challenges. Malcolm Johnson of the Hartford *Courant* gives the film a moderately good rating, writing, "While much of Petrie's film is instantly forgettable, its star's cross-dressing turn sustains it."[26] The title of Jay Boyar's review, "Star's Get-Up Is Only Funny Thing in *The Associate*," loudly proclaims the direction that the rest of the review will take. Boyar argues that "the first sight of Goldberg in her white-male outfit was the high point."[27] Others decried the film as a less-funny derivative of *Tootsie* (Sydney Pollack, 1982), *Mrs. Doubtfire* (Chris Columbus, 1993), or *The First Wives Club* (Hugh Wilson, 1996). Stephen Holden of the *New York Times* also cited the shortage of scenes of Laurel in whiteface as a shortcoming, writing, "*The Associate* is so nervous on the star's behalf that it keeps putting off the big moment."[28] The consistency of these reviews is telling, for they seem to ignore that the film is about Laurel's struggles as a smart, capable black woman who cannot get her talents recognized in the white patriarchal business world, no matter how hard she tries. By criticizing *The Associate* for not privileging her white, male creation, the reviewers inadvertently underscore how deep the problem truly runs. Roger Ebert, in a particularly telling review, faults Goldberg for apparently not making Robert Cutty warm and fuzzy enough. He demands, "Does she make the man into a character we like and care about? Not at all."[29]

Reviewers also consistently ignored the importance of race in the film. Stephen Holden's *New York Times* review even cites the film as "admirably if oddly color blind," noting that the few mentions of Laurel's blackness are made in passing.[30] Interestingly, *The Associate* does avoid talking about race, at least directly. Laurel often refers to the discrimination she faces as resulting from her status as a woman, not as a black woman. This may be because typical Hollywood treatments of employment discrimination have dealt with either sexism *or* racism, but rarely both simultaneously. Thus, Laurel's experience of sexist discrimination is more legible within the Hollywood story world. Indeed, when race is explicitly mentioned, it is usually the white female secretary, Sally, who makes the comments. For example, when Laurel initially disguises herself as Cutty, she tells the makeup artist to make her old and male. It is Sally who supplies the additional qualifier: white. The use of Sally to literally speak race into the film recalls the legal scholar Devon W. Carbado's discussion of privilege. Carbado explains how whiteness functions as a source of legitimation, writing, "There is a tendency on the part of dominant groups (e.g., males and heterosexuals) to discount the experiences of subordinate groups (e.g., straight women, lesbians, and gays) unless those experiences are authenticated or legitimized by a member of the dominant group."[31] Thus the white Sally functions as the "objective" voice within the film that is allowed to speak about racism.

Though *The Associate* may not frequently call out whiteness by name, the film does, in fact, construct whiteness and maleness as intertwined forces that quickly grow out of Laurel's control and threaten to wipe out her already tenuous existence, thus revisiting the monstrous quality of whiteness found in *Livin' Large*. In the film, she laments, "Even when I create the perfect man, he stabs me in the back." This view of whiteness deconstructs it as normal and benign and positions it as a very real and active threat. In her work, bell hooks elaborates on this sinister aspect of whiteness by exploring the complicated relationship that African Americans have to

FIGURE 2.11. Laurel as her creation, Robert Cutty.

FIGURE 2.12. Laurel and Sally discuss Robert Cutty.

whites and to whiteness more broadly. She writes, "Socialized to believe the fantasy, that whiteness represents goodness and all that is benign and non-threatening, many white people assume this is the way black people conceptualize whiteness. They do not imagine that the way whiteness makes its presence felt in black life, most often as terrorizing imposition, a power that wounds, hurts, tortures, is a reality that disrupts the fantasy of whiteness as representing goodness."[32]

The representation of whiteness and maleness as a two-headed Frankenstein that threatens to destroy Laurel disrupts the notion of whiteness as goodness and echoes the terror that is present in hooks's description. It also signals the larger problem of invisible norms of race and gender at work. At first, Laurel believes that she has created the monster of her own accord. She eventually comes to realize that what she has actually done is give independent life to the hidden forms of power that have been in operation all along. In her attempt to invoke whiteness, she mistakes access for control and finds herself at the mercy of the same forces that she attempted to escape in the first place.

The fact that the critics missed this aspect of *The Associate* may have as much to do with Goldberg's own star persona as the plot of the film. Bambi Haggins argues that Goldberg's physical appearance, choice in roles, and personal relationships have made her a prime target for charges of not being "black enough." In 1994, for example, Goldberg received a huge amount of negative publicity from black celebrities and the black press for defending then-boyfriend Ted Danson's blackface routine at Goldberg's Friars Club roast. In an interview with *Ebony* magazine in 1994, Halle Berry explained why she decided to walk out of Goldberg's roast as soon as Danson began his bit: "I can't ignore how it made me feel. Just as I respect Whoopi as a Black woman, I have to respect myself as a Black woman. And that means standing up for what I believe to be right. That night, I said what's right for me is to get the hell out of here."[33] Berry's words work to construct a positive/negative binary between herself and Goldberg. She presents herself as a specific type of black woman—the type who will not stand to be disrespected—in direct opposition to Goldberg, who went on the offensive in her defense of not only Danson's actions but also the principles of free speech that she claimed that his jokes represented.[34]

It is difficult to discern, however, how much of the vitriol directed at Goldberg was because of stunts like the one at the Friars Club or whether it was simply an attempt to demonize a woman who refused to stay in her predetermined "place" in society. Born Caryn Johnson, the star's name change to the Jewish "Goldberg" first signaled to the world a willful transgression of racial boundaries. Goldberg "flaunted" her very public relationship with Ted Danson (a white actor) when the couple starred together as onscreen lovers in the film *Made in America* (Richard Benjamin, 1993). And *Made in America* was only one of a number of other films in which Goldberg was paired with a white love interest. Other pairings include Sam Elliott in *Fatal Beauty* (Tom Holland, 1987) and Ray Liotta in *Corrina, Corrina* (Jessie Nelson, 1994). By breaking social taboos on interracial dating and what might be considered acceptable codes of behavior for African American women, I argue that the apparent lack of explicit discussion of race or racism cited in reviews of *The Associate* is not so much about the film itself as much as it is about the attitudes of a society that viewed Goldberg's own racial identification as suspicious in the first place.

In other words, the issue is not that *The Associate* ignores race, but that Goldberg was already positioned extratextually as someone whose blackness was in question. One wonders whether the critics would have charged a film starring a more avowedly "black" actress with color-blindness or if her mere presence would have stood as a testament to the film's engagement with race. Furthermore, such critiques take for granted that *The Associate* needs to announce Laurel's blackness explicitly in order to make race a recognizable issue in the film. By contrast, *The Associate* only mentions Cutty's whiteness once, a fact that does not stand in the way of understanding the significance of white identity in the corporate business world.

In fact, *The Associate* weaves gender and race into its story, but it chooses to foreground the former and to express the latter in coded ways.[35] For example, at the end of the film, Laurel lectures the all-white, male assembly about the consequences of their exclusivity. She says that the next great achievements in business could come from those individuals who are normally overlooked (e.g., invisible). As she speaks, the camera cuts to the figures of individual black men who work as servers at the club in which the event is taking place. Even though it has not been stated up until this point, the camera indicates that we are supposed to recognize that gender *and* race are factors contributing to invisibility.

The Associate also uses other elements to signal blackness even when Laurel's experiences do not explicitly speak to it. The film relies on black gospel music to punctuate sentimental moments. Black women artists provide most of the other music. The rap group Salt-n-Pepa's "What a Man" punctuates the moment when Laurel closes an important business deal, and Jean Knight's "Mr. Big Stuff" emphasizes her continued success. The in-joke, of course, is that the viewer hears a series of black women's voices telling stories about men, an amusing selection that fits with the theme of Laurel's experiences. In this way, *The Associate* employs a black aesthetic, perhaps even a womanist one, by privileging black women's voices to give meaning and context to the images that appear onscreen. This is in direct opposition to the white men who had up to that point dominated Laurel's professional life.[36]

The film uses coy techniques such as the musical soundtrack to stage Laurel's multiple sites of oppression within the white, male-dominated world of Wall Street. The ways in which the film constructs its narrative of dual oppression also speak to the issue of the invisibility of black women's perspectives in media representation. In her essay "Demarginalizing the Intersection of Race and Sex," the legal scholar Kimberlé Crenshaw discusses the problems that arise when black women's experiences are analyzed along a single axis of either gender oppression or racial oppression. She writes, "Because the intersectional experience is greater than the sum of racism and sexism, any analysis that does not take intersectionality into account cannot sufficiently address the particular manner in which Black women are subordinated."[37] She later continues, "The point is that Black women can experience discrimination in any number of ways and that the contradiction arises from our assumptions that their claims of exclusion must be unidirectional."[38] Thus, although the film wants to express that Laurel is victimized by both racism and sexism, it cannot conceive of a way to highlight both of these directly and equally while adhering to the standard representational methods of Hollywood cinema. Unable to render what Deborah K. King would call Laurel's multiple jeopardy and multiple consciousness into a conventional cinematic narrative, it foregrounds gender in the narrative while using music and cinematography to address race.[39]

Conclusion

Though they lack the social realism or the "ripped from the headlines" urgency of their hood counterparts, the films that I have surveyed here offer varying solutions to the problem of how to succeed in white corporate America. While missing the dramatic punch of something like *Menace II Society*, films such as *Strictly Business* deal with an aspect of black identity that continues to animate discussion today—namely, what it means to be "black enough" or what it means to "act white"—questions that have swirled, for instance, around Barack Obama ever since he first campaigned for the presidency in 2008. And while many of these films offer easy answers to these questions, ones that sometimes fall back on regressive models of masculinity, for instance, their exploration of these issues marks them as important artifacts of a time when racial identities and concerns about "selling out" dominated cultural and political spheres. The 1990s, after all, was the decade when hip hop gained traction outside of black spaces. It was also the decade when Spike Lee would score on the critical and commercial fronts with his film *Malcolm X* yet would face harsh criticism for his decision to market *X* merchandise. The 1990s was also the last decade in which individuals would have to choose a single race or ethnicity to identify with on the U.S. Census. Beginning in 2000 (based on a decision made in 1997), Americans would be able, for the first time, to mark multiple boxes to identify their racial identity. It is not surprising, then, that with these debates over cultural and racial authenticity in the air, the same anxieties would make their way into cinema.

Strictly Business, *Livin' Large*, *True Identity*, and *The Associate* question what it really means for African Americans to "make it" in a white man's world. While these films do not renounce capitalism or corporate America, they do understand it as an inherently foreign and hostile space for black culture and identity. While each film differs in the way that it represents the tension between personal identity and professional ambition, they all share certain important characteristics that link them as a countercanon to the more often-cited hood films of the same time period. Organizing their narratives around themes of "acting white," including the frequent literal depiction of whiteness, these sellout films question whether the prize of professional success is worth the risk of losing one's soul.

THE CIRCUMSTANTIAL NEGATIVITY
OF HALLE BERRY

This moment is so much bigger than me. This moment is for Dorothy Dandridge, Lena Horne, Diahann Carroll. It's for the women that stand beside me, Jada Pinkett, Angela Bassett, Vivica Fox. And it's for every nameless, faceless woman of color that now has a chance because this door tonight has been opened. —HALLE BERRY

Why Halle have to let a white man pop her to get a Oscar? —JADAKISS, "Why"

As I have already mentioned in my discussion of the "hood" versus the "sellout" films, critiques of certain models of blackness often run the risk of resurrecting other, equally troubling, images of black identity and behavior, particularly at the intersection of race and gender. Mark Anthony Neal argues that this particular moment of 1990s black culture can be identified by a constant renegotiation of past iterations of blackness. Yet black cinema proves to be a complicated object in this regard, given that there is no true "past" in the history of black media representations. Racial stereotypes are etched into both the social fabric of the nation and the celluloid of its films. Without the necessary distance between a sense of past and present, cinematic musings on blackness always run the risk of simply reanimating problematic modes of representation without reflexivity.

The actress Halle Berry proves insightful in this regard, as Berry has often struggled to escape the rigid cinematic tropes of black femininity throughout her career. Though her first attention-grabbing role was as a crack addict in *Jungle Fever* (Spike Lee, 1991), the former beauty queen's subsequent parts portrayed her as an alluring-but-accessible girl next door. Before making the jump to mainstream (read: white) films, Berry's early roles emphasized her good looks, highlighting her attractiveness without characterizing the young actress as too overtly sexual. She played beguiling dancers in both *Strictly Business* (Kevin Hooks, 1991) and *The Last Boy Scout* (Tony Scott, 1991), as well as Eddie Murphy's kindhearted love interest in *Boomerang* (Reginald Hudlin, 1992), leading a *New York Times* film reviewer, Janet Maslin, to refer to Berry as "the delectably sweet actress who looks and sounds as if she stepped right out of a teen-age girls' magazine."[1] In this early stage, Berry played unambiguously black characters located in predominantly black settings, a stark contrast to the roles that she would eventually take on later in her career.

Although Berry may have enjoyed relative freedom from stereotypes in the films and television programs in which she starred, publicity and press surrounding the actress marketed and categorized her within the same limited classifications that Hollywood has always used for black actresses. Regardless of her protests to the contrary, Berry became synonymous with preestablished models of black femininity, ones that had been cemented in Hollywood decades before her arrival. Though Berry seemed to break the color barriers that typically relegated black women to tired tropes such as the jezebel or the mammy, Berry's ascension to the Hollywood A-list did not result in her ability to transcend Hollywood's stereotypes.[2] Rather, at each star-making turn in Berry's career, the popular press and public opinion seemed to double down on shoehorning the actress into a premade category. Over the course of just over ten years, Berry would occupy three distinct categorical tropes that encompassed clear racialized and gendered connotations. These tropes include the "around-the-way girl," the "tragic mulatto," and "the white man's whore." Though Berry would fight against the latter two characterizations in both interviews and her selection of roles, the labels took on a life of their own, with Berry's own articulations about her identity taking a backseat. Tellingly, each shift in Berry's onscreen persona was accompanied by a change in the public's perception of the actress.

Whereas Berry had been a popular "It girl" during her early career, she suddenly became the butt of jokes and criticism, most notably around the time that she made *Monster's Ball* (Marc Forster, 2001), a film that won Berry a historic Academy Award for Best Actress and also a film in which she appeared in a graphic sex scene with a white actor, Billy Bob Thornton. But what is the relationship between Berry's ascent to box-office success and the hit that her public image took at roughly the same time? Though some may claim that Berry's personal life—two highly public and volatile relationships with the French Canadian model Gabriel Aubry and then the French actor Olivier Martinez (both white men)—damaged her cover-girl reputation, these turbulent affairs only confirmed a narrative that had been building around Berry for some time: Halle Berry as race traitor. But when and how did this transformation happen? The answer, I argue, lies with Berry's casting in the CBS television miniseries *Queen* (1993). It is Berry's appearance in *Queen* that marks the transition point for Berry from black-cast films to predominantly white ones. Given the buzz surrounding Berry at this early stage in her career, it is no surprise that she won the lead in the well-publicized miniseries, a sequel to Alex Haley's momentous 1977 miniseries *Roots*. Yet, prior to *Queen*, there was little about Berry's star persona to suggest that she fit the tragic mulatto trope of the titular character. As I have already mentioned, up to this point she had played decidedly black characters, and the bulk of her films had all-black casts. How, then, did Berry pull off a part where she played a woman passing for white? And how did appearing in *Queen* radically shift the types of films in which she would be cast from that point forward? In this chapter, I trace Berry's professional trajectory and intertextual celebrity persona, focusing primarily on her transformation into *Queen*'s "tragic mulatto," and I argue that the miniseries signals not only a turning point for the young actress's career but also a case study of the mutually constitutive nature of media and "real life."

The "Around-the-Way Girl"

Prior to *Queen*, nearly every interview or magazine article about Berry highlighted her inherent kindness, poise, and grace. Berry's well-publicized background as a beauty queen reinforced those qualities in the actress. While early press about Berry emphasized her attractiveness, it overwhelmingly concentrated on her sweetness and humility. Speaking of her beauty-pageant background with *People* magazine, Berry stated, "I learned to be a good winner—and a good loser. Which helps my acting; every day I face rejection."[3] The emphasis on Berry's beauty-pageant background—an industry with a long history of both intentional and circumstantial exclusion of African Americans—had another effect as well: it connoted Berry's ease in predominantly white spaces. Though, as I discussed in the previous chapter, 1990s Hollywood favored niche marketing over the promotion of a singular crossover star, Berry seemed to be the figure on whom both approaches converged.

This emphasis on sweetness and mainstream acceptability was crucial to Berry's appeal, but so was her blackness. Berry functioned in her early-career films as an "around-the-way girl": beautiful, grounded, kind, and culturally black. The rapper LL Cool J immortalized the notion of the "around-the-way girl" in his 1990 song of the same title. The opening verse—now famous—offers a description of the young woman in question: "I want a girl with extensions in her hair. Bamboo earrings, at least two pair. A Fendi bag and a bad attitude. That's all I need to get me in a good mood."[4] The young woman that LL Cool J describes in his song is at once an object of men's sexual desires while also being accessible and relatable, as the rapper captures in the line, "She can walk with a switch and talk with street slang." The core idea, then, of the "around-the-way girl" is one who seamlessly toggles between identities: casual attire vs. designer clothing, street slang vs. refined speech, lover vs. friend, sweet vs. fierce. Berry embodied this juxtaposition in the early phase of her career, nowhere more perfectly than in the film *Boomerang.* In that film, Berry's beauty and sweetness combined to win the heart of not only Eddie Murphy's lead character, but of audiences, too. Berry appeared as the sweet young woman to whom Murphy's character turns when his girlfriend breaks his heart. Even the name of Berry's character in that film—Angela—conveyed the innocence and goodness with which the actress herself was becoming associated.

Complicating the notion of the "around-the-way girl" further, the type is essentially a black play on the "girl next door" trope. Not unlike Hollywood's age-old habit of identifying black actors and actresses as "colored" versions of white stars—such as Lena Horne's early moniker, "the bronze Hedy Lamarr"—the press and her films subtly coded Berry as a decidedly black version of the girl next door/all-American girl. Early on in her career, the press latched onto this notion. And, while she unquestionably functioned

FIGURE 3.1. Halle Berry and Eddie Murphy in *Boomerang*.

as black in both her onscreen and offscreen existences, she became associated with a kind of "safe" blackness that was thoroughly rooted in black middle-class sensibilities, one that held appeal for white audiences.

Because Berry would later come to signify the exotic token black in white films, it is important to illustrate her performance of the black "girl next door" in this first stage of her career. In *Boomerang*, for instance, Berry's sweet-natured Angela is the foil to Robin Givens's man-eater Jacqueline. As Mia Mask puts it, "*Boomerang*'s conventional narrative resolution in the form of heterosexual union hinges on Angela's ability to make you believe the happily-ever-after fairy tale: that a lothario like Marcus would prefer nesting with Angela to casual sex with Jacqueline."[5] The film constructs Givens's Jacqueline as "acting white" in ways that are similar to *Strictly Business*'s Diedre (discussed in chapter 2): Jacqueline is professionally successful and ambitious (she is Marcus's boss) as well as sexually aggressive. While *Boomerang* explicitly plays on this idea of the reversal of gender roles between Jacqueline and Marcus, it is the contrast between Jacqueline and Angela that provides the more subtle racial undercurrent. Although the two characters share similar chocolate skin tones, Jacqueline has long, straight hair while Angela wears a short crop—the coif that would become Berry's signature style. In a scene where Angela confronts Marcus about sleeping with Jacqueline, this difference in hairstyles takes on a richer meaning: "I might not be all glamorous, and I don't have hair weaved all down my back,

FIGURE 3.2. Halle Berry as Angela in *Boomerang*.

FIGURE 3.3. Halle Berry (*left*) and Robin Givens in *Boomerang*.

but let me tell you one great thing about me, alright? I have a heart. And you know the bad thing about having a heart, Marcus? Is that it gets broken when you deal with people like you."

Angela's statement—in which she reveals Jacqueline's use of hair extensions—sets up a contrast between Jacqueline's phoniness and Angela's genuineness, signified by Angela's short hair. More than that, however, it is also a way of pointing out Jacqueline's emotional and racial inauthenticity. In other words, the distinction between the two hairstyles builds on previous characterizations of Jacqueline as "acting white." The film makes it clear that this distinction extends to the two women's cultural associations as well. While Jacqueline speaks French, wears her hair in a Eurocentric style, and dresses in conventional business attire, Angela, by contrast, displays African folk art in her home; wears colorful, ethnic-inspired outfits; and volunteers at an afterschool program where she teaches underprivileged children about black painters. Angela, the film suggests, is comfortable in her black skin and in her black heritage, thus making Marcus's eventual choice of Angela over Jacqueline an implied choice of Angela's Afrocentric identity over Jacqueline's Eurocentrism.

Halle's Haircut and Dorothy's Red Dress

The short haircut that Berry sports in *Boomerang* quickly became the young actress's signature look. Countless black magazines and newspapers raved about the starlet's bold hairdo. Berry's shorn locks stood out significantly in an industry where many actresses—black and white alike—maintain conventionally feminine long hair. Berry's haircut functioned as more than a stylistic choice, however. As press reporting on the actress's hair demonstrates, Berry's signature look operated as a proxy for the nuances of her "black girl next door" persona. After countless African American women streamed into beauty salons nationwide requesting "the Halle Berry cut," the journalist Mary Corey attempted to explain some of the style's charm: "Venel Brown wasn't looking to become a starlet when she copied Ms. Berry's cut. She simply wanted a change. 'What makes it so popular is that it's not an outrageous hairstyle. It's subtle, but it's still a little bit funky,' says Ms. Brown, a 30-year-old attorney who lives in Lochearn." Corey continues: "The look is particularly appealing to middle-class women, says Dr. Russell Adams, chair of Afro-American Studies at Howard University in Washington. 'The Afro-American middle class has not been comfortable with Afro-centric hairstyles. Middle-class sisters . . . don't want to do braids, but they don't want to be Cybill Shepherd, either. Halle's thing is a modest compromise,' he says."[6]

As the quoted article demonstrates, Berry's cut struck the perfect balance between 1990s black "edge" and 1980s mainstream appeal. It was, in the words of Dr. Russell Adams, "a modest compromise" between the Afrocentric ethos that was sweeping black cultural spaces in the 1990s and the constraints on physical appearance imposed by a society that still treated whiteness as the norm and where ethnic hairstyles were a source of heated debates and governmental legislation.[7] On the one hand, the short straight crop fit in well with the more adventurous hairstyles being worn by black female urban tastemakers such as the rap group Salt-n-Pepa.[8] On the other hand, the look was not "ethnic" in the way of hairstyles like braids or dreadlocks.

Like her hairstyle, Berry's persona struck a careful balance between being identifiably black but not so black as to threaten mainstream conventions of racialized femininity. As a black woman in Hollywood, Berry had to measure up to Eurocentric standards of beauty in order to appeal to a wide audience, while also having to be black enough in order to be marketable as the love interest of actors such as Eddie Murphy. This particular trope of black femininity was not new in Hollywood or specific to Berry but, in fact, had been in operation for decades, impacting stars such as Lena Horne and Dorothy Dandridge. Dandridge's career trajectory serves as an interesting point of comparison to Berry, and the two actresses' images would eventually intersect when Berry played Dandridge in the HBO biopic *Introducing Dorothy Dandridge* (Martha Coolidge, 1999).[9]

For both Dandridge and Berry, stories about the women's physical makeovers function discursively to signify something larger about their "girl next door" personae, and they became symbolic of the women's ascents to stardom. In Dandridge's case, the director Otto Preminger initially refused to consider the actress for the lead in his film *Carmen Jones* when she arrived at his office dressed beautifully but demurely. It was only when she returned costumed as the famed temptress that Preminger offered her the role. As the writer Anne Helen Petersen notes, "But Preminger thought she was way too 'high fashion.' As he purportedly told Dandridge, 'This Carmen is an earthy girl who's entirely different from you. Every time I look at you, I see Saks Fifth Avenue.'"[10] While an audition and a haircut are not equivalents, stories about both symbolically delineate the fine line between virgin and vixen. For Dandridge, her conversion from sweet girl to legendary tempt-ress was achieved through a simple outfit change, itself an indication that Dandridge's innocence was perhaps always predicated on the suggestion of repressed sensuality. In the case of Berry, her signature haircut signified similarly to Dandridge's famed audition for the lead role in *Carmen Jones.*

Like Dandridge's red dress, Berry's signature short haircut signaled a discursive shift from the wholesome ingénue to the sexy bombshell. Mary Corey recounts Berry's conversation with her agent: "At first, her agent wasn't so sure. When she showed up at his office minus her shoulder-length locks, he cringed. 'He said, "You're not apple pie anymore. You're exotic looking. It's never going to work," she recalls.'"[11] In both stories, the appearance shift in question—Dandridge's sexy red dress and Berry's shorn locks—marks the turning point at which the two actresses go from "nice girls" to bomb-shells. Given that the tales of both transformative moments have taken on a legendary quality, it is important to contextualize these stories as sym-bolic articulations about each star's inter- and extratextual personae, rather than factual accounts.

The edgy connotation created by the publicity around Berry's haircut—henceforth referred to in countless black hairstyling magazines as simply "the Halle Berry cut"—formed a counterpoint to the controlled image con-ferred by her beauty-queen status. In a broader sense, this juxtaposition was emblematic of Berry's appeal, an appeal that rested on her identity as a figure of in-betweenness: her hair was a compromise of black chic and mainstream respectability, her mediated racial identity was simultaneously niche blackness and crossover tokenism, and her persona was wholesome as well as erotic. Once Berry won the lead in *Queen*, the press would play up this aspect of in-betweenness in service of making her more credible in the role of a biracial woman caught between black and white worlds. Thus, while Berry's physical appearance and previous roles failed to make her believable in the part of Queen, her intertextual persona covered the gap between performer and character.

The Turning Point: *Queen*

Casting Berry in *Queen* was an attempt to capitalize on the young star's quickly growing fame as a means of drawing in viewers. Berry, fresh off of *Boomerang*, was an ideal candidate to bring some of her much desired "It girl" factor to the project. Deploying a casting strategy previously used by Haley's *Roots* sixteen years earlier, *Queen*'s cast was rounded out with recognizable black and white actors from film and television: Jasmine Guy (*A Different World*) is Queen's mother, Raven-Symoné (*The Cosby Show*) plays Queen as a child, Danny Glover appears as Queen's husband, and the legendary Hollywood film actress Ann-Margret is Queen's grandmother.

As an up-and-coming star at the time with some notable roles under her belt, Berry was in the midst of a booming publicity frenzy, with newspapers and media outlets chronicling her love life, film roles, and signature haircut. Indeed, Berry's casting in the well-publicized CBS miniseries appeared to have been motivated less by the actress's physical suitability for the role, and more by her current popularity and visibility in Hollywood. Therefore, it made perfect sense for the producers of *Queen* to choose Berry—an actress whom they reasoned would bring viewers to their television screens in droves—for the lead. This was of particular concern in 1993, given the waning popularity of the television miniseries as a genre, a marked difference from the "appointment television" status that *Roots* garnered in 1977. And though *Queen*'s supporting cast featured many prominent actors with more notable careers and more recognizable names than Berry's, the miniseries was clearly a star vehicle for Berry.

Queen marked the first time in Berry's career where she played a historical figure, and the first time where her real life and her character became enmeshed in popular discussion. And, because *Queen* was a resurrection of the passing narrative of an earlier era—stories that typically center around "tragic mulatto" figures—the miniseries was also Berry's first time playing such an immediately recognizable trope. Yet, though the tragic mulatto trope may have been instantly recognizable, Berry's herself was not physically recognizable as such. Berry's natural, brown skin did not "read" convincingly as a character that could pass for white. This disconnect between Berry's physical appearance and the character that she played had two important results. First, Berry's inability to convincingly play a passing character brings issues of racial performance to the forefront in ways that previous passing narratives (at least in film and television) have not done. Second, Berry's association with the tragic mulatto trope would forever alter her public persona and the lens through which she would be perceived.

Creating the Tragic Mulatto: Publicity and *Queen*

Berry's physical appearance and previous film roles did not make her the most likely actress to play the lead in a film about a young black woman struggling with her racial identity and passing for white in the antebellum South. Though Berry was herself biracial and had certainly never made a secret of her heritage, it did not figure significantly into the personal identity that she projected to the media, and it was not a feature of any of her onscreen roles. Though for some actresses, such as Jennifer Beals or Rae Dawn Chong, their biracial identity has been crucial to their casting across color lines, Berry's mixed-race background did not indicate that she was more suited to the role than any other nonbiracial black actress.[12] By contrast, Berry's body and skin tone presented the network with a challenge that had to be addressed in order for *Queen* to be believable to viewers.[13] Unlike Beals and Chong—who often played characters of ambiguous (or purposefully undefined racial backgrounds) in predominantly white casts—Berry had risen to stardom as an ingénue amid black-cast and black-directed films. Therefore, the factors that had marked Berry as unquestionably black in the earlier, *Boomerang* stage of her career would prove an impediment to her embodiment of Queen, the biracial slave passing for white in order to navigate a racially bifurcated Southern society. Before being cast in *Queen*, Berry's repeated and assertive insistence on her identity as a black woman (including her comments about Whoopi Goldberg, mentioned in chapter 2) was a necessary component of her success during the politically conscious 1990s. Her declarations of blackness, along with the unambiguously black characters that she played, allowed Berry to steer clear of the trap of typecasting that had plagued other "passing" narrative stars such as Fredi Washington in the 1930s and, in Berry's own time, an actress like Beals, who found herself trapped in a fetishized "tan Other" category.[14] Whatever Berry's own reasons were for identifying herself as black rather than biracial, it is clear that this choice and her decision to play black characters had an impact on her popularity among black audiences (in addition to white ones) early on in her career and protected her from charges of "selling out."[15]

Now, however, Berry needed to become believable as both biracial and white-appearing. According to *Entertainment Weekly*, Berry lobbied hard for the role, even shouldering the costs to fly from New York to Los Angeles for the audition, where she found herself up against more established, and also lighter-skinned, black actresses like Beals, Jasmine Guy, Vanessa Williams, and Lonette McKee.[16] Once cast, the challenge of Berry's physical appearance still remained, in spite of the attempts made by makeup artists and lighting specialists. The solution to this quandary took place outside of the film text: a reconstruction of Berry's image in the popular press that attempted to sell the idea of Berry as a tragic mulatto in order to make her believable for the role. If the makeup could not transform Berry into a tragic mulatto, then the press would do the work instead.

As the miniseries' airdate drew near, magazines and popular journals began to draw explicit connections between Berry's own background and that of Haley's grandmother, Queen. A story in the Los Angeles Times noted that "Berry looks uncannily like the real Queen. When George Haley, the late author's brother, came to the set, he looked up at the actress in costume and said, 'Hello, Grandmother.'"[17] In addition to this alleged physical resemblance, these stories most often focused on Berry's own biracial identity, drawing a direct connection between the actress's biography and that of the character that she was playing. Berry also provided support for these connections, referencing her own racial background to blur the lines between her life and that of the character she played. "Queen's life could have been my life," she said in an interview that ran in the Baltimore Sun.[18]

The stories about Berry's own racial background tapped into larger narrative concepts of the "tragic mulatto," embodied in films like Imitation of Life (John Stahl, 1934; Douglas Sirk, 1959), Pinky (Elia Kazan, 1949), and Lost Boundaries (Alfred Werker, 1949). According to the film scholar Donald Bogle, the tragic mulatto character as immortalized in Hollywood film is an African American—usually a woman—who is light enough to pass for white. The films' narratives typically present blackness as the main obstacle to the character's happiness, most often represented as romantic love with a white man.[19] Even in films that do not concentrate on the (always) tragic love story between the tragic mulatto and her white lover, the character's struggles over her racial identity usually play a significant role in the narrative. For example, the 1959 version of Imitation of Life includes a well-known scene where Sarah Jane affects an exaggerated Southern drawl while carrying a serving tray on her head, behavior that she explains as "acting colored." Though the scene is meant to convey Sarah Jane's ignorance and disrespect of her mother and white patron, it opens the door to another, more subversive interpretation as well—namely, that racial identity is itself a performance, one rendered more or less believable by the bodies that perform it.

FIGURE 3.4. Queen with her white family in *Queen*.

FIGURE 3.5. Queen with her black family in *Queen*.

Building on this notion, then, it becomes clear that Berry needed to be rendered believable for her role in *Queen*, in terms of both her body and her extratextual identity. Therefore, though Berry had not spoken much about her biracial identity before, from then on every story about the actress focused almost exclusively on this aspect of her personhood. Within the context of American media, the very mention of Berry's biracial heritage functioned to locate the actress within the cinematic tradition of the tragic mulatto figure and all of the narrative angst associated with it. Judith Lazarus of the *Los Angeles Times* quoted Berry as saying, "Being interracial myself, it dug up childhood feelings of not knowing who I was or where I belonged, and the hurt I felt at the things people said."[20] Interestingly, however, though Berry spoke candidly about her biracial heritage in interviews about *Queen*, she only talked about the difficulty of that identity when discussing her childhood, as the above quote articulates. She did not, however, suggest that being biracial posed an issue for her as an adult, in terms of her own racial subjectivity or in her dealings with black and white people. In other words, though Berry referenced her biraciality as a link to Queen, she did not portray it as an ongoing source of friction in her own life. Berry, in fact, rejected this characterization of herself as a tragic mulatto figure, constantly restating her identity as a black, not biracial, woman. While acknowledging her white mother, Berry was adamant about how she viewed herself and identified. As Lazarus described later in the same article, "When Berry was younger and wanted to know the truth about why she was 'different,' her mother, Judy, would put her in front of a mirror and ask her what she saw. '"You're white, I'm brown,"' Berry said. '"You're grown up, I'm little."' Mom said that was the reality: '"You are black; we're different colors but I'm still your mom."' I'm grateful for that, knowing who and what I am. It's easier if you accept reality and be proud of your heritage."[21]

Berry's careful delineation between her past hurts as a biracial child and her present identification as a proud black woman may have been too nuanced of a position in the face of an industry and a society committed to placing people of color in simplified categories. Though Berry's unquestionable blackness may have worked within Hollywood when she was appearing in the niche of black-cast films, her crossover into more mainstream fare necessitated, according to Hollywood logic, closer proximity to whiteness.[22] Yet this ran counter to Berry's own articulations of self and politics of identity. As time went on, Berry's statements on her identity became more forceful and straightforward. A few months after *Queen's* release, Berry once again discussed her biracial background, this time in a story in *Ebony* magazine. Explaining that her white mother had taught Berry to identify as black from an early age, Berry said, "I think if you're an interracial child and you're strong enough to live 'I'm neither Black nor White but in the middle,' then more power. But I needed to make a choice and feel part of this culture. I feel a lot of pride in being a Black woman."[23] Berry's frustration with trying to balance the tragic mulatto trope of the film that she was promoting against her own racial subjectivity became apparent in an interview that she gave to Lisa Jones of *Essence* magazine a year following *Queen*'s release. The actress attempted to set the record straight once and for all:

> I never once announced that I am interracial. I was never the one to bring it up. I've always said, "I'm Black, I'm African-American." But reporters constantly ask what childhood was like for an interracial person. And believe me, being interracial wasn't as big an issue as these articles might lead you to believe. Sure, there were problems, but there were other things in my childhood that caused me more pain than being interracial. Everyone wants to write about my having a White mother. I've shared every experience that I'm going to share about that. There's really nothing else for me to say.[24]

Emphasizing her racial identity as a "political choice," Berry's determination to take control of her own narrative comes across loud and clear in this quotation. And, it seems obvious, given the timing of the interview, that Berry was referring to the press around *Queen* when she mentions the "reporters" who "constantly ask what childhood was like for an interracial person." No matter her protests, however, the constant references to Berry's biracialism functioned to place the actress in the same tragic mulatto category as cinematic figures like *Imitation of Life*'s Sarah Jane.

Queen: From Script to Screen

Queen's narrative attempts to shoehorn a complicated story of an actual historical woman struggling with the very real social and political ramifications of her "in between" racial identity into a more conventional Hollywood tale of the tragic mulatto. Though Alex Haley had compiled a lengthy outline for his yet uncompleted book about *Queen*, the task fell to a white Australian screenwriter, David Stevens, to compile Haley's notes into a cohesive script. Though Stevens had experience in directing, producing, and writing for television, the process of converting Haley's seven hundred pages of notes into a television miniseries was a daunting one. As Stevens notes about Haley's existing work on *Queen*, "He had that outline and all his notes, . . . but no book. Haley was a hard man to pin down. There was always a little more research that needed doing."[25]

Stevens freely admitted that he lacked familiarity with black culture and the sociopolitical history around issues of American slavery and black racial identity. As he himself stated, "I was actually surprised that Haley chose me" and "I wasn't American. I wasn't black."[26] To address this, Haley and Stevens traveled together to the American South, where Stevens claims that Haley gave him "a crash course in African-American culture."[27] According to the journalist Tina Jordan, who interviewed Stevens about his experience working with Haley, the two did not go over the plot details of the book. Instead, Stevens notes, "We talked about historical background, contemporary attitudes, areas where the story takes place."[28]

Given the rather casual research that went into Haley and Stevens's collaboration, it made sense for Stevens to approach the screenplay as a work of fiction rather than as a historical account. Notes from Stevens's script (both the original version and first revision) show a writer undertaking the momentous task of creating a compelling narrative while attempting some degree of historical and cultural accuracy, with varying results. Reading through Stevens's notes reveals his building frustration as he ran into the practical difficulties of executing Haley's lofty vision. For example, Stevens initially intended for Queen's manner of speech to shift depending on whether she was addressing white or black characters in the film. In a note at the beginning of the first draft of the script, titled "The Way Queen Talks," Stevens says,

> As Queen is trying to find herself in this chapter, and what world she belongs in, her way of speech changes somewhat.
>
> At the plantation, she is still the educated slave, but her pattern can also vary, depending on the company she is in. With other slaves, or ex-slaves, she sounds a little more like them. When she's with whites, her speech takes on their tones.
>
> When she enters into Alice's world, she starts to sound more and more like a white Southern belle.

In Huntsville, befriended by blacks, she reverts to mild idiom, but tempered by what she has learned. So her speech becomes less and less of the slave, more and more of the contemporary black.[29]

Stevens's description of Queen's "code switching" would have gone a long way toward illustrating the performative aspects of race, but unfortunately, the writer found himself unable to encode these delicate shifts into his script. Frustrated by his inability to capture the nuances of the various linguistic vernaculars in the *Queen* story world, Stevens eventually made the decision to abandon these attempts altogether. In a follow-up note in the revised script, Stevens vents, "I spent many fruitless hours battling with Slave Idiom only to discover that I'm not very good at it. Since it seems to me more important, at this stage, to concern myself with what they say, rather than how they say it, I have abandoned any attempts at Idiom, apart from giving the Slaves some bad grammar. Alex [Haley] has promised to translate it for me later."[30] Unfortunately, Haley died before Stevens could finish the script, meaning that the final product lacked his authenticating touch.

In addition to the problems with the code-switching dialect, changes in the script on its journey to the screen also erased some of the racial complexities of the story. Stevens's script included several narrative episodes that highlighted Queen's "in between" status, made most evident in Queen's efforts to fit into black and white worlds. The script includes several scenes, for instance, which show Queen welcomed by black characters, usually at moments where she runs into direct conflict with the white world. After a scary attack at the hands of a few white bandits, Queen finds refuge with a slave community in the woods until it is safe enough for her to venture home. When she leaves the plantation that had been her home for her whole life, a young black boy provides her with a ride to town in his cart. Later on, when Queen's attempts at passing have failed and after she has been brutally raped by her white beau, Queen becomes involved with a black church community.

In fact, Stevens's script—for all of its linguistic issues—does a thorough job of demonstrating the amount of effort involved in Queen's attempts to correctly perform her racial identity. The script continuously emphasizes Queen's efforts through her behavior, speech, and stated politics to fit in with both black and white communities. To this end, Stevens's script contains several examples of Queen making deliberate attempts to "act black" and "act white," with varying levels of success. In one scene, Queen sits in front of a mirror and attempts to imitate the upper-class accent of her white employer. The script lets us know that Queen has been at this exercise for an hour. Later, Stevens describes Queen correcting her pronunciation from "axed" to "asked," in an attempt to "be the complete Southern gentlewoman."[31] In another scene, Queen takes a more direct approach to performing her whiteness by lashing out at a black man she encounters on the street. Queen, passing as white and on a date with her white suitor, encounters a black beggar. Stevens's script reads,

BLACK BEGGAR: Spare a little change, ma'am. I hungry—

QUEEN (SNAPS): Don't bother me nigger!

Disavowing her blackness by spewing a racist epithet, Queen engages in an act meant to reinforce her allegiance to whiteness—specifically the racism that she associates with whiteness in the antebellum South. In other words, in order for Queen to be accepted by whites as one of their own, she feels the need to distance herself from blackness as much as possible, or at least erase any suggestion of her own black identity. As the scholar and artist Adrian Piper argues in her essay "Passing for White; Passing for Black": "To look visibly black, or always to announce in advance that one is black is, I submit, never to experience this kind of camaraderie with white people, the relaxed, unguarded but respectful camaraderie that white people reserve for those whom they believe are like them: those who can be trusted, who are intrinsically worthy of value, respect and attention."[32]

Though Stevens does an admirable job of demonstrating the ways that Queen acts white in order to pass, the problem is that none of the abovementioned scenes appears in the final filmed version of the miniseries. The scene of Queen practicing her speech in front of the mirror is cut. The line where she adjusts her pronunciation from "axed" to "asked" is elided, so that Berry says only the latter, seamlessly integrated into the rest of the line. And, finally, the scene where Queen verbally attacks the black beggar is rewritten so that it is her white beau, not Queen, who angrily calls the man a racial slur.

These are important changes and omissions, as the absence of these scenes shifts the miniseries' focus away from the process of Queen's racial performance and back to the more conventional tragic mulatto narrative of the hidden secret of Queen's blackness. The former would have revealed the labor that goes into whiteness and, hence, would have shown whiteness itself to be a construction, thus denaturalizing its normativity. Without this important emphasis, however, scenes that would have originally demonstrated Queen's efforts to approximate whiteness take on a different meaning. Queen's linguistic code switching in black and white spaces barely registers (and this may be partly a result of John Erman's directing or Berry's acting). And, if it is Queen's lover rather than Queen herself who curses the black beggar, then the entire subtext of Queen's disavowal as a necessary requirement for her acceptance into whiteness disappears.

Even with these changes, however, *Queen* still retains some of this emphasis on racial performativity, most evident in Queen's relationship with fellow passer Alice as well as in the incredibly obvious makeup that Berry wears to make her believable as the character. These elements are particularly effective in creating space for viewers to grapple with the concept of whiteness and performativity throughout the miniseries. Queen's encounter with this other black woman passing for white supports a reading of the film as a commentary on the nature of racial performance in the media, specifically as it pertains to African American actresses and the roles available to them in Hollywood. In other words, *Queen*'s casting and narrative constitute a meta-discourse about larger issues of black women's visibility in film and television. After Queen leaves the plantation and finds herself homeless and hungry, she enters a whites-only soup line where a kind-hearted prostitute named Alice recognizes her as a kindred spirit. Alice, who has herself been passing as white, takes Queen under her wing, builds her self-confidence, and tutors her in the intricacies of believable passing. In one scene, Alice teaches Queen how to "talk white" in order to make her performance more believable. Though Alice has warned Queen never to disclose her true identity to the white men who court her, Queen reveals her blackness to a potential suitor who then brutally rapes her. Fearful that Queen's indiscretion will lead to her own outing, Alice kicks Queen out of her home and onto the streets.

Lonette McKee plays Alice, and the actress's own biracial identity and light-skinned appearance factor into her being cast as a number of specifically "light-skinned" black woman types throughout her career. She had appeared with Berry previously in *Jungle Fever* as a woman whose husband cheats on her with a white woman. McKee also starred in Julie Dash's 1983 independent short film, *Illusions*, as a 1940s Hollywood executive passing for white. With McKee as the representative of passing not only within

Queen's narrative but also within black popular cinema, and Berry as the newcomer, their interactions create an interesting meta-narrative that is based on both actresses' positioning within black popular culture.

ALICE: Tough, isn't it? Lookin' white?

QUEEN: Ma'am, I swear . . .

ALICE: It's alright. I understand, sister. We're lucky we can choose. Who'd choose to be black? White is so much easier.

The exchange, in addition to establishing a black feminine camaraderie between the two characters, can be creatively read as a contemporary discussion of racial politics. The use of the word "sista," anachronistic for the time in which *Queen* takes place, brings the conversation into the present. The word is clearly meant to indicate blackness, as an excised scene from the original script indicates. In the script, Queen, passing for white and working in the soup kitchen alongside Alice, serves a young woman who replies, "Thank you—sister." The direction reads: "CLOSE ON Queen. The last word had a frightening connotation to it. The Woman had guessed." It is clear, then, that Stevens used the word "sister" as a way to indicate racial recognition between black women.

McKee's history as an actress recognized for portraying light-skinned and biracial characters plays into her character's declaration of the ease of white identity; her character's perspective seems like a throwback not only to the Reconstruction-era South but also to the period just before the phrase "black is beautiful" swept through black communities. Alice is intended to be an anachronism and is rendered all the more out of date when associated with McKee, who literally represents the past in terms of black film. On the contrary, Berry, whose young career had already been defined by her very public declarations of black empowerment and pro-black identity, serves as the modern voice behind Queen, who repeatedly defies Alice's advice to hide her "authentic" identity.

Queen's reanimation of the tragic mulatto trope stuck to Berry long after the miniseries aired, mainly because the surrounding press insisted so strongly on equating the actress with the character that she played. For example, when *Jet* magazine ran a blurb to promote the film, the title read "Alex Haley's Epic Drama 'Queen' Stars Halle Berry as Mulatto Struggling with Her Identity in Six-Hour Mini-Series."[33] The article's use of the outdated term "mulatto" carried with it a knowing implication of the "tragic

FIGURE 3.6. Halle Berry (*left*) and Lonette McKee in *Queen*.

mulatto" trope, bringing its associations from the past into the present and into the discussion of the miniseries, and of Berry. Though *Queen* was one of the last of the traditional passing narratives onscreen, the basic issues that the miniseries raises—racial performance, the search for an identity, and the ways that society categorizes that identity—were far from being passé or limited to cinematic or televisual narratives. They were playing out in real life and in real time with Berry herself.

The White Man's Whore

Berry's role in *Queen* indeed signaled that the young actress had arrived as a Hollywood star: she began to perform in more and more big-budget mainstream films, moving from supporting cast member in predominantly white films to lead actress. Berry's film roles post-*Queen* prove that the television miniseries was indeed a transformative moment in the actress's career; after that point, the overwhelming majority of her films would consist of predominantly white casts. Indeed, many of Berry's early roles in this period of her career almost appear to be tokenized reboots of her pre-*Queen* roles. For instance, Berry played a crack addict battling a white family for custody of her child in *Losing Isaiah* (Stephen Gyllenhaal, 1995), a role that certainly recalled her first noticeable film part only a few years before in *Jungle Fever*. Whereas Berry had played a kind of accessible but mysterious dream girl in *Strictly Business*, she now played the sexy token black character in a string of white-cast films like *The Flintstones* (Brian Levant, 1994) and *The Rich Man's Wife* (Amy Holden Jones, 1996). And she seemed to resurrect her "around-the-way girl" persona in the film *Bulworth* (Warren Beatty, 1998), where her character Nina seemed to be almost a throwback to the types of characters that she played prior to *Queen*—the key difference being that her love interest was not Eddie Murphy or another black actor, but, instead, the white Warren Beatty. Though Berry still appeared in black-cast films from time to time, such as BAPS (Robert Townsend, 1995), *Why Do Fools Fall in Love* (Gregory Nava, 1999), and two Oprah Winfrey–produced miniseries, *The Wedding* (Charles Burnett, 1998) and *Their Eyes Were Watching God* (Darnell Martin, 2005), her public persona shifted once *Queen* aired.

From an industrial standpoint, Berry's appearances in these white-cast films were the result of color-blind casting, also known as blind-casting, a practice in which actors or actresses of color are cast in roles not explicitly specified for minorities. Though this practice was originally aimed at increasing the numbers of minorities in theater, film, and television, the result is the reinforcement of white normativity and the absence of cultural specificity in the media. As Herman Gray and Kristen Warner have convincingly argued, color-blind casting forces minority actors to perform "racially neutral" roles, which is really just a euphemism for "normatively white."[34] For Berry, the press around *Queen* had already begun the process of suggesting that she was less black than before. Now, with Berry playing parts typically associated with white women—or even originally written for them—her identity as the "around-the-way girl" slipped even further away.[35] With *Monster's Ball*, the film for which Berry would win an Academy Award for Best Actress (making her the first black woman to win in this category), public opinion around Berry would shift into an entirely new territory.

From a theoretical perspective, both Berry's crossover into predominantly white films and her Oscar win suggested that she had "transcended race." This idea of transcendence, as Ralina Joseph articulates, implies a person of color relinquishing their blackness in favor of whiteness. She writes,

On the one hand, multiracial blackness is disdained for its imagined primordially raced nature, with its tragic-mulatta lineage. On the other hand, multiracial blackness is desired for its imagined transcendent quality, where it is ahistorically divorced from racism and sexism in the United States with its troubling history of chattel slavery, Jim Crow racism, and entrenched misogyny. Because the popular conception that race means black, the end of race must mean the end of blackness. Whiteness, imaged as pure, invisible, and promise-laden, remains prized as the savior for multiracial African American figures from blackness, presented as sullied, hypervisible, and tragedy filled.[36]

Though Berry had never claimed anything even approximating a "tragic mulatta" identity—in fact, she had vehemently resisted such a categorization—the combination of the publicity around *Queen*, Berry's rising-star image, and the actress's transition from black- to white-cast films effectively thrust her into that role. It is easy to see, using Joseph's quote, how discourses around Berry's nonblackness dovetailed neatly with her new status as a crossover star.

Put another way, Berry's crossover success effectively transformed her into a "new millennium mulatta," or an "exceptional multiracial," to borrow Joseph's terms. Yet, as Joseph articulates, such representations often operate with antiblack sentiment. In other words, discourses that promote or reward "transcendence" for multiracial persons of color actually suggest that these persons are better positioned to relinquish the negative connotations associated with blackness in their "upward" journey to whiteness. Such political messages have a deeper history, such as debates surrounding the multiracial category on the 2000 census, which, not coincidentally, began in the mid-1990s, right around the time that Berry's racial identity became a topic.[37]

For black audiences, these thinly coded, antiblack discourses were nothing new. Nor was it a novelty to see a black star rise in the black community only to cross over into the mainstream (such has historically been the case with famous figures like the baseball player Jackie Robinson). Though Berry was certainly not responsible for the ways that the press constructed her as "multiracial," she was the image on which these various forces and discourses converged. Her appearance in *Monster's Ball*, then, must be understood within this very important social and political discourse.

Monster's Ball would become Berry's most controversial film to date because of the film's explicit sex scenes between the actress and Billy Bob Thornton. In *Monster's Ball*, Berry plays Leticia, a wife and mother whose ex-husband awaits execution on Death Row. Billy Bob Thornton plays Hank, a racist prison guard who is responsible for carrying out the execution. Leticia and Hank enter into a romance, unaware of this connection until the end of the film. Set in Georgia, the film raises questions about the nature of racism and its origins, and whether age, personal connections, and love are enough to dismantle it. The film is best remembered, though, for its graphic depiction of the lead characters' sexual relationship rather than the film's themes or performances. The role won Berry an Oscar, but many critics within black communities wondered whether the industry had rewarded Berry for playing a hypersexual jezebel. Already, Berry had drawn skepticism when she broke her long-standing rule against film nudity and appeared topless in Dominic Sena's 2001 film *Swordfish* opposite Hugh Jackman. Further, Berry's win for *Ball* accompanied Denzel Washington's Oscar that year for his portrayal of a villain in Antoine Fuqua's *Training Day*, leading many critical viewers to the conclusion that the Academy was rewarding black actors for playing "negative" roles, the types that groups like the National Association for the Advancement of Colored People had fought to challenge since D. W. Griffith's *The Birth of a Nation* in 1915.

Whether this criticism was justified or not, Berry's nudity and the sexually explicit love scenes set off a wave of discussion, particularly after Berry took home the Oscar. Word quickly spread that a number of prominent black actresses had turned down the part before it finally went to Berry because they found the role demeaning and stereotypical. Though the director Marc Forster denied that he had considered any other actress but Berry, the rumor—and its implications about Berry's politics—stuck. The actress Angela Bassett was particularly vocal in her condemnation of the part, telling *Newsweek* magazine, "I wasn't going to be a prostitute on film" and "I couldn't do that because it's such a stereotype about black women and sexuality." She continued: "It wasn't the role for me, but I told her [Berry] she'd win and I told her to go get what was hers. Of course I want one, too. I would love to have an Oscar. But it has to be for something I can sleep with at night."[38] Bassett's criticism—both of the part and of Berry for taking it—directly connected Berry to the legacy of negative stereotypes in Hollywood film.[39] And, like Berry's own comments about Whoopi Goldberg years earlier, Bassett's comments reiterated a positive/negative binary. This time, however, Berry was the negative representation.

In the film, however, Berry's character is far from a temptress or a pawn in a white man's seduction fantasy. And she is certainly far from the prostitute of Bassett's accusations. Leticia is a waitress and a single mother, who, within the film's diegesis, is only romantically connected to two men: her ex-lover and the prison guard. Yet what was it about the infamous sex scene that rankled so many who saw the film? Was it solely the broader, historical discourses around black female hypersexuality? Or did the film itself do something to provoke such a reactionary response?

The scene in question depicts the first sexual encounter between Leticia and Hank. After getting drunk together in Leticia's living room, the two engage in a frantic lovemaking session that Forster shoots using a cinema verité style, placing the camera behind furniture and around corners. The scene makes a perceptible shift, however, when the soundtrack introduces nondiegetic music to the scene, whose previous sounds had been limited to the grunts and groans of the two characters against a silent background. The shift transitions the interaction from one of desperate coupling out of mutual need to one of tenderness and mutual desire.

It is the way that Forster films the scene that adds to its controversial reception. Reviewing the film, few critics failed to mention either the scene or the frenzied discussions surrounding it. Nearly all of the critics—whether fans of the film or not—cited *Ball*'s realism, particularly in this first of the film's two sex scenes, as the film's distinguishing traits. Phillip French noted, "Their first bout of lovemaking begins tentatively as they get a little drunk. It's an extended, sweaty business, initially awkward but increasingly tender, and quite different from the soft-focus, slow fade-out treatment one customarily finds in Hollywood productions."[40] The film critic A. O. Scott observed, "This is one of those rare movies in which even people glimpsed only for a moment or two seem to have lives that ramify beyond the screen, as if the story were being witnessed rather than dramatized."[41]

This voyeuristic quality of the film, meant to convey the gritty realness of *Ball*'s story, creates the distinct impression that the viewer is viewing an illicit act, something with real-life connections to Hollywood's restrictions against representations of miscegenation as dictated by the famous (or infamous) Production Code.[42] In 1992, another film that depicted a romance between a black woman and a white man, *The Bodyguard* (Mick Jackson),

FIGURE 3.7. Halle Berry and Billy Bob Thornton in *Monster's Ball*.

notoriously cut its love scene between singer/actress Whitney Houston and Kevin Costner in favor of a few chaste kisses and a fade-out meant to imply, but not show, sex. Given this context of the existing taboo around inter-racial sex, the decision to film Berry and Thornton's lovemaking from the perspective of a voyeur simply reinforced the idea of their union as pro-hibited, yet simultaneously erotic, in its illicitness. In addition, Forster's close-ups on Berry's naked body were something that other film critics noted and responded to in less-than-glowing reviews. Roger Ebert wrote, "The film's only flaw is the way Marc Forster allows his camera to linger on Berry's half-clothed beauty; this story is not about sex appeal, and if the camera sees her that way, we are pretty sure that Hank doesn't."[43] Ian Grey went further in his critique, observing both the scene's voyeuristic qualities and the almost fetishistic attention to Berry's body: "Too much attention is spent on Berry's charms; the scene goes on too long, making a lecture of the idea of fleshy absolution, and it's sometimes shot disconcertingly like '70s soft-core, with the camera hiding behind furniture like a peeper."[44]

Though Berry's sensuality had been exoticized, objectified, and com-modified for most of her career, her new role as a crossover star raised the uncomfortable specter of "selling out," the phrase taking on a racialized and sexualized twist. Nowhere was this more apparent than in the rapper Jadakiss's 2004 song, "Why?" Mixing hip hop bragging with a healthy dose of social and political criticism, the rapper poses a number of rhetorical questions aimed at the institutions responsible for maintaining structural inequality for African Americans, such as the music industry, the Ameri-can political system, and Hollywood. For instance, he queries "Why is the industry designed to keep the artist in debt?" "Why did Bush knock down the towers?" "Why they stop letting niggas get degrees in jail?" Two of the most hard-hitting and oft-quoted lines of the song, however, are directed at Halle Berry and Denzel Washington, fresh off their Best Actress and Best Actor Academy Award wins for *Monster's Ball* and *Training Day*, respectively. In the last verse of the song, Jadakiss queries,

> Why Halle have to let a white man pop her to get a Oscar?
> Why Denzel have to be crooked before he took it?

The line about Berry, in its crudeness, reduces the entirety of the actress's career to this one moment. Yet Jadakiss's opinion does not exist in isolation, but echoes the sentiments expressed by Angela Bassett (and others) regarding Berry's choice to appear in the film.

For many, Berry's sex scene in *Monster's Ball* confirmed that the star had indeed finally, and definitively, crossed over into the mainstream. Her decision to play a racially problematic stereotype (as indeed many interpreted her role in *Monster's Ball*) followed by Berry's winning of the Oscar for the part only confirmed, for some, that she had indeed been paid handsomely for selling out, thus echoing Bassett's claims that the role of Leticia was one of a prostitute. It had been one thing for Berry to play the love interest opposite black actors, but her appearances in films such as *The Rich Man's Wife*, *Bulworth*, and *Swordfish* and as a "Bond girl" in *Die Another Day* (Lee Tamahori, 2002) tapped into uncomfortable historical discourses about black women's sexuality and white men.

Conclusion

Berry's personal and professional life post–*Monster's Ball* only seemed to confirm for many the idea that the transformation of her racial identity was complete. Critics panned her 2004 film *Catwoman* and the movie performed abysmally at the box office. A. O. Scott described it as "a howlingly silly, moderately diverting exercise in high, pointless style."[45] When the film won three Razzies, at the Golden Raspberry Awards, a ceremony intended to highlight the worst films of the year, Berry took it in good humor, showing up in person to accept her Razzie for Worst Actress and giving a funny take on her 2002 Academy Awards Best Actress speech.

Yet the scathing reviews of *Catwoman* and Berry's performance must have touched a nerve with the actress and could not have come at a worse time. Stories of infidelities committed by her second husband, the African American singer Eric Benét, filled the pages of the tabloids. Married in 2001, they finalized their divorce in January 2005, just a month before she took the stage to accept the Razzie for *Catwoman* and mocked the speech in which she had referred to Benét as "a manager, a friend, and the only father [she] had ever known."[46] Just prior to the finalization of their divorce, Berry appeared on the cover of *Ebony* magazine with the headline "Why I Will Never Marry Again."[47] For a woman who had launched her career playing love interests, Berry's statements on heartache and betrayal were a world away from her earlier onscreen persona.

The narrative around Berry's career and the subsequent backlash after *Monster's Ball* follow a narrative trajectory oddly reminiscent of some of the narratives of the "sellout" films that I discussed in chapter 2. Berry, the logic went, had decided to "sell out" her race in order to get ahead in the industry. In addition to her participation in *Queen*, part of the reason for the backlash against Berry seemed to be that she was now a bankable "crossover" star. In a relatively short time, she had gone from a little-known supporting actress in films like *Jungle Fever* to box-office star and *People* magazine's "Sexiest Woman Alive." Though Berry remained, and would continue to remain, outspoken on the subject of her own racial identity as well as on the tribulations of being a black woman in Hollywood, her seeming acceptance by white audiences seemed to confirm the worst-case suspicions about her racial betrayal.

EMBRACING THE RATCHET

Reality Television and Strategic Negativity

Most reality TV stars aren't famous for having a talent. . . . Instead, they're just famous for being famous. —**BOYCE WATKINS**

My job is to be a bad bitch. —**JOSELINE HERNANDEZ**

Love & Hip Hop Atlanta, a spinoff of VH1's popular New York–based *Love & Hip Hop*, has quickly risen to become one of the network's highest perform- ing shows, rated cable television's top reality show during the summer of 2015.[1] Part of the show's success is no doubt due to one of its cast mem- bers, Joseline Hernandez, an aspiring singer whose affair with her man- ager, Steven Jordan, and the resulting love triangle between Hernandez, Jordan, and his longtime girlfriend, Mimi Faust, constituted the season's main story line. During the premiere season, Hernandez quickly became the show's breakout star, both as a figure of ridicule and as a type of camp icon. Her unique speech patterns—resulting from a combination of African American Vernacular English (AAVE) and English as her second language— provided fodder for numerous Internet memes and jokes on social media.

FIGURE 4.1. Joseline Hernandez takes a pregnancy test on camera in *Love & Hip Hop Atlanta*.

More, her onscreen antics, such as taking a pregnancy test in front of the cameras, raised the bar for the kind of outrageous behavior possible on reality television.

Yet, as the season continued, the show revealed another, more complicated side of Hernandez's personality. She divulged that she had grown up with a drug-addicted mother and had run away from home at twelve; she then lived by seeking the "care" of several different men, a thinly veiled allusion to prostitution. Hernandez had worked as a stripper until she met Jordan, and she credited his support of her music career as the single factor that allowed her to leave the strip club. Though Hernandez spoke of her love for Jordan on the show, viewers could not help but notice that the dynamic between them—based on Jordan's power and Hernandez's indebtedness to him—replicated the troubled past from which he had ostensibly "saved" her. On the show, Jordan constantly leveraged his financial and emotional hold over Hernandez to compel her to yield to his demands in spite of her own desires. For example, Hernandez initially keeps their affair a secret because Jordan threatens to cut off professional support if she reveals the nature of their relationship to anyone. When she then becomes pregnant, he pressures her to abort the baby, claiming that it is in the best interest of her career, though he seems more concerned about placating his longtime girlfriend, Mimi Faust. And, throughout the season, whenever

Hernandez pushes back against Jordan's wishes, he callously threatens to send her "back to the strip club."

As a figure whose excesses inspire ridicule and yet whose fragility compels empathy, Hernandez embodies the central appeal of the types of "ratchet" reality television programs that I am examining in this chapter. In common parlance, "ratchet" connotes behavior that is crude, socially unacceptable, and, more often than not, associated with lower-class black vernacular culture. For many, then, *Love & Hip Hop* would be a textbook example of a ratchet reality show because the women curse, fight, and engage in seemingly indiscriminate sexual relationships. Kristen Warner attempts to nuance the definition of ratchetness, noting the necessity of "excess that is never disavowed" as a key component that delineates the "ratchet" from other related pejorative terms associated with blackness, such as "ghetto" or "hood."[2] Inherently performative in nature, Warner argues that ratchetness indicates "an awareness that one actively puts on this hyperexcessive performance" because, at its core, ratchetness "is performed to be seen and circulated through mediated channels."[3] Warner's assertion that the performance of ratchetness indicates not only awareness from women like Hernandez but also a degree of *agency* is extremely useful here, as it helps us to understand why many find these types of representations to be so odious. For it is one thing to acknowledge the structural and industrial pressures that lock black women into certain mediated tropes, but it is another thing altogether to grapple with the notion that these women actively *choose* to represent themselves in these ways. Moreover, when the show creator is herself an African American woman, and the bulk of viewers are also African American women, we must contend with matters of choice and agency on every level, from production to performance to reception. Let me be clear here: I am not suggesting that we ignore the ways that larger social, historical, and industrial factors constrain the kinds of options that these women have available to them. I am, however, proposing that we look at the various ways in which the women associated with these shows negotiate these limited choices within the system of reality television, and how they use the very behaviors labeled as "ratchet" to achieve a degree of autonomy regarding the representational and economic aspects of their lives.

By speaking of the autonomy of cast members like Hernandez, I again do not want to suggest that they make fully liberated choices among a sea of available options. But I do want to consider the ways that Hernandez and others exercise, in the words of Warner, a degree of "performative agency" in the way that they present themselves on camera and on social media, and that this agency is also connected to the labor and work that they put into the show. For while the conceit of *Love & Hip Hop* suggests that someone like Hernandez is simply acting outrageously because that is who she is, we must acknowledge that Hernandez's behavior is deeply embedded in negotiations of gender politics and tethered to her economic realities. Her popularity on the show has garnered increased followers on social media, which has in turn led to paid club appearances, product endorsements, and a spinoff series on VH1. These are, to put it simply, the fruits of her labor as a cast member. Therefore, when Hernandez says to Jordan on one episode, "my job is to be a bad bitch," her statement actually carries a commentary (perhaps unaware) about the value of her labor for *Love & Hip Hop*.

Yet, beyond the labor that women like Hernandez put into the show, there is also the way that she functions as a cipher for a host of issues and emotions facing women of color via her ratchet performance. For, though wrapped in a ratchet package and delivery, Hernandez's struggles on the show are ones that are not all that foreign or incomprehensible: she wants love and respect from the man in her life, she desires a professional career that will give her a sense of personal fulfillment, and she struggles to reconcile her private fears and insecurities with the hard-nosed exterior that she presents to the world. These characteristics, I would argue, find particular resonance among the black women who are the bulk of the audience for *Love & Hip Hop*. Therefore, while critics are quick to attribute these shows' massive success to the outrageous behaviors of their cast members, I am interested in exploring the nuanced means of identification that this type of behavioral excess creates. Moreover, I question the ways that the type of "bad" or "negative" behavior found on these shows connects to larger politics of respectability and representation, both in media depictions of women of color—particularly African American women—and in broader social discourse.[4]

Reality Television as the Ultimate Negative Text

While the past few chapters have focused on Hollywood comedies and the television miniseries, I turn my attention now to a genre that truly occupies the "gutter" within qualitative assessments of the media landscape. While awards shows, newspaper reviews, and academic books debate the artistic, industrial, and social merits of films and television, reality television—and specifically black-cast reality television—has not typically received such in-depth critical attention and close reading.[5] Instead, discussions of reality television, particularly in the public sphere, focus overwhelmingly on the behavior of the cast members and its presumed impact on viewers. These reality television shows are often cited as bad objects, with critics and scholars alike deconstructing the ways that they reflect or promote sexism, racism, and homophobia. This is particularly true in the realm of popular media criticism, where stereotypes in reality television are constant topics of discussion in the press and on talk news programs on both radio and television. In 2012, for instance, the cultural activist Michaela Angela Davis launched the Bury the Ratchet campaign, aimed at reducing the number of problematic stereotypes found on reality television shows featuring women of color.

Davis's Bury the Ratchet campaign took aim at media that, she claimed, promote and circulate problematic depictions of black women: "[Many women] find [that] when they say [that they] are from Atlanta the first image that comes to mind is mean, gold digging women."[6] The campaign rests on the implicit premise that such imagery supports and encourages sexist, racist beliefs about black women, treating them as objects and never as subjects. Further, the campaign and similar critiques presume that because reality television is seen as light and fun (as opposed to serious dramas), it is a genre particularly adept at disseminating their sexist and racist ideologies to the public at large while escaping scrutiny. In fact, some critics argue that these ideologies are precisely what make this genre so popular among viewers. Jennifer L. Pozner contends that the genre's appeal can be attributed to the way that it confirms normative social values for viewers. She writes, "But while the schadenfreude and escapism factors may get us to tune in, that's not what hooks us. On a more subconscious level, we continue to watch because these shows frame their narratives in ways that both play to and reinforce deeply ingrained societal biases about women and men, love and beauty, race and class, consumption and happiness in America."[7] Pozner's statement, like the arguments of Michaela Angela Davis, points out the ways that reality television—and, by extension, other forms of seemingly frivolous entertainment—can circulate deeply problematic stereotypes and narratives about race, gender, sexuality, and class, made all the more dangerous by these genres' oft-cited claims that they are just "harmless fun." These critiques are necessary, particularly in cases of allegedly unscripted realism, which often falls back on the defense of the apolitical and unmitigated capturing of "reality."

While these critiques are important, they do not account for the full complexity of this genre and its possibilities for representing complex or even radical aspects of racial identity and experience. As I have discussed elsewhere, this argument does not address a few key points: "First, it takes for granted the fact that reality television characters always perform their identities according to their preconceived roles. Second, it presumes that audiences straightforwardly accept the dominant version of 'reality' that the programs carefully assemble and present to them. Instead, the strategy of casting participants from diverse backgrounds in order to create an interesting program carries with it opportunities for moments that do not adhere to the expected norms or conventions concerning performance of racial identities, and that cannot be wholly controlled by the very sophisticated production methods that these shows employ."[8] For while reality television's instances of sexism and racism warrant scrutiny, we should not limit our discussion to just these, as if these are the genre's *only* salient features. While realism can function to pass off certain ideological structures as natural, it can also serve to take apart those same constructions.

Therefore, while some may view reality television's conventions as tools to mask its regressive politics, I am interested in exploring how reality television actually lends itself to contemplations of racial (and gender) identity that are specific to its genre conventions. In other words, I argue that, in contrast to critically attended-to genres such as the sitcom or the hour-long drama, reality television involves deeper considerations of race, gender, class, and sexuality precisely because it is perceived as frivolous, fun, and trashy. It is reality television's distance from respectability, its location in the gutter of television programming and critical regard, which allows it to delve into topics and issues that its respectable counterparts shy away from.

The boom in the production of ratchet reality shows matters because, in addition to the issues that I raise here, it occurs precisely at the point where the politics of racial representation and the dynamics of network programming logic intersect. As such, these programs reflect ongoing historical debates about where black representation fits into the larger schema of the sense of identity and society that television presents to the public and who stands to gain (both ideologically and monetarily) from these representations.[9] Beginning in roughly 2004, Bravo and VH1, in particular, have enjoyed a ratings bonanza when they began producing content aimed at African American women audiences. After the runaway success of *The Real Housewives of Atlanta*, the first predominantly black cast in Bravo's *Housewives* series, the network ordered three spinoff shows featuring series' regulars and also greenlit other black–themed shows set in Atlanta and elsewhere.[10] vH1 followed a similar trajectory, gaining high ratings from mostly African American audiences with shows like *Basketball Wives* and *Love & Hip Hop*, both of which were followed by spinoffs on the network.

Bravo's and vH1's interest in black shows and audiences is in direct response to these shows' high ratings as well as from increased projections for African American buying power. Michael O'Connell observes that the "National Association of Broadcasters projects African-American buying power rising 25 percent to $1.2 trillion between 2010 and 2015," making black shows and audiences a lucrative draw for advertisers.[11] But in spite of the African American audience's buying power, networks are reluctant to discuss their cash cow too openly, for fear of being labeled a "black" network and thus potentially alienating marketing aimed at white audiences, which still commands higher advertising rates than those aimed at African American ones. O'Connell notes, "Perhaps for this reason, networks remain careful not to outwardly identify the trend."[12] This treatment of black shows and audiences as profitable, but hidden, reinforces their identities as "guilty pleasures" and also glosses over the labor that these shows do for their networks by bringing in valuable ratings and advertising dollars.

And, indeed, there is a huge amount of invisible labor that goes into these unscripted television shows. Because producers seek out nonunion talent in order to save costs, casts and crews work tireless hours and lack the protections in terms of hours and wages that unions would guarantee. In fact, the reality television boom of the early 2000s rose partly due to a Writers Guild strike in 2001. Networks found that the easiest way to get around the demands of the Guild on behalf of its writers was simply to develop programming that did not require union writers.[13] As reality shows grew more popular and their narratives more involved, however, these new reality TV writers began to chafe at what they saw as exploitation of their labor. The situation came into public consciousness in 2006 when writers on Tyra Banks's reality television modeling competition, *America's Next Top Model*, replaced their pens with picket signs and went on strike outside of the Los Angeles production studio. The writers claimed that *Top Model's* management actively prevented them from joining the Writers Guild—the very organization whose efforts inadvertently led to the prevalence of non-unionized writing labor in the first place—which would offer them better compensation, health benefits, and pensions.

Whether one agrees or disagrees that reality show writers' efforts are tantamount to those of their scripted colleagues, there can be little debate that they do, in fact, produce a recognizable product. At the very least, reality TV writers compile hundreds of hours of raw unedited footage into weekly segments with well-defined characters and season-long narrative arcs. Jeanne McDowell, writing about the above-mentioned writers' strike, offers an explanation of the networks' motives and gestures toward a larger issue of networks and executives hiding the labor of reality TV crews. On the subject of why the networks blocked the writers' admission into the Writers Guild, she says, "For one thing, it would increase production costs in a genre that is considerably cheaper to produce than scripted shows. But there's also the recognition that granting writers union status would be admitting that 'reality' shows are more scripted than they appear to be. While the responses of contestants are allegedly spontaneous, the scenarios, plots and story lines on these shows are, in fact, crafted by writers—who often go by titles like 'show producer'—functioning in much the same capacity as writers on TV's more traditional scripted sitcoms and dramas."[14] Networks' deep investment in the façade of authenticity reminds us that the basic premise that viewers are watching authentic experiences with minimal producer interference rests at the heart of reality television. And, though it may seem redundant to note the expectation of the "real" in reality television, I highlight this point to call heightened attention to the very real labor that the shows themselves endeavor to conceal.

The issue of labor becomes slightly murkier, however, when it comes to the *casts* of reality shows, as their efforts are more deliberately rendered invisible in order to protect the fiction that the shows simply capture real people living their lives as they would without the presence of the cameras. Premised on the notion that the audience is gaining a voyeuristic look into the sometimes glamorous, sometimes stressful, but always extraordinary lives of women in rarefied spaces (e.g., high society, professional sports, and the music industry), these shows' emphasis on reality is then further complicated by the burden of authenticity placed specifically on the shoulders of their largely black casts. In other words, as I have already discussed in previous chapters, but particularly in chapter 2, there is an expectation that the women on shows like *The Real Housewives of Atlanta* will "keep it real," arguably even more than their white colleagues within the same franchise. This translates into a conflation of the women's interior and performative selves, as the facets of production strive to render invisible the labor that the women actually put into the show.

The important work that black women perform on reality television—challenging traditional notions of partnership and motherhood, troubling conventional models of femininity—is often obscured by the perception that reality television is simply capturing the unadulterated actions of its performers. Further, this emphasis on the shows' unscripted nature, itself a way of dismissing the actual labor and thought that goes into their production, closes off consideration of the shows' more interesting possibilities. Finally, because the dominant convention of the genre *is* reality, evidence to the contrary (such as cast members breaking the fourth wall by acknowledging the show *as* a show), is quickly incorporated back into the show itself.

Therefore, by turning the focus onto the labor that goes into producing these shows, I want to shift the analytical lens for race away from issues of visibility and representation and toward questions of possibility and affect. For, as I will argue in this next section, reality television shows engage in complicated explorations of black women's experiences and nonnormative identities—explorations that are actually encouraged by the soap opera format of the shows—yet much of this work is buried under discourses about representation, respectability, and quality. Moreover, the insistence on authenticity creates a particular type of critical engagement with the shows that is markedly different than the approaches that a critic or scholar might take with regard to scripted television. In other words, while the shows' generic conventions encourage these nonnormative identity performances on the one hand, they also function to discourage critical acknowledgment of these practices. Though these ratchet reality shows offer some of the most interesting explorations of black women's experiences and identities (and those of women of color more broadly) currently on television, concerns about the women's images and criticisms of the reality TV genre itself bury the more significant and progressive aspects of the shows.

To put it more clearly, I argue that these shows' melodramatic conventions enable the nonnormative identity performances of the cast members and their legibility to viewers, while the conventions of the reality TV genre simultaneously work to naturalize and hide the labor that undergirds these performances. This means that though programs like *The Real Housewives of Atlanta*, *Basketball Wives*, and *Love & Hip Hop* offer unprecedented and intimate looks at the ways that black women push back against the social and institutional forces that attempt to lock them into limiting tropes and categories, the design of reality television actively endeavors to conceal these aspects of their struggles. Complicating matters is the perception of both soap opera and reality television as disreputable genres, making the shows in question "double negatives" in the truest sense of the term. As Michael Z. Newman and Elana Levine have argued, feminized soap operas often function as the "bad objects" against which critics measure the rise of the male-oriented, so-called quality television, even if the latter owes much in the way of format and narrative to the lambasted genre. Add to that the oft-repeated criticism that reality television traffics in only the most debased, stereotypical types of black representations, and it becomes clearer how the ratchet reality shows, which focus almost entirely on black women, are doubly implicated in the notion of "bad" television in the eyes of many critics.

I stress the issue of genre here, because genre conventions also figure prominently into the perception of these programs. These shows, and particularly *Love & Hip* Hop, may be categorized as reality television, but their aesthetic, narrative, and thematic structure more closely approximate the soap opera. *Love & Hip Hop*'s executive producer, Mona Scott Young, embraces the connection, saying, "What we've tried to do from a production standpoint is not just throw a camera up and show people talking. It's cinematography. There is storytelling. It's woven in a way that I like to call 'Hip-Hopera.' It's the new age soap opera."[15] As a hybrid of reality television and soap opera, *Love & Hip Hop* employs soap opera conventions in its production, as Young notes. Yet, as reality television, the show is open to criticisms regarding its authenticity and presumed effect on viewers in ways that differ from the soap opera.

Yet it is precisely this double bind, the one that relegates these shows to the absolute gutter of media taste hierarchies, that enables the rich negotiations of identity and labor that I want to explore in this chapter. For, rather than simply being evaluative markers, labels related to taste and, more specifically, "quality" also carry prescriptive and proscriptive norms, particularly when it comes to matters of gender and sexuality. In other words, it is *because* these shows operate in the televisual gutter that they are able to play with norms of behavior and identity. Whereas some critics of the genre might view these women's distance from traditional modes of acceptable femininity as troublesome or stereotypical, I contend that these kinds of negative behaviors and representations—understood as ratchetness in the context of this iteration of reality television—enable liberatory possibilities not always enjoyed by their respectable counterparts.

Moreover, an understanding of these shows as connected to the soap opera also helps us to see the economic and consumerist elements that thread throughout the shows at every level. As Lynn Spigel and Lynne Joyrich remind us, television has, since its introduction, been associated with women as consumers. Soap operas were, as their name makes clear, programs inextricably connected to the sale of domestic products to female viewers. To discuss ratchet reality shows *solely* in terms of a rhetoric of "quality" is to ignore the extent to which concerns about work, labor, and financial independence motivate women's desires to participate in these shows and guide the form that their participation takes.

Black Women, Labor, and Work on Reality Television

Most obviously, ratchet reality television challenges social norms governing personal conduct and identity for the women who inhabit their diegetic worlds, a point that I will return to later in this chapter. Less apparent, however, are the ways that these shows walk a tightrope regarding the concealment versus the reveal of these women's labor and of their work. I draw a distinction between work and labor that borrows from Matthew Tinkcom's scholarship on the work of camp and from Hannah Arendt's distinction between labor and work.[16] In this chapter, I understand "labor" in economic terms: the hours of filming time that the women contribute, the products that they promote, and the other professional ventures in which the women participate. Their labor benefits both the networks and the women themselves. By contrast, "work" occurs at the level of culture and ideology: the women's resistance to dominant norms of black femininity and the new models of subjectivity that they offer in their place. Or, to put it another way, labor might be understood as the professional activities that the women engage in on and off camera, whereas work involves their negotiation of broader conceptions of identity and social expectations.

Labor: Performance and Extratextuality

The women's labor takes two forms: the women as employees of the production company, and the shows as platforms for business opportunities. Regarding the first form of labor, the women who appear on reality television are compensated financially for their time, and they sign contracts that govern their filming schedules and locations. In order to guarantee their continued employment, the women must decide which aspects of their personal and professional lives they want to share on camera, in the interest of creating entertaining and compelling story lines.[17] Like professional actors, the women who appear on reality television are expected to perform for the camera. In terms of the second form of labor, many of the cast members use their screen time and resulting fan bases to promote their own career endeavors. However, matters of labor in these shows are complicated. The structure of the shows themselves functions to make labor invisible. Producers, writers, and editors work tireless hours and engage in any number of manipulations to present the most seamless, naturalistic narratives possible. Resting at the core of reality television is the premise of an unadulterated look into the real lives of people whom the audience would not typically have access to; therefore, those working behind the scenes endeavor to conceal the extent to which the presentation of these lives is planned, orchestrated, and choreographed. Consequently, producers work hard to pass off scheduled filming times between various cast members as happenstance gatherings of friends, and they negotiate cuts of the profits from cast members' business ventures in exchange for showcasing the business as part of the "natural" story lines.

Complicating matters is the fact that reality television of the past few years has grown progressively meta to account for the increasingly savvy viewers who are well attuned to the tricks and manipulations of production. Whereas the logic of reality television used to dictate that the show never acknowledge itself *as* a show in order to maintain the illusion of unadulterated, fly-on-the-wall reality, more recent programs have begun to incorporate extratextual components into their diegeses. For example, when a fight breaks out on *Love & Hip Hop*, it is not uncommon to see security and other staff intervening on camera. And a significant story line during season four of *Basketball Wives* involved the deterioration of the friendship between the cast members Evelyn Lozada and Jennifer Williams because of a radio interview and blog post by Williams that occurred prior to filming.

These acknowledgments of the behind-the-scenes activity do not mean, however, that the shows' producers have given up the conceit of the "realness" inherent in the reality television genre. Instead, they indicate a recognition of the new ways that audiences are engaging with the shows, as well as an effort to fold these means of engagement back into the formula of the shows' narratives. For instance, at the conclusion of the second season of *Love & Hip Hop*, Mona Scott Young eschewed the traditional reality-show reunion format (where a host and cast members assemble on a stage to discuss the season's events) in favor of sitting down with each cast member separately and offering them the opportunity to weigh their account of situations against what had aired. Young continuously provided unaired footage that supported the show's version of events, particularly whenever a cast member attempted to blame editing for how they came across. In this way, Young purposefully acknowledged the constructedness of her show but did so in order to maintain control over the images and narratives, especially in the face of the articulated criticism by cast members and the presumed criticism by viewers at home.[18]

All of this would seem to suggest that those in charge of these shows—the networks, production companies, and individual producers—wield total control over the ways that the women's labor and work is represented, to the extent that it is represented onscreen at all. Or, to be more accurate, it would seem that those in charge of production easily erase any signs that would point to the *existence* of the women's labor in the first place. Yet what we see on shows like *The Real Housewives of Atlanta*, *Basketball Wives*, and *Love & Hip Hop* are constant slippages and ruptures where the reality of the women's labor breaks through the constructed façades. While many aspects of reality television are certainly embellished or even fabricated for the sake of creating a compelling television show, there are indeed real women, real lives, and real labor that undergird the carefully manufactured pretense.

One of these moments of slippage occurred on the season five reunion show of *The Real Housewives of Atlanta*, where the women broke the fourth wall by openly discussing the show *as* labor. The intersection of race, gender, and labor came to the forefront as the black cast members interrogated a white castmate, Kim Zolciak (the only nonblack cast member on the show), for routinely missing scheduled filming days and, most significantly, for refusing to go on the mandatory filmed "vacation" that the entire cast attends each season. Zolciak claimed that she backed out of the trip to the Caribbean island of Anguilla because of medical concerns (she was pregnant at the time): "I'm not delivering my son anywhere but in the United States, honey, in Atlanta, Georgia. So take it as an excuse or not, but my priority stems [sic] at home with my children and with my family, and that's it."[19] The reunion show host and then-executive vice president of development and talent, Andy Cohen (thus making him the women's employer), pressed Zolciak more, questioning not only her absence from the trip but also her season-long refusal to film with the other women. Zolciak replied, "I think I had a lot going on with my move, and I'm having pregnancy problems; my husband's at work; I'm moving; like, I can't deal; like, I was just like, 'I can't deal anymore.'"[20] Zolciak's response is noteworthy in that she subtly reveals the pressures of filming the show, and while she stops short of referring to it as work, her statement clearly juxtaposes the demands of the show against her domestic responsibilities. In response, Cohen and cast members Cynthia Bailey and Phaedra Parks emphasize that *all* of the women on the show "have a lot going on," questioning why Zolciak's issues warrant her excused absence from job-related activities. The concept of the show as workplace comes up again when Bailey subtly turns the question to Cohen and the show's producers when she wonders aloud why Zolciak is *allowed* to miss filming (and still get paid) while the others are not.

The situation carries thinly veiled racial undertones that, though none of the women mention race directly, connects to broader historical realties regarding women, race, work, and motherhood. Of *The Real Housewives of Atlanta*'s seven cast members, five are married and four have children. Zolciak's comments, therefore, implied that *her* domestic obligations, and hers alone, should warrant a release from the professional demands of the show in a way that clearly did not apply to her castmates. And, further, her implication that her role as a wife and mother is somehow incompatible with her duties to the show only served to anger her fellow cast members, who no doubt viewed filming as a work obligation to be upheld as an effort toward financially supporting *their* families. When Bailey criticizes Zolciak, therefore, for failing to be a "team player," she is referring to their collective need to produce a show that will continue to generate revenue for each of them. It should come as no surprise, then, that the women who demonstrate the most frustration with Zolciak's poor work ethic are Bailey, Kandi Burruss, Nene Leakes, and Phaedra Parks: those cast members with the primary responsibility for financially supporting their households. This calls to mind Deborah K. King's assertion that "labor, whether unpaid and coerced (as under slavery) or paid and necessary employment, has been a distinctive characteristic of black women's social roles."[21] Phaedra Parks articulates the difference between how the white Zolciak and the black women function on the show: "You know, at the end of the day, you're married, you've got a new baby, you're pregnant. I understand. I mean, obviously,

I'm pregnant now. I had my first child on air. And I worked. Never missed a day. I mean, I went into labor many a times and they [Bravo's crew] came right to that hospital with those cameras. I never took off one day with my baby."[22]

Parks's statement refutes Zolciak's distinction between public and private forms of labor, offering in its place a version of motherhood that black feminist thinkers such as Patricia Hill Collins details in her concept of "motherwork." Arguing that motherhood has traditionally been defined through the experience of white, middle-class (heterosexual) women, Collins explains that, for women of color, divisions between public and private labor have never existed as they have for their white counterparts: "Whether because of the labor exploitation of African-American women under slavery and its ensuing tenant farm system, the political conquest of Native American women during European acquisition of land, or exclusionary immigration policies applied to Asian-Americans and Hispanics, women of color have performed motherwork that challenges social constructions of work and family as separate spheres, of male and female gender roles as similarly dichotomized, and of the search for autonomy as the guiding human quest."[23] Without necessarily being aware of it, Zolciak and her cast members play out this long-standing dichotomy between privileged versus nonprivileged motherhood traditions. In her continuous mentions of her home, her children, and her family as reasons for why she cannot work, therefore, Zolciak attempts to invoke white privilege vis-à-vis her castmates, who, lacking such privilege—and possibly sensing the dynamics at play—hold Zolciak accountable to the standards of motherwork.[24]

Beyond the coded forms of labor that occur on the show, reality television also offers an excellent platform for cast members to launch and promote their own products and business ventures. Women on *The Real Housewives*, *Basketball Wives*, *Love & Hip Hop*, and countless other reality television programs pitch a wide variety of merchandise, including T-shirts, lingerie, lip gloss, hair extensions, and even specialty cognac. And this practice is not limited to the women of color who appear on these shows. As Bethenny Frankel of *The Real Housewives of New York City* bluntly put it, "I went on the show single-handedly and exclusively for business."[25] Some of the women use their screen time to drum up publicity for existing products, such as *The Real Housewives of New York City* cast member Heather Thompson, who joined the cast to promote her already successful shapewear business Yummie. Still, the vast majority of cast members launch their ventures only

FIGURE 4.2. *The Real Housewives of Atlanta* cast reunion.

after joining the shows. In this category, there are Theresa Giudice (*The Real Housewives of New Jersey*), who stands out for her *New York Times* best-selling cookbooks, and Frankel, who may be the biggest success story of all reality TV–launched businesses with her line of Skinnygirl alcoholic beverages (and now lifestyle products), which she reportedly sold to Jim Beam for $120 million in March 2011.[26]

Reality television stars without a specific product to promote often attempt to brand their individual selves, with the goal of extending their reality television careers beyond their initial "fifteen minutes of fame" or to transition into a more legitimate sphere of the entertainment industry. Nene Leakes from *The Real Housewives of Atlanta* is a prime example of this. Leakes has managed to translate her larger-than-life persona and penchant for coming up with memorable catchphrases into a legitimate career beyond *Housewives*. While still appearing on *Housewives*, Leakes also appeared on the Bravo spinoff *I Dream of Nene: The Wedding* and other popular non-Bravo reality programs, such as *Dancing with the Stars* and *The Apprentice*. Beyond the world of reality television, Leakes caught the attention of the television producer Ryan Murphy, who first cast her as the recurring character Roz Washington on his popular musical dramedy *Glee* (FOX), and then later as Rocky Rhoades on his sitcom *The New Normal* (NBC). When *Normal* was canceled after only a season, Leakes appeared on Broadway as the wicked stepmother in a production of *Cinderella* and then as Mama Morton in

Chicago. In addition, Leakes has cohosted entertainment programs like *The View*, *Live with Kelly and Michael*, and *Fashion Police*; has made guest appearances on a variety of sitcoms, talk shows, and other TV programs, including *The Real Husbands of Hollywood*, *Jimmy Kimmel Live!*, and the *Ellen DeGeneres Show*; and toured the country in a one-woman standup show.

Of course, success stories like those of Frankel, Leakes, and, most recently, Cardi B are the exception rather than the rule. In general, products, businesses, and endeavors launched on reality shows rarely provide much more for their innovators than a story line for the duration of the season. For every Skinnygirl, there are dozens of failed cosmetics, clothing, and liquor lines, yet the promise of financial independence beyond the paycheck earned on the show is enough to keep the women trying to launch the Next Big Thing. In fact, the women's insistent attempts to launch their products, coupled with their appearance on the shows in spite of the often less-than-flattering portrayals that they receive, suggest that they are indeed thinking about their participation as revenue-generating opportunities rather than simply about chances for temporary fame.

This comes into focus with those reality TV cast members who are decidedly far below the popularity and recognition of someone like Leakes. Though they may not be able to make the leap from reality television notoriety to legitimate celebrity, these women capitalize on their fame— most often, their social media presence—to create sources of income outside of the shows. Many of the women regularly host parties in cities around the country, with promoters relying on the women's popularity to draw in attendees hoping for a "real-life" glimpse or encounter with the reality stars. Others use their Twitter and Instagram accounts to endorse products for other companies, making thousands of dollars to tweet their support of a particular teeth-whitening tool or to post a photo drinking a specific protein shake. Predictably, the women who appear on the "ratchet" reality shows tend to endorse products aimed at women, and specifically women of color, such as waist trainers, dietary teas, and hair vitamins. While these women may not rake in as much money per endorsement as famous celebrities with more recognizable names, such opportunities provide the women with an independent revenue stream that grants them a degree of financial autonomy, itself a contradiction to their performative identities on the shows as *Wives*, girlfriends, "baby mamas," and so forth, who depend on men for their economic well-being.

Of course, reality television shows are not charities. They do not exist as altruistic platforms for women to launch products and businesses and pursue financial independence. Networks such as Bravo and VH1—where the bulk of the ratchet reality shows appear—have honed strategies to maintain control over the women's work and labor.[27] These strategies generally include fitting labor into another story line, taking a share of the profits generated by the women's behavior and professional efforts, and completely erasing the women's labor from the show's diegesis.

On the shows themselves, as was the case with the motherwork that I described on *The Real Housewives of Atlanta*, labor can only be a story line to the extent that it fits into the shows' larger melodramatic narrative arcs. For example, on the second season finale of VH1's *Basketball Wives*, Evelyn Lozada reveals that she had slept with castmate Tami Roman's former husband years before the two women met. The episode reaches a dramatic high point when Roman physically attacks Lozada before tearfully exiting the scene alone, upset by the betrayal at the hands of her ex-husband as well as the seeming callousness from the woman (Lozada) with whom she had been developing a friendship. The third season opens with yet another confrontation between Lozada and Roman. This time, the audience discovers that Lozada is selling a line of T-shirts emblazoned with the words that she said to Roman at the height of the previous season's confrontation: "You are a non-motherfucking factor, bitch." Roman, feeling that Lozada is capitalizing off a shameful and hurtful event, seeks to prevent the sale of the shirts via legal injunction. The women have a second confrontation but eventually reach a mutually satisfactory resolution to the conflict, thus wrapping up this particular story line.

Basketball Wives presents the clash between Lozada and Roman as a typical, melodramatic narrative of two women fighting over the actions of a no-account man. Yet reading between the lines reveals that much of the women's conflict is actually about the invisible labor on the show itself. When Lozada first decides to confess her prior relationship with Roman's ex-husband, it is at the prompting of Shaunie O'Neal, a fellow cast member, and also, more importantly, an executive producer of *Basketball Wives*. The women are at dinner together, ostensibly to celebrate cast member Jennifer Williams's birthday, but it is clearly the finale party for the season.[28] Roman leaves the table to smoke a cigarette, at which point O'Neal takes advantage of Roman's absence to encourage Lozada to go outside and discuss the matter with Roman. "Now?" asks Lozada, clearly aware of the inevitable awkwardness and potential fireworks on the horizon, not to mention the inappropriateness of the timing. Yet, as executive producer and, hence, Lozada's employer, O'Neal is not suggesting so much as commanding. We must understand Lozada's decision to initiate the conversation with Roman, therefore, as embedded within an employer/employee dynamic. Once outside with Roman, Lozada's language also refers to the production of the show, albeit in carefully coded language. She demonstrates clear trepidation as she initiates the subject with Roman, opening with "I didn't know that you were going to come into this situation." Clearly, though, what Lozada means is "I didn't know that you were going to get cast on this show." That Lozada begins her confession with this statement indicates her awareness of the larger framework of what is about to follow: she will divulge the infidelity of Roman's then-husband, then confess her own sexual relationship with a married man, all on camera. In fact, "on camera" is the subtext that floats around the entire conversation, escalating the exchange to verbal and physical violence, and which explains Roman's subsequent tearful breakdown. When Roman angrily expresses her sense of betrayal at Lozada's actions and confession, the show would have us believe that her reaction is based on a sense of betrayal at the actions of her newfound friend. But I contend that Roman feels betrayed not by the confession, but by the fact that it is taking place on camera, thus making her personal life the unwitting source of the season finale drama. As she states in a talking-head interview segment, "It really makes me wonder if the entire time that we've been hanging out, and chilling and talking, and getting to know each other—was it real, or was it like some fraudulent bullshit?" To translate, Roman wonders whether Lozada was genuinely interested in developing a friendship, or if she was simply baiting Roman in an effort to create good television. After the confrontation turns violent and security separates Roman and Lozada, Roman tearfully admits her feelings of betrayal to O'Neal: "I thought everything was cool. I'm sitting up here saying nice things about her [Lozada], trying to be cool with her, being a friend to her, not disrespecting her." Once again, the looming but absent subtext is "on camera." In other words, Roman has been offering complimentary statements about Lozada in her interview segments and following what she *believed* her story line to be: getting back into the social scene and making new friends. It is the realization that Lozada and O'Neal have been discussing the situation on camera throughout the entire season, thus making

Roman look like a naïve fool in the eyes of viewers, that is the deception that leads to Roman's tears. As she concludes in a talking head, "I can't trust any of these bitches. That's really how I feel."

Once the third season begins and Lozada and Roman begin to fight over the production of the former's "You Are a Non-Fucking Factor, Bitch" shirts, the show once again frames the conflict as one of unresolved tensions over the previous season's confession. Certainly, this is partially true. But more than that, the new fight is about who has the right to profit from that ratchet performance. Though the phrase is one that Lozada uttered in the midst of the fight, Roman is completely aware that it came about at the expense of her dignity, and therefore she objects to Lozada profiting from her embarrassment. Again, *Basketball Wives* would have us believe that it is solely a matter of Roman's pride, but the mise-en-scène of their confrontation alerts us to the fact that this is just as much about who has the right to profit from whose performances. When Roman enters Lozada's boutique to serve her with a cease-and-desist order, she arrives wearing a T-shirt with the words "It Wasn't Not Funny" imprinted on the front. The phrase is a direct quote from Roman's days on her first reality show, *The Real World*, eighteen years before. Roman had screamed the line when a male cast member attempted to pull a blanket off her, revealing her half-naked body in spite of her vehement protests. The result was the expulsion of the offending cast member from the show. By wearing the shirt to her confrontation with Lozada, Roman demonstrates that she does not have a problem with the idea of turning a negative situation into a memorable catchphrase and profiting from it. Instead, it is the fact that it is Lozada who stands to benefit from Roman's embarrassment and pain that is the issue. In other words, Roman has not only suffered public humiliation, but also stands to endure the additional insult of watching the instigator of this humiliation make money off it.

In addition to the cast members, the networks also have a vested interest in profiting from the women's actions on the shows as well as from the products that they create. Especially in the wake of Frankel's unprecedented success with her Skinnygirl line, of which Bravo reportedly did not receive a share of the sales, producers quickly amended cast members' contracts in order to guarantee that networks, too, benefit from product sales. Bravo, for instance, allegedly receives an undisclosed percentage of the profits made from any *Housewives*-endorsed product in exchange for the "free" advertising that the network provides to the women, who

FIGURE 4.3. Evelyn Lozada (*left*) and Tami Roman in *Basketball Wives*.

often use the launch of their various product lines as narrative material for the season. And Bravo even has a store on its website where viewers can purchase apparel and merchandise with some of the more popular catchphrases from the various *Housewives*. For example, the Bravo website currently sells a T-shirt that says "Who Gon' Check Me, Boo?," a line spoken by *Atlanta* housewife Sheree Whitfield amid a heated verbal altercation with a party planner on the second season's premiere. Whitfield's calm, perfectly timed delivery of the line—complete with black-girl neck roll while wearing designer sunglasses and oversized Chanel earrings (the large size a seeming "ratchet" or "ghetto" riff on the Chanel brand's typical delicate, understated aesthetic)—resonated with viewers immediately, who created memes and animated gifs to capture and recirculate the ratchet moment, echoing Warner's argument that "the excess of the performances depends on them being viewed as spectacles that not only must be watched but must be watched repeatedly."[29] Bravo, however, quickly capitalized on the popularity of Whitfield's ratchet performance, selling the "Who Gon' Check Me, Boo?" T-shirts well after Whitfield's departure from the show

FIGURE 4.4. The "Who Gon' Check Me, Boo?" shirt for sale on Bravo's website.

at the conclusion of season four. Thus, Bravo benefited from Whitfield's performative labor on the show in the form of viewership and ratings, and then later, from the merchandising of her performance.

While Bravo has a clear way of making money off its cast members—either by receiving a share of product sales or by marketing the women's memorable phrases and moments on its website—VH1 is different because of the nature of that network. Formerly a channel dedicated exclusively to music videos, the Viacom-owned VH1 continues to play music in its early morning broadcasts and maintains ties to the music industry in spite of its foray into scripted and unscripted programming. VH1 still actively promotes music artists, whether by showing their videos or by including their music in the episodes of the network's television shows. Much of this promotion occurs through the reality shows that air on the network. Yet, ironically, even though VH1's top-rated series—*Love & Hip Hop*—is premised on the personal and professional connections between black women and the hip hop industry, the artists within *Love & Hip Hop*'s world are rarely the ones whose music is featured in the episodes.[30] Thus, though the show may capitalize on the name recognition of musicians such as K. Michelle, Teairra Marí, Remy Ma, and male rappers like Jim Jones and Joe Budden, the show more frequently highlights their personal dramas rather than their professional endeavors. And when *Love & Hip Hop* does address their identities as professional or even aspiring musicians, the story lines still emphasize the interpersonal conflicts with producers, collaborators, and so on, rather than the music itself. For example, during the first season of *Love & Hip Hop*, when would-be rapper Somaya Reece revealed her single in a live showcase, the camera largely ignored Reece's performance in order to focus on the mean-spirited comments that her castmates made while sitting in the audience and in their talking-head interviews.[31]

Therefore, when shows like *Love & Hip Hop* largely erase their cast members' work and labor in order to highlight the melodramatic story lines instead, these women must find innovative ways to make their labor visible. Often, they turn to social media to do the work that they cannot do on the shows. Yet beyond simple promotion, the women rely on the audience's intertextual engagement across media to draw connections between what the show merely references but that Instagram, Twitter, and Facebook can flesh out more fully. *Love & Hip Hop*'s musical married couple, Amina Buddafly and Peter Gunz, demonstrated this strategy during the fourth season. In one scene, Amina and Peter discuss the status of their rocky marriage and Gunz's desire to keep the union a secret, an ongoing story line that also involved Gunz's ex-girlfriend and Buddafly's fellow castmate, Tara Wallace. As their discussion comes to a close, the pair lay the matter to rest temporarily, take out their guitars (which they have brought with them), and begin playing a song together. They get through the song's rap intro and chorus before the show cuts to a commercial. Notably, Gunz wears a T-shirt promoting Buddafly's upcoming single during the scene, a means of promoting the music even though there are no direct references to what the song is or where it comes from during the actual broadcast. And, a few weeks earlier, Buddafly posted a video of the pair performing the song in its entirety on her YouTube page. In this way, Buddafly and Gunz use social media and mise-en-scène in order to create awareness around their professional activities in a way that *Love & Hip Hop* wants to make secondary to the love triangle story line.

Nonmusical cast members likewise employ this approach when it comes to marketing themselves and their products. On the second season of *Love & Hip Hop Hollywood*, one plotline involves the rapper Lil' Fizz

FIGURE 4.5. Nikki Mudarris in *Love & Hip Hop Hollywood.*

and his attempt to cut things off with former girlfriend Kamiah Adams in order to pursue a relationship with his cast member, Nikki Mudarris. In one scene, Fizz and Mudarris appear in his kitchen as a lingerie-clad Mudarris cooks breakfast, presumably after spending the night together. Fizz has arranged for Adams to come by to pick up the remainder of her belongings. In a deliciously over-the-top moment that fully embodies the show's soap opera–esque aspects, the scantily attired Mudarris sits on the kitchen counter, patiently shaping her nails with a bedazzled nail file as she waits for Adams to enter the house. Once Adams arrives, the three get into a heated verbal altercation, which, unsurprisingly, escalates into physical violence. Again, moments such as these gesture toward the ratchetness of the performances on *Love & Hip Hop*, yet the memorable takeaway from the scene is not necessarily the fight, but the visual of Mudarris, wearing nothing more than a lace negligee and heels, calmly filing her nails while sitting serenely on Fizz's kitchen counter. The episode aired on September 28, 2015, and a quick scan of Mudarris's Instagram account shows that she posted a photo from the set while shooting the scene prior to the air date. Mudarris, whose lingerie line would become a story line later on in the season, also reposts the photo once the show reveals the name of her line, "Nude by Nikki." Like Amina Buddafly and Peter Gunz, Mudarris employs the melodramatic, ratchet stage of the show as a platform from which to highlight her own business venture. And though the show itself manages Mudarris's performance in order to fit into the designated story lines for the season, Mudarris's control over her social media interactions allows her a way of complementing the show's limited presentation of her endeavors.

Work: Feeling Some Type of Way

In many ways, it is easy to identify the labor that these women perform on reality television once one makes an effort to look for it. For, in spite of the shows' designs to conceal it, the women's efforts have material evidence: contracts, salaries, products, and the media texts themselves. Less apparent, and lacking in the same kinds of signs, is the work that these same women do in terms of identity politics. Teasing out the women's work and its larger significance becomes complicated because those moments where these shows do "work" (in the vein of Tinkcom and Arendt) tend to occur at the same moments where reality and respectability collide. Cast members utter feminist sentiments within sentences laden with curse words; acknowledgments of queer identity come in the midst of a story line about sexual threesomes; questions about gender roles are raised immediately preceding a fistfight. Because critics of black media have often taken up the task of policing against so-called negative images, only the latter half of each of these scenarios seems to catch their attention, leaving the more interesting work of identity performance unacknowledged and unexamined.

Yet, in contrast to Jennifer Pozner's assessment that reality television's appeal rests in schadenfreude and confirmation of hegemonic norms, I argue that these so-called negative images provide viewers with a cathartic space for the exploration of complicated emotions. I use Lauren Berlant's concept of the intimate public as well as Laurie Ouellette and Susan Murray's notion of reality television as an "unstable text that encourages viewers to test out their own notions of the real, the ordinary, and the intimate against the representation before them," as a means of thinking about how black-cast reality shows create spaces for affective engagement and collective experience for black audiences.[32] I argue that these shows provide viewers with pleasures stemming not from schadenfreude (as many in the academic and popular spheres might quickly offer), but, instead, from the collective experience of being systematically denied access to the aspects of the American Dream and/or neoliberal notions of success that most mainstream media offer. In addition, the intimate publics created by these shows are engaged in empathy, which as Kathleen Billman argues, is not necessarily about identification through shared experiences. She writes, "In much common parlance it [empathy] implies an easy ability to feel what others feel because we have experienced something similar. But empathy, which is so much a part of listening to forgotten stories and conspiring and collaborating with individuals and congregations, is that point where otherness captures our interest and attention, and where we seek to understand what we do not yet know."[33] If, then, as Nicole Fleetwood argues, the process of deciphering media images is itself a performative act, then the act of viewing should be understood as a push back against gendered and racialized norms, and a decision to "feel" along with the women on the screen.[34] Perhaps audiences derive pleasure from these negative texts precisely because of their distance from "quality" and "positivity," if we understand these terms in quotes and presume that the audiences do as well.

What I want to offer here is the idea that shows like *Love & Hip Hop*, *Basketball Wives*, and other unapologetically trashy reality TV programs provide a safe space for emotional and psychological catharsis and the exploration of complicated, messy, or "negative" feelings. These feelings are particularly complicated because of black women's intersectionality and, thus, the ways that they experience everyday life from specifically gendered, racialized (but also classed and sexualized) points of view. Shows like *The Real Housewives of Atlanta*, *Basketball Wives*, and *Love & Hip Hop* focus on the joys and tensions of messy interpersonal relationships and—unencumbered by an emphasis on respectability—are therefore free to present the raw emotions that black women experience in these situations.

Adding to Berlant's conception of the intimate public, I contend that the ratchet reality shows make viewers "feel some type of way." The phrase, which can mean that one is jealous, angry, happy, melancholy, or confused (in addition to multiple other emotions), has been crystallized in numerous black-cast reality television shows, rap songs, and popular black vernacular. The murkiness of its definition is evident from these two entries from Urban Dictionary:

1 A phrase used to describe sexual needs, disgust, or even happiness. Usually a feeling that is so heightened it elicits confusion and raw emotion.
2 A phrase meaning I'm unable to express the complexity of the emotion at the moment. Can be used seriously or in jest.[35]

The very ambiguity of the phrase "feel some type of way" leads to the charge that it is a lazy expression for people unable or unwilling to articulate their exact sentiments. But what is particularly useful about it within the context of this discussion is that it captures the myriad feelings that do not fit neatly into socially recognizable categories. It allows for emotional messiness and complexity. The ratchet reality shows, I argue, dwell in this emotional chaos. It is this that resonates in particular with black women viewers who, because of their own intersectional identities, seek not only representations of their bodies in the images onscreen but also representations of the complex experiences of living under what Deborah K. King calls "multiple jeopardy and multiple consciousness."[36]

Further, to paraphrase a point that Berlant suggests, the pleasure that one derives from viewing a performer onscreen need not necessarily indicate identification with that person, but rather, a desire to inhabit that body and its privileges, even if just temporarily. In discussing Nella Larsen's novel *Passing*, Berlant describes the protagonist Irene's emotions toward Clare as "a desire to occupy, to experience the privileges of Clare's body, not to love or make love to her, but rather to wear her way of wearing her body, like a prosthesis or a fetish. What Irene wants is relief from the body she has: her intense class identification with the discipline of the bourgeois body is only one tactic for producing the corporeal 'fog' in which she walks."[37] I find the description of Irene's desire to escape her middle-class subjectivity to be quite apt in thinking through the appeal that a show like *Love & Hip Hop* might have for women of various socioeconomic backgrounds. Thinking about the specific pleasures that shows like *Love & Hip Hop*, *The Real Housewives*, and *Basketball Wives* provide for viewers who certainly do not imitate the actions of the cast members, Berlant's suggestion of temporary *habitation* rather than identification offers a different paradigm for sorting through the messy interplay of black representations and audiences. The intimate public created by these reality shows, then, provides its women of color viewers with a space to work out the complicated issues of living an intersectional existence.

An episode from the fourth season of vh1's *Love & Hip Hop*, where rapper Joe Budden proposes to his longtime on-again, off-again girlfriend, Tahiry Jose, emblematizes the work that I see these shows doing to provide this space for viewers. The show spends two seasons chronicling the tumultuous relationship between the two, including recovery from drug addiction, breakups, relationships with other people, a tentative reconciliation, and an ensuing split due to suspicions of infidelity. Offscreen, rumors and allegations about the couple's turbulent history popped up in gossip blogs and on social networking sites, the most troubling being the claims that Budden had a history of domestic violence with Jose as well as other prior girlfriends.[38] Although these stories did not enter into the television show's diegesis, they certainly added extratextual information to the relationship's onscreen narrative arc for fans of the show that trafficked the online spaces where information about the show circulated.

The actual scene of Budden's proposal is quite impressive from a production standpoint. It opens with shots of busy New York City streets at night, and then transitions to Budden, sitting in the back seat of a limousine as he rides to Times Square, the site of his proposal. The scene alternates between shots of the glittering nighttime cityscape and close-ups of Budden's introspective face and the red box containing the engagement ring. Then, after focusing exclusively on Budden, the scene transitions to a slow-motion shot of Tahiry Jose walking to their prearranged meeting place. The form of the scene would recall for viewers a moment from the previous season of *Love & Hip Hop* where rapper Jim Jones proposed to his girlfriend, Chrissy, with similar shots of Jones getting dressed, the ring box, and the journey to the proposal site. The glossy aesthetics of Budden's proposal demonstrate the extent to which reality television has moved away from its cinema verité roots: gone are the voyeuristic fly-on-the-wall visuals shot with handheld cameras, such as in the early days of MTV's *The Real World*. Now, shows like VH1's *Love & Hip Hop* look just as well produced and well shot as any "quality" television program that might be found on other networks known for "respectable" programming, such as AMC or HBO.

One might argue that the high production quality moves the show up along one axis and that its aesthetics approach respectability. And yet what follows—Jose's rejection of Budden's proposal—not only critiques Budden but also works to undo the formal elements of the love story that the show has thus far crafted: "So you think that you giving me a ring, I'm supposed to be like, 'Yeah, you know what? Yeah, two weeks ago he was at the strip club with the next bitch on my bed. And, now he brings me a ring.' And I'm supposed to be like, 'Yes, I do'? Nobody gives a fuck about the clarity of a stone or your nice fucking velour jacket. Get your shit right." Upon watching, Jose's blunt dismissal and use of crass language appear at odds with the proposal's glossy and romantic setup. Yet this juxtaposition actually uses the clash of the positive/quality/respectable aesthetics and the negative/trashy response in service of making a broader, feminist-infused statement about marriage and women of color. Jose not only declines the offer of marriage—and hence the thing that would make her respectable according to conventional gender norms—but calls out the elements of that respectability (the ring, the suit) as inherently undesirable. Thus, by rejecting Budden's offer in a decisively "negative" manner, Jose also refuses to accept the value typically assigned to these particular signifiers of respectability.

We should understand, however, that the proposal/rejection scenario that *Love & Hip Hop* sets up is not an either/or proposition for viewers. Instead, Jose's criticisms of Budden's intentions and actions fall into what Berlant labels the mode of "female complaint" and are inherently ambivalent. Writing about the texts that function within this mode, Berlant says, "They foreground witnessing and explaining women's disappointment in the tenuous relation of romantic fantasy to lived intimacy." Female complaints, Berlant continues, are inherently ambivalent, which translates in a particular way within the sphere of popular culture. She continues: "But in popular culture ambivalence is seen as the failure of a relation, the opposite of happiness, rather than as an inevitable condition of intimate attachment and a pleasure in its own right (as evidenced in the affectionate ironies toward personality of the situation comedy and the thrilling re-encounter with pleasure, foreboding, and disappointment familiar to fans of the soap opera and the melodrama)."[39] Thus, Jose's female complaints on *Love & Hip Hop* allow audiences both to criticize gendered structures (identifying with her rejection of Budden) and simultaneously take pleasure in the act of the proposal itself (assisted by the high production quality).

The women watching the show, therefore, get to "have it all" with this scene: the fairy tale proposal, the fantasy that the love of a good woman can actually change a bad boy into a good man, and the declaration of independence and agency that Jose proclaims via her refusal. The scene does not show Jose at first, and this structured absence allows the viewer to imagine herself as the waiting recipient of Budden's meticulous preparations. Next, the viewer identifies with Jose when she finally comes into the scene, temporarily allowing the viewer to inhabit Jose's body as she rejects Budden's ring and offer of marriage. It is a fantasy where the viewer

FIGURE 4.6. Joe Budden proposes to Tahiry Jose in New York's Times Square on *Love & Hip Hop.*

gets to enjoy the subject position of being object of desire as well as agent. This is particularly important when placed in the context of the recent onslaught of books, newspaper articles, and blog posts seeking to "explain" black women's alleged inability to marry, thus pathologizing them as inherently undesirable as well as positioning unmarried women as "failures."[40] This echoes the Berlant statement that I quoted earlier, which claims that popular culture often translates ambivalence as failure. Thus, it is crucial to acknowledge how *Love & Hip Hop* reconfigures Jose's "failure" to marry as a feminist choice: a conscious and willful rejection of Budden's advances in favor of her own emotional well-being.

THE QUEER AND WOMANIST NUANCES OF
LOVE & HIP HOP AND *BASKETBALL WIVES*

Tahiry Jose's rejection of Joe Budden's proposal is just one example of the way that *Love & Hip Hop* pushes back against heteronormativity, but it is not the only one. Take, for instance, the exploration of both feminist and queer identity on *Love & Hip Hop* (and its spinoffs, *Love & Hip Hop Atlanta* and *Love & Hip Hop Hollywood*), a reality series that ostensibly chronicles the lives and relationships of women romantically connected to men in the hip hop music industry, but that also regularly features women (and, more recently, men) whose sexual identities would be best categorized as queer. For example, on *Love & Hip Hop*, cast member Erica Mena's story line has featured her girlfriend, a development that may have surprised some viewers given Mena's previous on-air relationship with a man.[41] Some social media users even suggested that Mena's new relationship with a woman was simply a way for her to create an interesting story line for the show. Yet Mena has been quite vocal about her bisexuality and her relationships in interviews and other press materials. Most interestingly, in explaining her sexuality to interviewers, Mena shuns conventional labels like "lesbian," claiming that she finds categories such as that one to be too restrictive. At first glance, it might seem as if Mena's rejection of a lesbian identity is in service of maintaining some kind of heterosexual privilege. But in an interview with the New York radio station Hot 97, Mena states that although she does not want her relationship referred to as a "lesbian relationship," she would most certainly marry her girlfriend, Cyn Santana, adding that she would wed Santana in New Jersey because the state recognizes the legality of same-sex marriages.[42] The second season of *Love & Hip Hop Hollywood* features a season-long story line about the relationship between Miles and Milan, the former struggling to reveal his sexuality to his family, friends, and former girlfriend. The following season of the same show saw Nikki Mudarris leave Fizz (but not her bedazzled nail file) behind and enter into a relationship with another woman. Chris, Mimi Faust's love interest on *Love & Hip Hop Atlanta*, identifies as genderqueer.[43] And these are but a few examples of the numerous queer characters and relationships that are featured across all of the *Love & Hip Hop* shows.

Here, I want to take a closer look at one such story line in the series. On *Love & Hip Hop Atlanta*, Kalenna Harper articulates her nonheteronormative feelings and identity when she describes her relationship with another woman, a relationship that continues in spite of Harper's marriage to a man: "It's always been my dream to have a wife and a husband. But I know that that don't work like that. But damn it feels good to have a best friend with a fat ass that's beautiful, that smiles pretty."[44]

Over the course of three episodes, Harper's story line leads the viewer to believe that she is interested in bringing her best friend and lover, Ashley, into town in order to have a sexual threesome with Harper's husband, Tony.[45] This is reinforced by Harper's frequent statements on camera implying as much to her husband. In his interviews, Tony expresses his excitement at the possibility of sleeping with both women. But when

FIGURE 4.7. Kalenna Harper (*center*) with her girlfriend, Ashley, and husband, Tony, in *Love & Hip Hop Atlanta*.

Tony broaches the subject upon Ashley's arrival, the women shut down this idea. One episode ends with Harper and Ashley heading to the bedroom together, leaving Tony to wash their dinner dishes. This turn of events subverts Tony's (and the viewer's) expectations of a sexual encounter in which the women's bodies would serve the purpose of fulfilling his fantasies and desires. Had the story followed this more conventional path, Harper's sexuality and her relationship with Ashley would be subsumed by an emphasis on the man's sexual pleasure. This is not the case, however, and the ending of the episode leaves the women's desire for one another unquestioned and unchallenged.

Though the women do not always actively claim lesbian, bisexual, or queer identities, this does not mean that they are not involved in challenging heteronormativity on the show or for their viewers. Mena, for instance, is well aware of the fact that her actions reverberate throughout larger social discussions about sexuality. In an interview with *Vibe* magazine, she responds to those who might take issue with her fluid sexuality on the show: "It makes me laugh because whether they believe it or not this is what you have to accept, this is what is going to be on your TV every Monday night. I think what people have to just naturally give me the respect for is the fact that me being a woman and no matter what I've done, fault to mistakes or right to wrong, that I'm able to step out and be like, 'This is who I am and this is who I love to be with. This is what it is, this is my life. I'm on a reality show so you get what you get.'"[46]

Though some might criticize the women's refusal to actively claim politicized identity markers such as "lesbian" or "queer," E. Patrick Johnson, Cathy Cohen, and others argue that while these labels challenge heteronormativity in certain ways, they often fail to recognize markers of difference within nonheterosexual identities. Johnson writes, "While offering a progressive and sometimes transgressive politics of sexuality, the seams of queer theory become exposed when that theory is applied to identities around which sexuality may pivot, such as race and class."[47] For women like Erica Mena and Kalenna Harper, identifying themselves solely in relation to their sexuality closes off considerations of their race and class, factors that operate significantly both in front of and behind the camera.

More accurately, then, we might think of their identities as "quare." In his offering of "quare" as a distinctly black form of queerness, Johnson's definition overlaps with the characteristics that I have already identified as emblematic of "negative" texts:

> **Quare** (Kwâr), *n.* **1.** meaning *queer*; also, opp. of *straight*; odd or slightly off kilter; from the African American vernacular for queer; sometimes homophobic in usage, but always denotes excess incapable of being contained within conventional categories of *being*; curiously equivalent to the Anglo-Irish (and sometimes "Black" Irish) variant of queer, as in Brendan Behan's famous play *The Quare Fellow.*[48]

The excessiveness that characterizes Mena's and Harper's (and the other women's) quare sexuality, I would argue, then, is part of the same excess that renders the women's behavior ratchet (to quote Warner) or negative, as I have been using the term.[49]

Indeed, the idea of queerness/quareness extends to the identity of these ratchet shows themselves, as they are partly defined in juxtaposition to their respectable counterparts. To borrow from Alexander Doty, "I am using the term 'queer' to mark a flexible space for the expression of all aspects of non- (anti-, contra-) straight cultural production and reception."[50] The case for the show as embodying elements of a queer/quare politics becomes stronger when we look at the language that critics use to denounce the show and others like it. I already discussed the NAACP's boycott of *Amos 'n' Andy*, as well as the example of how Bill Cosby explicitly compared his sitcom to previous "negative" television representations of blackness. In the case of *Basketball Wives*, I noted the language of Star Jones's appeal to "high profile" and "conscious" black people whose duty, as she saw it, was to be part of the "solution" rather than the "problem." Boyce Watkins launched perhaps the most vehement condemnation of the reality shows that I discuss in this section in his essay titled "7 Ways VH1 is Destroying the Black Community."

In this regard, the denigrations of these shows, including the charge that these shows are little more than "modern day minstrelsy" (meant to convey the shows' trafficking in negative stereotypes), prove instructive. As I have previously noted,

> Mel Watkins and Arthur Knight have argued that African American participation in blackface minstrelsy both on stage and on celluloid were marked by a complicated set of meanings among performers and audiences. Watkins argues that the negative critique of African American minstrel performers by African American critics is deeply connected to politics of uplift and respectability during times of racial inequality. Writing about the tendency of middle class African Americans to disparage black folk culture seen as "low," he notes that these criticisms had less to do with the formal qualities of the performances themselves and more to do with how they were assumed to operate in larger discussions of race in society.[51]

In fact, looking at the language of the harshest criticism of reality television reveals much about its power to destabilize hegemonic norms, a point that Lee Edelman makes in his discussion of the conservative right's vitriolic campaign against LGBTQ rights. He writes, "The right, that is, better sees the inherently conflictual aspect of identities, the constant danger they face in alterity, the psychic anxiety with which they are lived."[52] Similarly, those critics that denigrate ratchet reality TV, for promoting negative family values, for instance, reveal anxieties about the shows' depictions of nonnormative sexuality, and the power of those representations to destabilize conventional concepts of family and gender roles. Complicating matters, however, is that black politics of respectability and uplift do not map as easily along political lines as Edelman's right vs. left comparison. While those African Americans who advance respectability politics tend to echo conservative rhetoric, they also do so in an effort to counter the racism that has historically and politically been a tool of the conservative right. In spite of this, however, Edelman's reminder that all politics, regardless of ideological affiliation, is complicit in the policing and shaping of identities is well taken. As he persuasively argues, politics'—whether liberal or conservative, ratchet or respectable—emphasis on futurism (in the case of reality television, the perceived impact of the shows on young viewers' behavior and morality) demonstrates an investment not in social change, but in the idea of the promise of social change as a moderating force for the present. Put another way, this focus on the future not only promotes a particular vision of the ideal future but also shapes the contours of discourse in the current moment. As he writes, this "serves to regulate political discourse—to prescribe what will count as political discourse—by compelling such discourse to accede in advance to the reality of a collective future whose figurative status we are never permitted to acknowledge or address."[53]

Applied to my analysis, this focus on the alleged impact of reality TV on young people is a coping mechanism aimed at alleviating feelings of helplessness or frustration in a world where structural racism still has material and political effects by assuring black people that the end of racism and oppression is as close as one "good" black character on television. Or, seemingly more accessibly, that the end of stereotypes in film and on television is as close as one positive representation. And yet, as Edelman cynically reminds us, we must remember that certain structures, whether they be political parties, media representations, or American society, have, from their birth, been designed around the inclusion of certain identities and the exclusion of others. He writes about queer identity, but his words might just as easily apply to African Americans, in the media as well as in society:

> We might like to believe that with patience, with work, with generous contributions to lobbying groups or generous participation in activist groups or generous doses of legal savvy and electoral sophistication, the future will hold a place for us—a place at the political table that won't have to come at the cost of the places we seek in the bed or the bar or the baths. But there are no queers in that future as there can be no future for queers, chosen as they are to bear the bad tidings that there can be no future at all: that the future, as Annie's hymn to the hope of "Tomorrow" understands, is "always/A day/ Away."[54]

Let us turn now to more closely examine Watkins's "7 Ways VH1 Is Destroying the Black Community" to see what the language of the article reveals about the subversive potential of reality television. Purposefully incendiary and hyperbolic in his pronouncements, Watkins outlines the specific ways that the "Evil Empire," as he dubs VH1, damages the black community. He accuses the network of (1) promoting sloppy and tragic decision making; (2) assisting in the sale of sex tapes; (3) launching "unhealthy, self-destructive" individuals into positions as role models in the black community; (4) promoting violent behavior; (5) turning viewers into passive consumers; (6) normalizing "broken" families; and (7) encouraging "dysfunctional" relationships.[55] Closer analysis of Watkins's complaints reveals that the overarching theme connecting each of the items on his list is a concern that lingers on the characters' excessive, nonnormative behaviors, particularly those concerning their romantic and sexual habits. Indeed, rather than rightfully criticize the ways that VH1 and other reality TV—heavy networks exploit women of color (taking advantage of cast members' financial need by encouraging them, whether explicitly or implicitly, to "up the drama" in order to remain employed by the shows), Watkins takes aim at the sexual and moral "looseness" of the women in question, holding them responsible for the social values of the entire black community. Particularly troubling is the way that Watkins's arguments align with a tradition of right-wing conservative politicians who, from Daniel Patrick Moynihan to Ronald Reagan and beyond, have sought to pathologize black women and cite their failure/refusal to adhere to normative gender roles as the cause of structural inequality within black communities.[56] Though he does not come right out and say it, the rhetoric in Watkins's article emphasizes white, middle-class, heteronormative family structure and appropriate gender roles as the standards by which the shows and the women on them should be judged. He promotes a masculinist vision of gender roles when he states, "This deforming of the black male psyche is making us the weakest in our communities when we should be the strongest. High-testosterone women who grow up expecting to be both the mother and the father of their kids don't help the problem either."[57] And, later, his attack on the title of the show *Basketball Wives* quite clearly invokes respectability politics: "Seriously, can you please explain what talent most of the members of *Basketball Wives* possess other than being able to get a rich athlete to sleep with them? Wait . . . maybe that is a special talent . . . the kind that men pay for on street corners late at night. From what I understand, most of the 'Basketball Wives' were never wives at all. Shouldn't they just be called 'Basketball Baby's mamas' instead?" In other words, Watkins expresses his displeasure that the women that he views as "hoes" are essentially allowed the title of, or are passing as, "housewives." His objection, I would argue, is not a semantic issue, but rather an attempt to relegate black women into categories as he (and society) deems fit. Olivia Cole fruitfully articulates the perceived dichotomy between "ho" and "housewife" and the ways that it contributes to the erasure of black women from public discourse, arguing,

> Once I (whoever "I" may be) perceives a woman as unworthy of respect, then her inhumanity is permanent, a systematic erasure of worth in which one by one, woman by woman, all of us lose our humanity over time: with every rape, every short skirt, every leaked photo, every rumored blowjob, every former stripping career, with every incident where patriarchy and its many, many gazes deems us no longer worthy of respect, we are no longer worthy of having one toe in the Madonna camp. We are delegated to whore, and with every one of these things, we are stripped, demoted, erased.[58]

Of course, in Watkins's world, there is no criticism made, or category created, for the male athletes who have children outside of marriage—only for the women who raise them outside of the conventional family structure.

Basketball Wives, the show that Watkins takes as his "bad object," provides another example of the ways that respectability politics operate invisibly, here attaching itself to the concept of what it means to be a "wife." As I have argued elsewhere, traditional definitions and media imagery of "wives" tend to make the term synonymous with upper-middle-class, heterosexual white femininity.[59] Therefore, any criticisms about the specific cast members of shows like *Basketball Wives* must be understood as stemming from assumptions about how a "wife" looks and acts.

On *Basketball Wives*, the title of "wife" is conferred on a woman whether she is or has been legally married or not. Therefore, the "wives" on the show consist of longtime and former girlfriends, ex-fiancées, and recently divorced or currently divorcing women, leading one blogger to observe, "One has to be curious as to why this show is called *Basketball Wives* rather than *Unhappy Ex-Wives and Girlfriends of Basketball Players*."[60] Interestingly, many of the show's physical confrontations occur when a woman's status is directly challenged, such as when Roman insults Lozada by indirectly referring to her as a "ho" and a "jumpoff," labels that the women offer as the polar opposite of a "wife." In another episode, the women, led by cast member Jennifer Williams, confront a known "groupie" who was possibly romantically involved with Williams's husband. The scenario is a tired cliché: the women misdirect their ire toward the "other woman" as a way of concealing their insecurities about their men's fidelity. At the same time, however, the scene embodies the tensions that surround black women and their relationship to normative gender roles, particularly the idea of what it means to be a "wife."

The irony of the women's antigroupie pearl clutching is that many of them could just as easily be classified as "groupies," "jumpoffs," or "baby mamas" by their own narrow definitions. However, within the context that I have already discussed, Williams's insistence on her identity as "the wife" (complete with ring display) in her confrontation with her husband's alleged mistress is laden with meaning. Rather than merely describing marital status, "wife" is a strategic subject position that confers respectability and value upon its bearer.

Perhaps the reason that the women on *Basketball Wives* cling so tightly to their "wife" status is because black women have always been excluded from an understanding of what it means to be one. The characteristics that define the very image of a "wife" in our society (white, middle class, appropriately feminine) have been defined in contrast to the lived experiences of black women, and have often been used to exclude them from the social, political, and financial privileges associated with its status. The Moynihan Report and its scathing condemnation of the black single mother is a notable example, as are the recent flurry of books, articles, and news reports that focus on the "problem" of unmarriageable black women.

On *Basketball Wives*, the women's assertion that they are "wives" signifies an attempt to appropriate a privilege typically denied to black women. In this way, the show functions as a site of privilege for its cast. Within the world of VH1, fiancées, girlfriends, ex-girlfriends, and baby mamas all get to claim the title of "wife" by virtue of their being cast. Interestingly, on Internet message boards, Jennifer Williams is often referred to as a "gold-digger," proving that even a wife can't be a "wife" if she happens to be black.

Conclusion

Rather than indulging in bad behavior, reality shows like the ones highlighted in this chapter provide a respite from the politics of respectability that not only dominate media representations of black women and women of color but also permeate the everyday experiences of living while black.

Thus, rather than believing that the gratification in watching these shows comes from schadenfreude, which implies emotional distance between performer and viewer, I contend that these shows function as a type of virtual reality, allowing viewers to inhabit these "bad" actors and work through the everyday tensions, contradictions, and frustrations that characterize life for black women across class, educational background, and professional achievement. Put another way, these shows and the intimate publics that they produce generate space for what Frantz Fanon describes as "collective catharsis," which he defines as "a channel, an outlet through which the forces accumulated in the form of aggression can be released." [61] In other words, shows such as *Love & Hip Hop* provide an emotional release from the social pressures placed on black women to "correctly" perform their gender along white, patriarchal norms. There is no need to "wait to exhale" with these shows, built as they are on a pneumatic smorgasbord of cathartic moments.

I would wager that many of the viewers watching these shows at home desire a break from the politics of respectability long enough that they might be able to get "real" for a moment without fearing what it might cost them (I am reminded here of Dave Chappelle's famous "When Keeping It Real Goes Wrong" sketches on Comedy Central's *Chappelle's Show*). And that is precisely the conundrum that leads to reality television's criticism and its appeal. In many ways, it is simply too real. I don't mean to suggest that "real" is synonymous with "authentic," or to imply that these explosions of anger, violence, or other bad behavior are somehow more authentic than the perfect composure and outfits of either *The Cosby Show*'s Clair Huxtable or *Scandal*'s Olivia Pope. By contrast, I view both of these types of shows as mirror images that capture the complicated nature of *being* while black. But if Pope's perfection—or, rather, the pressure to represent oneself as perfect—is one aspect of black women's experience, then the flip side is its equally relevant other. However, it is the latter that connects to problematic tropes of blackness historically promoted by Hollywood and mass media and, thus, the form that results in the type of image policing that we regularly see from popular critics and scholars alike.

As I have detailed, the structures of power in ratchet reality TV attempt to co-opt and control the labor as well as the work of the black women who inhabit these melodramatic, unscripted worlds. But as sophisticated and effective as these efforts of control often are, they are not the end of the story. For these women's performances of self hold a powerful attraction for the audiences of these shows. Indeed, it is the messy, over-the-top, "ratchet" worlds of shows like *The Real Housewives of Atlanta*, *Basketball Wives*, and *Love & Hip Hop* that provide viewers with an opportunity to linger in the emotional messiness that characterizes everyday life. And at the same time, they also provide the cast members with opportunities to seek out various degrees of personal and professional agency, even while they seemingly do little more than reinvigorate historically problematic tropes of black femininity. True, they may not really be *Housewives*, but they play them on television.

EMPIRE A False Negative?

Witness as Empire becomes synonymous with American culture. —LUCIOUS LYON

You lose your soul when you feel like the world's forgotten you. —COOKIE LYON

I know Cookie been taking some lessons from me.
I mean, where do you think she got it from? —JOSELINE HERNANDEZ

Though the buzz for the FOX Network's new show *Empire* started to build well before its premiere on January 7, 2015, nothing could have predicted the runaway success of the program, a nighttime soap opera about a hip hop music empire run by the fictitious Lyon family. The first season finale drew in a groundbreaking 17.6 million viewers, "making it the highest-rated episode of a broadcast drama to air in the last seven seasons."[1] It wasn't just *Empire*'s finale that broke records. The show gained viewers and increased in the ratings from week to week, a significant feat given that most television shows have a drop-off in their numbers between the pilot and the second episode.[2]

Immediately, and prematurely, online news outlets began predicting that *Empire*'s success would usher in sweeping changes for diversity on network television. Citing *Empire* alongside shows like *black-ish* (ABC, 2014–) and *Fresh Off the Boat* (ABC, 2015–), a *Deadline* writer, Nellie Andreeva, hyperbolically announced the explosion of "ethnic castings" during the 2015 television season.[3] *Variety*'s Debra Birnbaum praised *Empire*'s diversity both in front of and behind the cameras by noting that the show employed a large number of writers of color.[4]

The show's success reverberated outside of the conventional viewership model, too. With a heavy emphasis on diegetic musical performance that made *Empire* as similar to the television musical *Glee* as to its soap opera predecessor *Dynasty*, the show's music quickly became an additional site of fandom. The *Empire* soundtrack quickly rose to #1 on the Billboard 200 chart when it debuted on March 10, 2015, edging out Madonna's latest album release.[5] The show's costars Jussie Smollett and Bryshere "Yazz" Gray participated in album signings in the Chicago area (where *Empire* is filmed) and performed their songs on the 2015 BET awards, blurring the line between their identities as actors and their onscreen personas.

It is little surprise that, with a stellar cast led by Terrence Howard and Taraji P. Henson, musical numbers written by celebrated hip hop producer Timbaland, and fast-paced story lines that upped the ante for drama week after week, the show, created by executive producers Lee Daniels and Danny Strong, would rise to such heights in every possible aspect. And yet, with a narrative that centers on a mogul, Lucious, who made his career as a gangster rapper, and his drug-dealing ex-wife, Cookie, who returns from prison to claim her share of Lucious's fortune, it was a given that *Empire* would also stir up controversy as an example of a "negative" representation of blackness. In this regard, *Empire*'s immense popularity and impressive ratings seemed to intensify debates over the nature of its images, particularly as online news sites such as *Vulture*, *Slate*, and *The Root* talked about "the *Empire* effect": the presumed impact of the show on network executives' decisions about the types of blackness that they wanted to push forward in future programming. Whether they explicitly stated it or not, *Empire*'s detractors clearly understood "the *Empire* effect" within a media effects context, fearing that networks, show runners, and writers would hasten to duplicate *Empire*'s "negative" formula in the hopes of creating the next big media phenomenon.

As might be expected, criticism of *Empire* took the usual form by focusing on the types of African Americans and the kind of blackness portrayed on the show. Boyce Watkins, who had previously claimed that VH1 and reality shows were destroying the black community, now turned his attention to FOX and *Empire*. Employing the same dysfunctionality argument that he used to attack VH1, Watkins did not mince words when discussing the new show. He laid into the fan favorite on CNN *Tonight*, in a lengthy YouTube diatribe, and on his *Financial Juneteenth* website: "If you do some research, you might notice some of the same things I've seen in this ghetto-fied hood drama: Pimps, hoes, thugs, gangsters, emasculated black men, and all kinds of other kinds of stereotypical coonery that many of us have grown tired of seeing portrayed on-screen."[6]

Given the politics of representation that I have described in the preceding chapters, this reaction to *Empire* (as exemplified by Watkins) came as little surprise to me. Yet what I could not have anticipated would be the large-scale defense of the show by both scholars and popular critics alike. Don Lemon, the CNN journalist whose respectability politics had been on full display throughout his coverage of Trayvon Martin's murder and during the civil rights protests against police brutality in Ferguson, Missouri, provided one of the most unexpected arguments in support of *Empire*. In a radio segment on the *Tom Joyner Morning Show*, Lemon attempted to remove the burden of representation from the show's back when he argued that "no show is reflective of the entirety of our community, and I don't think *Empire* is even trying to be that."[7] A month later in a panel discussion on his CNN show, Lemon continued his defense of *Empire* and his disagreement with Watkins. In response to Watkins's charge that *Empire* shows "dysfunctional families," Lemon attempted to navigate away from a discussion of representation and toward one of genre instead: "Did you watch *Dynasty*? Did you watch *Dallas*? Did you watch *Falcon Crest*? Did you watch every soap opera that's come along?"[8] Lemon's point was that *Empire* exists within the world of fictional soap operas, and, therefore, it should be judged according to genre conventions rather than by racial tropes.

I admit to being flabbergasted at hearing Lemon use the same genre argument to defend *Empire* that I had been using to explain the affective pleasures of *Love & Hip Hop*. Moreover, I was rather amazed to see that Watkins's anti-*Empire* sentiments were in the minority among Lemon's panel. Lemon's other two guests—an *Entertainment Tonight* reporter, Nichelle Turner; and an editor for *theGrio*, Chris Witherspoon—sided with Lemon in defending the show for its representation of the nuances of black lives and black families. Given the nearly universal condemnation of *Love & Hip Hop* that I had been observing for some time, I simply could not comprehend the almost perfectly inverse reaction that *Empire* was garnering, in spite of the fact that the two shows share similar themes, characters, and story lines. What was going on? Was the praise for *Empire* a sign that the positive/negative binary had finally, at long last, been dismantled? And, if not, what was *Empire* doing that made it exempt from the usual criticisms launched at its reality TV cousins? The relatively simple answer is that, in spite of *Empire*'s somewhat stereotypical representations, melodramatic story lines, and excessive characters, it does not actually function as a negative text at all. It is, in fact, a positive text masquerading as a negative one.

A closer look at Lemon's defense of the show reveals this. Listing the reasons that he "hates" *Empire* (a play on his expected reaction given his well-known politics), Lemon directly addresses some of Watkins's more classist and homophobic criticisms of the show's representations. Watkins had cited the gay *Empire* character Jamal, played by Jussie Smollett, as an example of the mainstream media's preference for "emasculated" black men.[9] Lemon counters, "I hate that it took so long for a show like this one to come around which unapologetically shows *positive* images of Black gay men and Black gay women to the masses."[10] Lemon's use of the word "positive" is the first clue that *Empire* might not exactly be quite the negative text that Watkins claimed it to be.

Taking a closer look at Smollett's Jamal and his positioning on the show, it is easy to see why Lemon cited him as a positive character. On the show, Jamal is most often paired with and against his brother Hakeem (played by the actor-musician Bryshere Gray), and the comparison proves insightful. Jamal is fairer skinned and is an R&B songwriter-singer, in contrast to his browner-skinned brother Hakeem, a rapper and, initially, the father's favorite to take over the multimillion-dollar family business. Jamal's relationship with their father is strained and makes him the black sheep of the family (one scene in the pilot episode shows the father, Lucious, angrily dumping a young Jamal into a trash can). While Hakeem is spoiled, immature, and indulgent, Jamal is a musical genius who takes inspiration from his surroundings, channeling his frustrations and passions into his music. These assorted narrative and aesthetic associations work to present Jamal as the quite obviously exceptional, "positive" brother in comparison to Hakeem. Further, a third brother, Andre, who is characterized along the lines of the "sellout" that I described in chapter 2, functions to round out Jamal's characterization. Suit wearing, Ivy League educated, with a white wife and with no musical inclinations or abilities, Andre is the CFO of the family company. The pilot episode shows Andre standing on a staircase landing with his wife, literally looking down on his two younger brothers as they collaborate musically. With Hakeem as the most "hood" of the brothers and Andre as the sellout, Jamal essentially embodies the Goldilocks principle of black masculinity on the show. Neither excessively black nor deficient in his blackness, Jamal is just right.

Jamal is just one example of *Empire*'s careful, deliberately positive spin on a negative text. The show's elements of "quality" establish an even more persuasive case for *Empire* as a positive representation, for it is a show buffered by markers of quality at every level: from its show runner, Lee Daniels, to the Academy Award–lauded cast, and, finally, by the network on which it airs. Though *Empire* may flirt with the metaphorical gutter, discussed in the introduction of this book, the show retains a "quality" safety net that allows for a particular type of representational exploration. In other words, *Empire* is, in sum, a show that gets to play at being ratchet because of the buffering effects of "quality," as opposed to the ratchet reality shows whose negativity is simply taken as a given.

On the surface, *Empire* is a negative text. It employs the same excesses as something like *Love & Hip Hop*, with characters that we might just as easily find on that show. This is nowhere as clear as with *Empire*'s star character, Cookie Lyon, superbly acted by Henson. Brassy, sexy, calculating, and incredibly fierce, Cookie is a woman who wears her heart on her sleeve but whose emotions get the better of her, often resulting in verbal and physical outbursts. In the pilot, she promptly beats her son Hakeem with a broom when he disrespects her. In a later episode from the same season, she initiates an all-out brawl with a romantic rival, Anika, leading many viewers to make an immediate association between *Empire*'s scuffle and the legendary Krystle-Alexis catfights on *Dynasty*.

Watching Cookie fight, love, and seduce (all while wearing skintight dresses and a dizzying array of fur coats) immediately conjures up the gloriously excessive women who make up the casts of *Love & Hip Hop* and *Basketball Wives*. And yet those very qualities, which inspired some to boycott the shows made known by women like Tahiry Jose and Evelyn Lozada, suddenly became examples of "nuance" and "emotional complexity" when embodied by a fictional character on a scripted television show. These similarities did not go unnoticed by *Love & Hip Hop Atlanta*'s Joseline Hernandez, who straightforwardly claimed credit as the inspiration for Cookie's character in an online video, stating, "I know Cookie been taking some lessons from me. I mean, where do you think she got it from?"[11] Unsurprisingly, Hernandez's statement was met with backlash and denial across the Internet. This is perhaps the best evidence of the fact that *Empire*, and Cookie, are indeed "positive" representations: the impulse to disavow any connection to either Hernandez or *Love & Hip Hop* suggests the binary opposition that I have been arguing exists between positive and negative texts, and reveals the assumption that a negative image has the power to "taint" its positive counterpart by association.

Cookie Lyon gets to be a multilayered woman while Joseline Hernandez is merely "ratchet" because Taraji P. Henson is buffered by a certain type of quality taste culture, and it is this aspect that also marks *Empire* as belonging to the category of positivity rather than negativity, contrary to all outward appearances. For, as I have argued throughout this book, negativity is not just a static label that we can apply to texts outside of their historical and cultural context. True, *Empire* may traffic in elements that often connote negativity, but these should not obfuscate the ways that markers of quality constitute a large portion of the show's character. First, with the exception of music producer Timbaland, nearly all of *Empire*'s significant players come from the world of Hollywood film, rather than from television or the hip hop music industry, in spite of the show's emphasis on music. Lee Daniels is best known for directing films such as *Precious* (2009) and *The Butler* (2013), and for producing *Monster's Ball* (2001), the film for which Halle Berry won an Oscar. *Empire*'s cast features a veritable cornucopia of Academy Award nominees and winners, including Terrence Howard and Taraji P. Henson in leading roles, Gabourey Sidibe in a supporting role, and guest stars such as Courtney Love, Cuba Gooding Jr., and Jennifer Hudson. And the show packed in star power from all areas of entertainment in its first season, including cameos from music artists like Mary J. Blige, Estelle, Gladys Knight, Patti LaBelle, and Snoop Dogg.[12]

Empire's "quality" designation is further reinforced by its home on FOX, a big network not particularly known for its diverse racial programming.[13] As I already mentioned, *Empire*'s ratings bonanza created a firestorm of articles and commentary about the formula for the show's success, much of which was attributed to the racial diversity in front of and behind the camera. And yet the praise heaped on the show for its "diversity" speaks volumes about

FIGURE C.1. Joseline Hernandez in *Love & Hip Hop Atlanta*.

FIGURE C.2. Taraji P. Henson as Cookie in *Empire*.

the context within which *Empire* operates, as there is precious little commendation for the "diverse" programming on predominantly black networks like BET and TV One. In other words, the very mention of "diversity" suggests a white framework against which blackness provides a supposed added value—the pepper that spices up the dish—to put it another way. To push further, I offer that the main reason that *Empire*'s diversity becomes noteworthy is because it is (implicitly) presumed to exist on a white network and in a white genre. When Ilene Chaiken, also one of the show runners, boldly announced to *Variety* that "there's never been a drama that has told these stories," what she actually meant was that there has never been a black-cast drama on a major noncable network showing a wide range of black experiences and emotions.[14] However, that observation—I would argue—should warrant indignation rather than celebration.[15]

What is missing in Chaiken's (and others') assessment of *Empire* is the acknowledgement of a show like *Love & Hip Hop*. Indeed, as Kristen Warner observes, programs like *Basketball Wives* and *Love & Hip Hop* paved the way for *Empire* by demonstrating to networks that there was a ready market for nighttime melodramas aimed at black viewers.[16] Would the network have gambled on a show that so heavily features the type of woman that Cookie Lyon embodies (the polar opposite of Kerry Washington's perfectly coiffed and composed Olivia Pope on *Scandal*) if not for the verified popularity of figures like Evelyn Lozada and Joseline Hernandez? Would FOX have risked putting a black-cast show in a coveted primetime slot if Bravo, VH1, and other reality-heavy cable networks had not first revealed that there were highly lucrative African American TV audiences hungry for programming?[17]

While I cannot answer these questions with absolute certainty, television and film history tells us that mainstream media rarely takes chances with untested products, preferring instead to capitalize on products with a measurable degree of proven success. And it is this process that, like the many others that I have explored throughout this book, has the power to render certain texts invisible—hidden from critical discourse and robbed of the credit that they rightly deserve for the labor, the work, that they do. For the overwhelming similarities between *Empire* and *Love & Hip Hop* and their wildly divergent positions within public discussion alert us to their interconnectedness, to their relationship as a positive/negative pairing. Though *Empire* may appear to be a negative text on the surface, its function as a text that erases the complex work of a show like *Love & Hip Hop* is the surest indication that it is not.

As I write this, *Empire* continues in its popularity. In 2016, Taraji P. Henson won a Golden Globe for her performance as Cookie, cementing the mainstream recognition of both her and the show. Like many others, I will continue to tune in to see what new developments each season brings. But more than that, I am curious to see what scholars, critics, and audiences will have to say about *Empire* once the initial euphoria has worn off and scholars and fans alike have had time to process and analyze the various aspects of the show's production, circulation, and reception. I wonder whether the unabashed praise for the show will continue, or if a shift in context will result in displacement from its throne. Perhaps *Empire* will push too hard against the politics of respectability, become too excessive, too dramatic, too black, in its subsequent seasons. What then? For, if my analysis has demonstrated anything, it is that the fluctuations of taste are contingent on a myriad of factors that exist both inside and outside of the texts themselves. It is possible, then, that by next season *Empire* could descend from its lofty perch as the media darling du jour and fall into the gutter of negative representations. I, for one, have my fingers crossed.

INTRODUCTION

Epigraphs: Chris Rock, *Chris Rock: Kill the Messenger—London, New York, Johannesburg*, stand-up special, H BO, September 27, 2008. Public Enemy, "Fight the Power (Flavor Flav Meets Spike Lee)," on *Do the Right Thing: Original Motion Picture Soundtrack* (Motown, 1989). Katt Williams, *It's Pimpin' Pimpin'*, Comedy Central, November 11, 2008.

A portion of this chapter appeared in an earlier form in "Activating the Negative Image," *Television & New Media* 16, no. 7 (2015): 616–630.

1 Within R&B and hip hop music traditions, a hype man usually functions to get the crowd excited for the lead performer, often serving as an entertaining foil to the lead. For example, a regular routine for the funk group the Time involved a backup singer and dancer, Jerome Benton, producing and holding a large mirror for the lead singer Morris Day while onstage. Similarly, James Brown's famous "cape act," in which a band member draped a cape over the exhausted singer's shoulders, only for Brown to triumphantly cast it off and continue performing, could work only with the assistance of the band member as pseudo-hype man. In the case of Public Enemy, Flavor Flav's comical antics operated as a counterpoint to the explicitly political material of the lead rapper, Chuck D, thus using "buffoonery" as a way to prime the audience for the upcoming critical message.

2 Racquel Gates, "Keeping It Real(ity) Television," in *Watching While Black: Centering the Television of Black Audiences*, ed. Beretta Smith-Shomade (New Brunswick, NJ: Rutgers University Press, 2013), 141–156.

3 Throughout this book, I generally use the term "African American" when referring to specific individuals and people. I use "black" when describing more abstract concepts such as those pertaining to images and culture.

4 Lewis Gordon draws on Alfred Schutz's idea of "anonymity" and Jean-Paul Sartre's and Frantz Fanon's concepts of "overdetermination" to contextualize society's complex relationship to blackness. Lewis Gordon, "Existential Dynamics of Theorizing Black Invisibility," in *Existence in Black: An Anthology of Black Existential Philosophy*, ed. Lewis Gordon (New York: Routledge, 1997), 75.

5 I do not mean that stereotypical behaviors are synonymous with blackness; rather, I want to acknowledge that certain tropes have long been associated with

blackness. Problematic and inaccurate though this may be, this connection would certainly be comprehensible to Williams's audience.

6 Comedians Keegan-Michael Key and Jordan Peele played on this concept with their character Luther, "Obama's Anger Translator," in their comedy show, *Key & Peele* (VH1, 2012–2015).

7 Devon W. Carbado and Mitu Gulati, *Acting White? Rethinking Race in Post-racial America* (New York: Oxford University Press, 2013).

8 Many thanks to Jane Gaines for giving me the opportunity to present a portion of this chapter at Columbia University's Sites of Cinema seminar.

9 Rock's persona captures the "homeboy cosmopolitanism," a concept that Manthia Diawara describes and that Mark Anthony Neal utilizes to describe the rapper/mogul Jay-Z as a figure of both racial authenticity and global consumer appeal. See Manthia Diawara, "Homeboy Cosmopolitan," in *In Search of Africa* (Cambridge, MA: Harvard University Press, 1998), 238.

10 The leather ensemble visually connects Rock to other well-known black comedians' concert-film attire, most notably Eddie Murphy's leather jumpsuits in *Delirious* and *Raw*. I am especially grateful to Michael Gillespie for his helpful feedback on the comparison between Rock and Williams and for framing the meaning of Rock's wardrobe changes.

11 Williams carries the pimp motif throughout his specials, always entering wearing a floor-length fur coat, another reference to the pimp attire from the blaxploitation era.

12 Here I draw on Kara Keeling's use of black common sense (drawn from Wahneema Lubiano's use of the term), which posits common sense as something that can both uphold and challenge hegemony: "Common sense contains elements that consent to dominant hegemonies, as well as to aspects that are antagonistic to them. It can be understood as a record of a group's survival, incorporating compromises to dominating and exploitative forces while retaining challenges to those forces." Kara Keeling, *The Witch's Flight: The Cinematic, the Black Femme, and the Image of Common Sense* (Durham, NC: Duke University Press, 2007), 21.

13 Williams's recorded comedy specials typically take place in cities with significant African American populations and significance in African American history, such as Williams's hometown of Cincinnati, just after the police shooting of a nineteen-year-old unarmed African American man (*Katt Williams Live*, 2006); Atlanta (*The Pimp Chronicles, Pt. 1*, 2006); Chicago (*American Hustle*, 2007); and Los Angeles (*Kattpacalypse*, 2012).

14 Coincidentally, the song prominently features a sample from Willie Hutch's "I Choose You," which appears on the soundtrack for *The Mack*.

15 Williams's use of the word "nigga" implies black fellowship and functions differently from the pejorative "nigger."

16 Later, he relays that he asked Flav whether or not he cares about what the racist jokes indicate about how people perceive Flav, to which Flav responds (according to Williams), "I don't give a fuck what they think. They got to pay me, boyyyy!"

17 See, for example, the listing for the doll on Amazon: http://www.amazon.com/dp/B018DWZ6AU.

18 Many thanks to Kyra Hunting for alerting me to the existence of GoldieBlox's Movie Machine app.

19 Stuart Hall, "The Spectacle of the 'Other,'" in *Representation: Cultural Representations and Signifying Practices*, ed. Stuart Hall (London: Sage, 2003), 274.

20 Linda Williams, *Playing the Race Card: Melodramas of Black and White from Uncle Tom to O.J. Simpson* (Princeton, NJ: Princeton University Press, 2001), 276.

21 Hall, "Spectacle of the 'Other,'" 274.

22 Here, I use the dictionary definition of the word "negative" taken from http://dictionary.reference.com.

23 Most of this "unladylike" behavior comes in the form of physical aggression and sexual promiscuity, a topic that I explore in depth in chapter 4.

24 Kristen J. Warner, "They Gon' Think You Loud Regardless: Ratchetness, Reality Television, and Black Womanhood," *Camera Obscura* 30, no. 1 (2015): 129–153.

25 Stefan Martin and Walt Wolfram, "The Sentence in African American Vernacular English," in *African-American English: Structure, History, and Use*, ed. Salikoko S. Mufwene, John R. Rickford, Guy Bailey, and John Baugh (New York: Routledge, 1998), 17.

26 Yuval Taylor and Jake Austen, *Darkest America: Black Minstrelsy from Slavery to Hip-Hop* (New York: W. W. Norton, 2012), 128–131.

27 Louis Chude-Sokei, *The Last "Darky": Bert Williams, Black-on-Black Minstrelsy, and the African Diaspora* (Durham, NC: Duke University Press, 2006), 8–9.

28 Chude-Sokei, *Last "Darky."*

29 Pierre Bourdieu, *Distinction: A Social Critique of the Judgment of Taste* (Cambridge, MA: Harvard University Press, 1984), 3.

30 Here, I mobilize Matthew Tinkcom's argument that camp is queer labor whose work is disguised as play. Matthew Tinkcom, *Working Like a Homosexual: Camp, Capital, Cinema* (Durham, NC: Duke University Press, 2002), Kindle edition.

31 Bourdieu, *Distinction*, 3.

32 Henry Louis Gates Jr., *The Signifying Monkey: A Theory of Afro-American Literary Criticism* (New York: Oxford University Press, 1988), xxi.

33 Crunk Feminist Collective, "Disrespectability Politics: On Jay-Z's Bitch, Beyonce's 'Fly' Ass, and Black Girl Blue," *Crunk Feminist Collective*, January 19, 2012, http://www.crunkfeministcollective.com/2012/01/19/disrespectability-politics-on-jay-zs-bitch-beyonces-fly-ass-and-black-girl-blue/.

34 "Pharrell Williams," *Oprah Prime*, OWN, April 13, 2014.

35 Fredrick C. Harris, "The Rise of Respectability Politics," *Dissent* (Winter 2014), http://www.dissentmagazine.org/article/the-rise-of-respectability-politics.

36 Willa Paskin, "Shonda Rhimes: 'Calling a Show a "Guilty Pleasure"—It's Like Saying It's a Piece of Crap,'" *Salon*, February 10, 2013, http://www.salon.com/2013/02/10/shonda_rhimes_calling_a_show_a_guilty_pleasure_%E2%80%94_it%E2%80%99s_like_saying_its_a_piece_of_crap/; "Remarks by the President at the National Urban League Convention," White House, July 25, 2012, http://www.whitehouse.gov/the-press-office/2012/07/25/remarks-president-national-urban-league-convention.

37 Jeffrey Sconce, "Introduction," in *Sleaze Artists: Cinema at the Margins of Taste, Style, and Politics*, ed. Jeffrey Sconce (Durham, NC: Duke University Press, 2007), 4.

38 Richard Wright, "Between Laughter and Tears," *New Masses*, October 5, 1937, 25.

39 Carla Kaplan, *Zora Neale Hurston: A Life in Letters* (New York: Doubleday, 2002), 6.

40 Van Peebles has claimed in various publications that *Shaft* was a remake of his own *Sweetback*, with the more radical elements removed in favor of making the film marketable to white audiences. Given the amount of time that it took to shoot, cut, and distribute *Shaft*, it is unclear whether Van Peebles's claims are entirely accurate. However, as Jon Hartmann argues, "Sweetback's success at splitting off a Black and youth audience from the proto-typical cinematic spectator likely accelerated the marketing of American movies to Americans of African descent and gave indirect impetus to the movies' targeting of other minority groups." Jon Hartmann, "The Trope of Blaxploitation in Critical Responses to 'Sweetback,'" *Film History* 6, no. 3 (Autumn 1994): 391.

41 "Tyler Perry to Spike Lee: 'Go Straight to Hell,'" *Huffington Post*, April 20, 2011, http://www.huffingtonpost.com/2011/04/20/tyler-perry-spike-lee-go-to-hell_n_851344.html.

42 Melvin Patrick Ely, *The Adventures of Amos 'n' Andy: A Social History of an American Phenomenon* (Charlottesville: University of Virginia Press, 1991).

43 Ethel Waters, Louise Beavers, and Hattie McDaniel played Beulah over the course of the series.

44 "'Julia': Television Network Introduces First Black Family Series," *Ebony*, November 1968, 56.

45 Bob Lucas, "A 'Salt Pork and Collard Greens' TV Show," *Ebony*, June 1974, 50.

46 Herman Gray, *Watching Race: Television and the Struggle for "Blackness"* (Minneapolis: University of Minnesota Press, 1995), 80.

47 "Bill Cosby Returns to TV in Family Series," *Jet*, August 13, 1984, 57.

48 Sergio Mims, "Star Jones Calls for Boycott of 'Basketball Wives' and Other Reality Shows," *Shadow and Act*, April 27, 2012, http://blogs.indiewire.com/shadowandact/star-jones-calls-for-boycott-of-basketball-wives-and-other-reality-shows.

49 Liane Membis, "It's Time to Bury the Ratchet," *Clutch Magazine*, December 2012, http://www.clutchmagonline.com/2012/12/its-time-to-bury-the-ratchet/.

50 Joshua Gamson, *Freaks Talk Back: Tabloid Talk Shows and Sexual Nonconformity* (Chicago: University of Chicago Press, 1999).

51 Alex Abad-Santos, "The Only Gay Story Hollywood Is Telling Is One That Belongs to White Men," *Vox*, November 1, 2014, http://www.vox.com/2014/7/7/5860980/the-only-gay-story-hollywood-is-telling-is-one-that-belongs-to-white.

52 Gamson, *Freaks Talk Back*; Laura Grindstaff, *The Money Shot: Trash, Class, and the Making of TV Talk Shows* (Chicago: University of Chicago Press, 2002); Eric Schaeffer, *Bold! Daring! Shocking! True: A History of Exploitation Films, 1919–1959* (Durham, NC: Duke University Press, 1999).

53 Sconce, "Introduction," 4.

54 Phillip Brian Harper, "The Evidence of Felt Intuition: Minority Evidence, Everyday Life, and Critical Speculative Knowledge," in *Black Queer Studies*, ed. E. Patrick Johnson and Mae G. Henderson (Durham, NC: Duke University Press, 2005), 106–123.

55 Pauline Kael, "Trash, Art, and the Movies," *Harper's Magazine*, February 1969.

56 Bourdieu, *Distinction*; Theodor W. Adorno, *The Culture Industry: Selected Essays on Mass Culture* (New York: Routledge, 1991); Walter Benjamin, *The Work of Art in the Age of Mechanical Reproduction* (New York: Classic Books America, 2009); Raymond Williams, *Marxism and Literature* (Oxford: Oxford University Press, 1977).

57 Jeffrey Sconce, "'Trashing' the Academy: Taste, Excess, and an Emerging Politics of Cinematic Style," *Screen* 36, no. 4 (Winter 1995): 371–393.

58 I am indebted to Kristen Warner for the very enlightening Facebook discussion that she prompted on the subject of what constitutes a black cult film. As posters offered their suggestions, it became clear that we were simply listing every black film that we could think of that had gained some modicum of fame since its release. This led to the natural question "How do we define a black cult film?" We determined that cult status can only exist in relation to a widely accepted definition of high/low culture, which itself implies an area where "high" culture receives widespread validation from the society at large. The casual conclusion that we reached is that barely any black films have achieved this status, thus rendering the distinction, and hence the designation of "cult" status, effectively moot.

59 Gene Demby, *"All My Babies' Mamas* Won't Be Happening, But What If It Had?," NPR, January 17, 2013, http://www.npr.org/blogs/monkeysee/2013/01/16/169535025 /all-my-babies-mamas-wont-be-happening-but-what-if-it-had.

60 Jacqueline Stewart, *Migrating to the Movies: Cinema and Black Urban Modernity* (Berkeley: University of California Press, 2005); L. Williams, *Playing the Race Card.*

61 Donald Bogle, *Toms, Coons, Mulattoes, Mammies, and Bucks: An Interpretive History of African Americans in American Films*, 4th ed. (New York: Continuum, 2001), 15, 102–103.

62 Stuart Hall, "What Is This 'Black' in Black Popular Culture," in *Black Popular Culture*, ed. Gina Dent and Michele Wallace (New York: New Press, 1998), 28.

63 There are several examples of how the film continues to circulate in black popular culture. For instance, in 1998, a decade after the release of *Coming to America*, the rapper Busta Rhymes re-created the film in the music video for his song "Put Your Hands Where My Eyes Can See." In 2010, a black cultural website called "The Hillman Alumni Association" (for the fictitious historically black college on the television programs *The Cosby Show* and *A Different World*) ranked *Coming to America* #2 on its list of "Movies Every Bougie Black Person Should Have Seen."

64 Lawrence W. Levine, *Black Culture and Black Consciousness: Afro-American Folk Thought from Slavery to Freedom* (Oxford: Oxford University Press, 1978), 338.

65 Racquel Gates, "Bringing the Black: Eddie Murphy and African American Humor on *Saturday Night Live*," in *Saturday Night Live and American TV*, ed. Ron Becker, Nick Marx, and Matt Sienkiewicz (Bloomington: Indiana University Press, 2013), 151–172.

1. Eddie Murphy and Formal Negativity

Epigraphs: Steve Weintraub, "The Collider Interview: John Landis, Part II," *Collider*, September 2, 2005, http://collider.com/the-collider-interview-john-landis-part-ii/. "Eddie Murphy on His Legacy, the Oscars, and 'Saturday Night Live,'" *Rolling Stone*, October 26, 2011, http://www.rollingstone.com/movies/pictures/photos-eddie-murphy -on-his-legacy-the-oscars-and-saturday-night-live-20111026.

    A portion of this chapter appeared in an earlier form in "Bringing the Black: Eddie Murphy and African American Humor on *Saturday Night Live*," in *Saturday Night Live and American TV*, ed. Ron Becker, Nick Marx, and Matt Sienkiewicz (Bloomington: Indiana University Press, 2013), 151–172.

1 Quincy T. Mills, *Cutting across the Color Line: Black Barbers and Barbershops in America* (Philadelphia: University of Pennsylvania Press, 2013).

2 According to the makeup artist, Rick Baker, the makeup was so convincing that executives at Paramount actually complained that their young star had been rendered unrecognizable. Therefore, at the behest of the studio, Baker made Murphy's other characters more recognizable as Murphy. See the special feature "Character Building: The Many Faces of Rick Baker," on *Coming to America*, dir. John Landis (Burbank, CA: Warner Home Video, 2007), DVD.

3 Racquel Gates, "Subverting Hollywood from the Inside Out: Melvin Van Peebles's *Watermelon Man*," *Film Quarterly* 68, no. 1 (September 2014): 20.

4 Saul's Jewish identity marginalizes him from white hegemony, thus helping to establish his presence in the black community of the barbershop. At the same time, though he is ethnically white, he takes on the "white" point of view during the racial debates with the black barbers.

5 "*Coming to America* Segment from Eddie Murphy's Bio with Arsenio Hall on Biography," YouTube.com, accessed October 26, 2015, https://www.youtube.com/watch?v =3N755yrXcos.

6 "Eddie Murphy Signs Pact with Paramount," *New York Times*, August 27, 1987, http://www.nytimes.com/1987/08/27/movies/eddie-murphy-signs-pact-with -paramount.html.

7 For a more in-depth discussion of Murphy's time on SNL, see Gates, "Bringing the Black."

8 J. Fred MacDonald, *Blacks and White TV: Afro-Americans in Television since 1948* (Chicago: Nelson-Hall, 1983), 240.

9 Donald Bogle, *Toms, Coons, Mulattoes, Mammies, and Bucks: An Interpretive History of Blacks in American Films*, 4th ed. (New York: Continuum, 2001), 281.

10 I explore this concept of the black "sellout" in depth in chapter 2.

11 Bambi Haggins, *Laughing Mad: The Black Comic Persona in Post-soul America* (New Brunswick, NJ: Rutgers University Press, 2007), 74.

12 Nelson George, *Post-soul Nation: The Explosive, Contradictory, Triumphant, and Tragic 1980s as Experienced by African Americans (Previously Known as Blacks and before That Negroes)* (New York: Viking, 2004), 13.

13 George, *Post-soul Nation*, 23.

14 Elvis Mitchell, "Spike Lee: The *Playboy* Interview" (July 1991), in *Spike Lee: Interviews*, ed. Cynthia Fuchs (Jackson: University Press of Mississippi, 2002), 41.

15 Jimmie Lynn Reeves and Richard Campbell, *Cracked Coverage: Television News, the Anticocaine Crusade, and the Reagan Legacy* (Durham, NC: Duke University Press, 1994), 74.

16 Reeves and Campbell, *Cracked Coverage*, 53.

17 Herman Gray, *Watching Race: Television and the Struggle for "Blackness"* (Minneapolis: University of Minnesota Press, 1995), 34.

18 Sut Jhally and Justin Lewis, *"Enlightened" Racism: "The Cosby Show," Audiences, and the Myth of the American Dream* (Boulder, CO: Westview, 1992), 95.

19 Jhally and Lewis, *"Enlightened" Racism*, 97.

20 According to Nelson George, this shift in language was aimed at increasing sales among nonblack consumers. George, *Post-soul Nation*, 55.

21 George, *Post-soul Nation*, 14.

22 Weintraub, "Collider Interview."

23 John Landis, interviewed by Jeremy Kagan, "Visual History with John Landis," Directors Guild of America, http://www.dga.org/Craft/VisualHistory/Interviews/John-Landis.aspx.

24 Donald Bogle writes, "Predictable comedies . . . assured the mass audience that African Americans and whites could laugh together without fretting about social issues." Bogle, *Toms*, 268.

25 Mel Watkins traces the African American practice of using comedy to criticize social inequality back to its roots in West African cultural traditions. Watkins, *On the Real Side: Laughing, Lying, and Signifying—the Underground Tradition of African-American Humor That Transformed American Culture, from Slavery to Richard Pryor* (New York: Simon and Schuster, 1994), 41.

26 Marvin McAllister argues that the black penchant for parody as a way to put people and situations into a black-oriented context dates back to the theater in the years just after the American Revolution, when "New World Africans crafted complex, contradictory, and multilayered performances that celebrated, parodied, and even historicized Indian, African, and European others." In the days of slavery, for instance, African Americans created the cakewalk as a means of poking fun at the airs put on by their white owners. Marvin McAllister, *White People Do Not Know How to Behave at Entertainments Designed for Ladies and Gentlemen of Colour: William Brown's African and American Theater* (Chapel Hill: University of North Carolina Press, 2003), 7.

27 David Rensin, "Playboy Interview: Eddie Murphy," *Playboy*, February 1990, 61.

28 Rensin, "Playboy Interview," 58.

29 Rensin, "Playboy Interview," 61.

30 Monica Ndounou, *Shaping the Future of African American Film: Color-Coded Economics and the Story behind the Numbers* (New Brunswick, NJ: Rutgers University Press, 2014), Kindle edition, location 4247.

31 Ndounou, *Shaping the Future*, location 4247.

32 Rensin, "Playboy Interview," 68.

33 Rensin, "Playboy Interview," 61.

34 Rensin, "Playboy Interview," 61.

35 Weintraub, "Collider Interview."

36 For an extensive analysis of color-blindness in media, see Kristen J. Warner, *The Cultural Politics of Colorblind TV Casting*, Routledge Transformations in Race and Media (New York: Routledge, 2015).

37 *Siskel and Ebert at the Movies*, July 9, 1988.

38 "*Coming to America* Segment," Biography channel.

39 Vincent Canby, "African Prince in Queens," *New York Times*, June 29, 1988, http://www.nytimes.com/1988/06/29/movies/review-film-african-prince-in-queens.html.

40 Haggins, *Laughing Mad*, 107.

41 Notably, Landis has been quite eager to talk about his rift with Murphy and the tensions on the set of *Coming to America*. Murphy, on the other hand, demonstrates far more restraint, limiting his comments to vague allusions and without going into detail. One of the exceptions to Murphy's reserve is in the February 1990 *Playboy* interview with David Rensin, which I draw on extensively for his account of the events connected to the making of the film.

42 "Eddie Murphy Signs Five-Film Contract," *New York Times*, June 28, 1983, http://www.nytimes.com/1983/06/28/movies/eddie-murphy-signs-five-film-contract.html.

43 "Eddie Murphy Signs Pact with Paramount."

44 Rensin, "Playboy Interview," 56.

45 Weintraub, "Collider Interview."

46 Rensin, "Playboy Interview," 56.

47 Rensin, "Playboy Interview," 56.

48 Rensin, "Playboy Interview," 56.

49 James McBride, "Eddie Murphy Comes Clean," *People*, August 8, 1988.

50 McBride, "Eddie Murphy Comes Clean."

51 "Eddie Murphy on His Legacy, the Oscars, and 'Saturday Night Live.'"

52 Moreover, Ndounou argues that studios are more likely to use box-office performance as a justification for not producing black films, while continuing on with white-cast films and franchises with similar or worse box-office returns. "The mystery of Hollywood accounting affects all films but is particularly troubling for evaluating black films when the process has been used to suggest that the highest-grossing African American film to date was an economic failure in Hollywood." Ndounou, *Shaping the Future*, location 4414.

53 Similarly, fellow "Black Pack" director Robert Townsend includes a hilarious Jheri curl reference in *Hollywood Shuffle* that pokes fun at the greasy "activator" spray necessary to maintain the hairstyle.

54 Mekado Murphy, "Talking Comedy with John Landis," *New York Times*, November 21, 2011, http://artsbeat.blogs.nytimes.com/2011/11/21/talking-comedy-with-john-landis/.

55 Janet Maslin, "Nick Nolte and Eddie Murphy in *48 Hours*," *New York Times*, December 8, 1982, http://www.nytimes.com/movie/review?res=980DE7D71038F93BA357 51C1A964948260.

56 Bogle, *Toms*; Ed Guerrero, *Framing Blackness: The African American Image in Film*, Culture and the Moving Image (Philadelphia: Temple University Press, 1993);

Richard Schickel, "Review of *48 Hours*," *Time*, December 20, 1982; Canby, "African Prince in Queens."

57 Henry Jenkins, *What Made Pistachio Nuts? Early Sound Comedy and the Vaudeville Aesthetic* (New York: Columbia University Press, 1992), 22.

58 Bruce Babington and Peter Evans, *Blue Skies and Silver Linings: Aspects of the Hollywood Musical* (Dover, NH: Manchester University Press, 1985), 15.

59 Author conversation with Kevin Jerome Everson.

60 Richard Schickel, review of *Coming to America*, *Time*, July 4, 1988; Watkins, *On the Real Side*, 569.

61 I argue that Murphy operates similarly in the SNL short film *White Like Me* in my essay "Bringing the Black."

62 For an extended analysis of *White Like Me*, see Gates, "Bringing the Black."

63 In the essay "Affirmative Action and White Rage," Dwight McBride argues that the political right emphasized cultural whiteness and "reverse discrimination" as a response to discourses of multiculturalism and affirmative action. Dwight McBride, *Why I Hate Abercrombie and Fitch: Essays on Race and Sexuality* (New York: New York University Press, 2005).

64 Canby, "African Prince in Queens."

65 Tambay A. Obenson, "When Paramount Withheld *Coming to America* from the Press, Not Knowing What They Had," *Shadow and Act*, March 29, 2016, http://www.indiewire.com/2016/03/when-paramount-withheld-coming-to-america-from-film-critics-worried-about-box-office-not-knowing-what-they-had-135327/.

66 *Oprah Winfrey Show*, May 1988.

67 Ndounou, *Shaping the Future*, location 122.

68 In the DVD commentary for *Coming to America*, Landis reveals that Arsenio Hall based the character on his own father, a Baptist preacher.

2. Relational Negativity

1 Devon W. Carbado and Mitu Gulati, *Acting White? Rethinking Race in Post-racial America* (New York: Oxford University Press, 2013).

2 Ed Guerrero, *Framing Blackness: The African American Image in Film* (Philadelphia: Temple University Press, 1993), 164–165.

3 Donald Bogle argues that the diffusion and acceptance of black popular music opened the door for the favorable reception of black-themed films in the 1990s. Donald Bogle, *Toms, Coons, Mulattoes, Mammies, and Bucks: An Interpretive History of African Americans in American Films*, 4th ed. (New York: Continuum, 2001).

4 Bogle, *Toms*, 347.

5 Guerrero, *Framing Blackness*, 158.

6 Keith M. Harris, *Boys, Boyz, Bois: An Ethics of Black Masculinity in Film and Popular Media*, Studies in African American History and Culture (New York: Routledge, 2006), 82.

7 Herman Gray, *Watching Race: Television and the Struggle for "Blackness"* (Minneapolis: University of Minnesota Press, 1995), 81.

8 Wahneema Lubiano, "But Compared to What? Reading Realism, Representation, and Essentialism in *School Daze*, *Do the Right Thing*, and the Spike Lee Discourse," *Black American Literature Forum* 25, no. 2 (Summer 1991): 262.

9 Monica Ndounou, *Shaping the Future of African American Film: Color-Coded Economics and the Story behind the Numbers* (New Brunswick, NJ: Rutgers University Press, 2014), Kindle edition, locations 4339–4340.

10 Suzanne Leonard, *Fatal Attraction* (Malden, MA: Wiley-Blackwell, 2009), 81.

11 Armond White, *The Resistance: Ten Years of Pop Culture That Shocked the World* (Woodstock, NY: Overlook, 1995), 230.

12 At the end of *Working Girl*, the head of the company is the one who fires the villain and offers a promotion to Tess.

13 Derald Wing Sue, Christina M. Capodilupo, Gina C. Torino, Jennifer M. Bucceri, Aisha M. B. Holder, Kevin L. Nadal, and Marta Esquilin, "Racial Microaggressions in Everyday Life: Implications for Clinical Practice," *American Psychologist* 62, no. 4 (May–June 2007): 271–286.

14 Hal Hinson, "*Strictly Business*," *Washington Post*, November 8, 1991, http://www.washingtonpost.com/wp-srv/style/longterm/movies/videos/strictlybusinessrhinson_a0a715.htm.

15 Hinson, "*Strictly Business*."

16 Dwight A. McBride, *Why I Hate Abercrombie and Fitch: Essays on Race and Sexuality* (New York: New York University Press, 2005), 157.

17 Island World produced the film, but Warner Brothers distributed it.

18 Mark Anthony Neal, *Soul Babies: Black Popular Culture and the Post-soul Aesthetic* (New York: Routledge, 2002).

19 Bambi Haggins, *Laughing Mad: The Black Comic Persona in Post-soul America* (New Brunswick, NJ: Rutgers University Press, 2007), 76.

20 This is similar to the "off-white" version of white identity that Eddie Murphy portrays with his character Saul in *Coming to America*, as discussed in chapter 1.

21 Valerie Smith, *Not Just Race, Not Just Gender: Black Feminist Readings* (New York: Routledge, 1998), 59.

22 Racquel Gates, "Subverting Hollywood from the Inside Out: Melvin Van Peebles's *Watermelon Man*," *Film Quarterly* 68, no. 1 (Fall 2014): 9–21.

23 When Miles goes to read for the title character in *Othello*, he is disappointed to learn that he is actually auditioning for the part of understudy, with the lead being played by the famous actor James Earl Jones. Here, Jones serves as the example for the type of black actor that Miles aspires to be.

24 Neal, *Soul Babies*, 3.

25 Mia Mask describes Goldberg's performance in *The Associate* as an example of Goldberg's carnivalesque transformation (drawing on Chris Straayer's work on the "temporary transvestite film"). While I agree with Mask's assessment that the film works to reveal the performativity of both white masculinity and black femininity, I would argue that Goldberg's relatively scant time actually spent in drag on camera makes the film less like other cross-dressing comedies such as *Mrs. Doubtfire* and more like the "career women" films of the 1980s such as Colin Higgins's *9 to 5*

(1980) and *Working Girl*. Mia Mask, *Divas on Screen: Black Women in American Film* (Champaign: University of Illinois Press, 2009).

26 Malcolm Johnson, "Goldberg Does the Guy Thing in *The Associate*," *Courant*, October 25, 1996, http://articles.courant.com/1996-10-25/features/9610250083_1 _robert-w-cort-hollywood-pictures-frederic-golchan.

27 Jay Boyar, "Star's Get-Up Is Only Funny Thing in *The Associate*," *Orlando Sentinel*, October 25, 1996.

28 Stephen Holden, "Whoopi Goldberg's Turn to Try a Gender Bender," *New York Times*, October 25, 1996.

29 Roger Ebert, *"The Associate,"* *Chicago Sun-Times*, October 25, 1996, http:// rogerebert.suntimes.com/apps/pbcs.dll/article?AID=/19961025/REVIEWS /610250301/1023.

30 Holden, "Whoopi Goldberg's Turn."

31 Devon Carbado, "Privilege," in *Black Queer Studies: A Critical Anthology*, ed. E. Patrick Johnson and Mae Henderson (Durham, NC: Duke University Press, 2005), 207.

32 bell hooks, *Black Looks: Race and Representation* (New York: Routledge, 1992), 169.

33 Laura B. Randolph, "Halle Berry: Hollywood's Hottest Black Actress Has a New Husband, a New Home and a New Attitude," *Ebony*, April 1993, 114.

34 Berry's own identity politics as a biracial woman and social pressure for her to constantly proclaim her "authentic" blackness to the public may have had something to do with her strong statement about Goldberg.

35 This strategy recalls the background/foreground analogy that I referenced in chapter 1, where *The Cosby Show* placed the explicit signs of blackness in the "background" as elements of mise-en-scène.

36 Alice Walker popularized the term "womanist" to describe a black woman-oriented perspective of gender and sexuality. Sometimes described as "black feminism," "womanism" addresses black women's (and men's) experiences with the interconnected issues of race, class, and gender. Alice Walker, *In Search of Our Mothers' Gardens: Womanist Prose* (Orlando: Harcourt, 2004).

37 Kimberlé Crenshaw, "Demarginalizing the Intersection of Race and Sex: A Black Feminist Critique of Antidiscrimination Doctrine, Feminist Theory and Antiracist Politics," *University of Chicago Legal Forum* 1989, no. 1: 140.

38 Crenshaw, "Demarginalizing the Intersection," 149.

39 Deborah K. King, "Multiple Jeopardy, Multiple Consciousness: The Context of a Black Feminist Ideology," *Signs* 14, no. 1 (Autumn 1988): 42–72.

3. The Circumstantial Negativity of Halle Berry

Epigraphs: Halle Berry, speech at the seventy-fourth Academy Awards ceremony, ABC, March 24, 2002, broadcast. Jadakiss, "Why?," on *Kiss of Death* (Ruff Ryders/ Interscope, 2004).

1 Janet Maslin, "The Tables Are Turned on a Smug, Sweet-Talking Don Juan," *New York Times*, July 1, 1992, http://www.nytimes.com/1992/07/01/movies/reviews-film -the-tables-are-turned-on-a-smug-sweet-talking-don-juan.html.

2 Donald Bogle, *Toms, Coons, Mulattoes, Mammies, and Bucks: An Interpretive History of African Americans in American Films*, 4th ed. (New York: Continuum, 2001).

3 "Halle Berry," *People*, May 4, 1992.

4 LL Cool J, "Around the Way Girl," from the album *Mama Said Knock You Out* (Def Jam, 1990). More recently, the Dream's 2007 single "I Luv Your Girl" and August Alsina's 2013 "Ghetto" invoke nouveau versions of the "around-the-way girl."

5 Mia Mask, *Divas on Screen: Black Women in American Film* (Champaign: University of Illinois Press, 2009).

6 Mary Corey, "Hair Like Halle: A Cut above the Rest," *Baltimore Sun*, August 21, 1992, http://articles.baltimoresun.com/1992-08-21/features/1992234014_1_halle -berry-hairstyle-afro.

7 In the early 1990s, African American women took action—sometimes in the form of class action lawsuits—in response to workplace discrimination against "ethnic" hairstyles. Some of the companies that changed their antibraid policy as a result of these efforts included the Marriott Hotel corporation, the District of Columbia Police Department, the Smithsonian Institution, American Airlines, and the United States Navy. Pamela Ferrell, *Let's Talk Hair: Every Black Woman's Personal Consultation for Healthy Growing Hair* (Washington, DC: Cornrows and Co., 1996), 20.

8 The singer Toni Braxton also sported a short haircut. Interestingly, Braxton first appeared as a nationally recognized performer as a result of her single "Love Shoulda Brought You Home" on the soundtrack for *Boomerang*. The title is taken from a line that Berry's character, Angela, says in the film. In the video for the single, Braxton acts out the part of a cheated-on lover. This and her haircut create strong aesthetic and thematic connections to Berry's character.

9 In *Divas on Screen*, Mia Mask discusses the similarities and the symbiotic relationship between Berry's and Dandridge's careers in the chapter "Halle Berry: Charismatic Beauty in a Multicultural Age."

10 Anne Helen Petersen, "Scandals of Classic Hollywood: Dorothy Dandridge vs. the World," *Hairpin*, June 20, 2012, http://thehairpin.com/2012/06/scandals-of-classic -hollywood-dorothy-dandridge-vs-the-world.

11 Corey, "Hair Like Halle."

12 Donald Bogle discusses how Beals and Chong were typically cast as "exotics and non-racials" during their careers in the 1980s and 1990s. Bogle, *Toms*, 291.

13 Berry's appearance stands in sharp contrast with the actresses most recognized for playing iconic passing roles: Fredi Washington in Stahl's 1934 production of *Imitation of Life*, Jeanne Crain in *Pinky*, Ava Gardner in *Showboat* (George Sidney, 1951), and Susan Kohner in Douglas Sirk's remake of *Imitation of Life* in 1959. With the exception of Washington, all of the actresses playing these characters were white, a condition influenced as much by social taboos on scenes of interracial romance as by believability. In the case of *Queen*, Berry's unbelievable body serves as a distinct break from these earlier representations.

14 Bogle argues that Beals's ambiguous racial appearance led to her appearance in films where she could function as a "tan Other," a figure exoticized without

being explicitly coded as black. In films such as *Flashdance* (Adrian Lyne, 1983) and *The Bride* (Franc Roddam, 1985), Beals plays characters with no family and a fuzzy past. In *Devil in a Blue Dress* (Carl Franklin, 1995), she plays a biracial character, but Bogle notes that there was no onscreen kiss between the actress and Denzel Washington for fear that it would appear to be an interracial kiss. Bogle, *Toms*.

15 In "Faking the Funk," Caroline Streeter argues that this avowed affiliation with the black community (whether by choice of project, hairstyle, or other cultural marker) is crucial for acceptance and marketability in popular culture. Contrasting the public hostility aimed toward Mariah Carey, whose ethnic background remained ambiguous or tacitly white early in her career, with the adoration of Alicia Keys, coded as black through choice of music genre and personal style, Streeter argues that biracial, hybrid female bodies occupy "a complex node of privilege and stigma in the American racial imaginary." Caroline Streeter, "Faking the Funk: Mariah Carey, Alicia Keys, and (Hybrid) Black Celebrity," in *Black Cultural Traffic: Crossroads in Global Performance and Popular Culture*, ed. Harry Justin Elam and Kennell A. Jackson (Ann Arbor: University of Michigan Press, 2005), 185–207.

16 Jasmine Guy and Lonette McKee would eventually be cast in the miniseries as Queen's mother and friend, respectively.

17 Judith Lazarus, "The Woman Who Would Be Queen," *Los Angeles Times*, February 14, 1993, http://articles.latimes.com/1993-02-14/news/tv-225_1_halle -berry.

18 David Zurawik, "'Queen' for a Day—or Three: Miniseries Star Halle Berry Likes Exposure as Opinions Surface about Haley Saga," *Baltimore Sun*, February 17, 1993, http://articles.baltimoresun.com/1993-02-17/features/1993048135_1_halle -berry-queen-miniseries.

19 Bogle, *Toms*.

20 Lazarus, "Woman Who Would Be Queen."

21 Lazarus, "Woman Who Would Be Queen."

22 Mia Mask discusses Berry's biraciality and color privilege in *Divas on Screen*.

23 Laura B. Randolph, "Halle Berry: Hollywood's Hottest Black Actress Has a New Husband, a New Home and a New Attitude," *Ebony*, April 1993, 19.

24 Lisa Jones, "The Blacker the Berry," *Essence*, June 1994, 60.

25 Tina Jordan, "In 'Queen,' Alex Haley's Roots Are Showing," *Entertainment Weekly*, May 14, 1993, http://www.ew.com/ew/article/0,,306562,00.html.

26 Jordan, "In 'Queen,' Alex Haley's Roots Are Showing."

27 Jordan, "In 'Queen,' Alex Haley's Roots Are Showing." One wonders what a "crash course" in African American culture could have possibly consisted of.

28 Jordan, "In 'Queen,' Alex Haley's Roots Are Showing."

29 David Stevens, *Queen*, first draft of script, April 19, 1991, 1, UCLA Film and Television Archive, Los Angeles, CA.

30 David Stevens, *Queen*, second draft of script, January 17, 1992, 2, UCLA Film and Television Archive, Los Angeles, CA.

31 David Stevens, *Queen*, first draft of script, 46.

32 Adrian Piper, "Passing for White; Passing for Black," in *Out of Order, Out of Sight* (Cambridge, MA: MIT Press, 1996), 23.

33 "Alex Haley's Epic Drama 'Queen' Stars Halle Berry as Mulatto Struggling with Her Identity in Six-Hour Mini-Series," *Jet*, February 15, 1995.

34 Kristen J. Warner, "A Black Cast Doesn't Make a Black Show: City of Angels and the Plausible Deniability of Color-Blindness," in *Watching while Black: Centering the Television of Black Audiences*, ed. Beretta E. Smith-Shomade (New Brunswick, NJ: Rutgers University Press, 2012), 49–62; Herman Gray, *Watching Race: Television and the Struggle for "Blackness"* (Minneapolis: University of Minnesota Press, 1995).

35 Interestingly, Berry was rumored to have turned down the role of Annie Porter in the highly successful action film *Speed*, later played by a white actress, Sandra Bullock.

36 Ralina Joseph, *Transcending Blackness: From the New Millennium Mulatta to the Exceptional Multiracial* (Durham, NC: Duke University Press, 2012), Kindle edition, location 319.

37 Joseph, *Transcending Blackness*, location 345.

38 Allison Samuels, "Angela's Fire," *Newsweek*, June 30, 2002, http://www.newsweek.com/angelas-fire-145863.

39 Berry herself understood the historical significance of her win, albeit in a more positive way. In her acceptance speech, the actress dedicated the award to both legendary African American actresses like Dorothy Dandridge and Lena Horne and contemporary African American actresses as well.

40 Phillip French, "*Monster's Ball*—Review," *Observer*, June 8, 2002, http://www.theguardian.com/theobserver/2002/jun/09/features.review67.

41 A. O. Scott, "Courtesy and Decency Play Sneaky with a Tough Guy," *New York Times*, December 26, 2001, http://www.nytimes.com/2001/12/26/movies/26BALL.html.

42 The Production Code, also known as the Hays Code, was a set of moral protocols that filmmakers and studios had to adhere to if they wanted their films to be distributed in the United States. The Production Code was adopted in the early 1930s and was finally abandoned in the 1960s.

43 Roger Ebert, "Review of *Monster's Ball*," RogerEbert.com, February 1, 2002, http://www.rogerebert.com/reviews/monsters-ball-2002.

44 Ian Grey, "Love and Death: *Monster's Ball* Takes Its Characters into Hell," *Baltimore City Paper*, February 13, 2002.

45 A. O. Scott, "Not-So-Cuddly Cat: This One Packs a Mean Whip," *New York Times*, July 22, 2004, http://www.nytimes.com/movie/review?res=9804EEDD1E3AF931A1 5754C0A9629C8B63.

46 Berry, speech at seventy-fourth Academy Awards, ABC, March 24, 2002.

47 Aldore Collier, "Why I Will Never Marry Again," *Ebony*, August 2004, 64.

4. Embracing the Ratchet

Epigraphs: Boyce Watkins, "7 Ways VH1 Is Destroying the Black Community," *Financial Juneteenth*, April 22, 2014, http://financialjuneteenth.com/dr-boyce-watkins-7 -ways-vh1-is-destroying-the-black-community/. *Love & Hip Hop Atlanta*, "She Loves Me Not," VH1, April 29, 2013.

Portions of this chapter appeared in an earlier form in "Activating the Negative Image," *Television & New Media* 16, no. 7 (2015): 616–630; and "You Can't Turn a Ho into a Housewife: *Basketball Wives* and the Politics of Wifedom," *In Media Res*, September 26, 2011.

1 Damian Bellino, "VH1 Announces Stevie J and Joseline Spinoff and New Season of *K. Michelle: My Life*," VH1.com, August 27, 2015.

2 Kristen J. Warner, "They Gon' Think You Loud Regardless: Ratchetness, Reality Television, and Black Womanhood," *Camera Obscura* 30, no. 1 (2015): 130.

3 Warner, "They Gon' Think You Loud," 132, 133.

4 Though Joseline Hernandez is not African American, I argue that her character is still framed within the same representational model that characterizes African American women.

5 I do not mean to imply that no scholars are addressing the complexities of reality television at all. In particular, this chapter draws heavily from the work of scholars like Elana Levine, Michael Newman, Laurie Ouellette, and Kristen Warner. Further, Mark Anthony Neal's thoughtful considerations of the complexities of black popular culture, Bambi Haggins's and Mel Watkins's work on black comedy, and Herman Gray's analyses of the politics of black representation have contributed much to how I think through reality television and negative texts more broadly.

6 Liane Membis, "It's Time to Bury the Ratchet," *Clutch Magazine*, December 2012, http://www.clutchmagonline.com/2012/12/its-time-to-bury-the-ratchet/.

7 Jennifer L. Pozner, *Reality Bites Back: The Troubling Truth about Guilty Pleasure TV* (Berkeley, CA: Seal Press, 2010), Kindle edition, location 281.

8 Racquel Gates, "Keeping It Real(ity) Television," in *Watching While Black: Centering the Television of Black Audiences*, ed. Beretta Smith-Shomade (New Brunswick, NJ: Rutgers University Press, 2013), 143.

9 As Herman Gray reminds us, television has traditionally been a site of contested racial politics, precisely because the nature of television itself has been, since its origins, invested in the promotion of a singular American nation, one that has historically normalized whiteness as the desired subject/goal. Herman Gray, *Cultural Moves: African Americans and the Politics of Representation* (Berkeley: University of California Press, 2005), 96.

10 Michael O'Connell, "Race and Reality: The Quiet Success of the Black Unscripted Boom," *Hollywood Reporter*, April 3, 2014, https://www.hollywoodreporter.com /news/black-reality-shows-quiet-success-692844.

11 O'Connell, "Race and Reality."

12 O'Connell, "Race and Reality."

13 Drew Grant, "10 Year Time Capsule: When Reality TV Took Over," *Salon*, April 26, 2011, http://Bravo.salon.com/2011/04/26/10_year_time_capsule_writers_strike/.

14 Jeanne McDowell, "Strikers on the Catwalk," *Time*, July 27, 2006, http://content .time.com/time/arts/article/0,8599,1220040,00.html.

15 Ray Cornelius, "Up Close with 'Love & Hip Hop's' Mona Scott Young," RayCornelius.com, April 1, 2013, http://raycornelius.com/up-close-with-love-and-hip-hops -mona-scott-young/.

16 Matthew Tinkcom's excellent scholarship on cinema and camp proves instructive here. He notes that camp is a form of queer work that often masquerades as fun, and it is often dismissed as frivolous because of the ways that camp aesthetics deviate from standard genre conventions, as is particularly evident in recognizable genres such as the Hollywood musical and melodrama. By drawing on Hannah Arendt's concept of work as "the acts by which humans create for themselves something recognizably outside of themselves by which they can know their relation to labor," Tinkcom argues that the work of queer men "is often disguised . . . precisely through what Arendt calls its 'playfulness' and through other forms of negation to labor—laziness, lack of seriousness, indifference to the formal logics of the popular commodity of the motion picture." Tinkcom, using Arendt, differentiates between work and *labor*, where "labor is characterized as the ongoing, repetitive, dull task of scratching out a life from the world." Matthew Tinkcom, *Working Like a Homosexual: Camp, Capital, Cinema* (Durham, NC: Duke University Press, 2002), Kindle edition, location 237.

17 Interestingly, on the season two reunion for *The Real Housewives of Atlanta*, the women were noticeably subdued and civil during their interactions, a contrast with the usual combative tone and argumentative stances that typically characterize these reunions. It was rumored that the women were protesting the fact that the show had gone into syndication but that they were left out of the profits. In other words, they protested by refusing to provide the outrageous, dramatic behavior that they knew brought in ratings, a clear demonstration that the women understood the value (in a literal sense) of their actions for the network.

18 *Love & Hip Hop: Reality Check*, episode 211, VH1, February 8, 2012.

19 *The Real Housewives of Atlanta* Reunion Part II, season 5, episode 22, Bravo, April 14, 2013.

20 *Real Housewives of Atlanta* Reunion Part II, season 5, episode 22.

21 Deborah K. King, "Multiple Jeopardy, Multiple Consciousness: The Context of a Black Feminist Ideology," *Signs* 14, no. 1 (Autumn 1988): 42–72.

22 *Real Housewives of Atlanta* Reunion Part II, season 5, episode 22.

23 Patricia Hill Collins, "Shifting the Center: Race, Class, and Feminist Theorizing about Motherhood," in *Mothering: Ideology, Experience and Agency*, ed. Evelyn Nakano Glenn, Grace Chang, and Linda Rennie Forcey (New York: Routledge, 1994), 47.

24 For a more detailed analysis of the intersection of race, motherhood, and reality television, see Racquel Gates, "What Snooki and Joseline Taught Me about Race, Motherhood, and Reality TV," *Los Angeles Review of Books*, October 21, 2017, https://lareviewofbooks.org/article/what-snooki-and-joseline-taught-me-about-race -motherhood-and-reality-tv/.

25 Lizzie Widdicombe, "Perfect Pitching: Bethenny Frankel and the New Breed of Celebrity Entrepreneur," *New Yorker*, September 21, 2015, https://www.newyorker.com/magazine/2015/09/21/perfect-pitching.

26 Widdicombe, "Perfect Pitching."

27 VH1 has even co-opted the intellectual labor of black Twitter by finding the funniest memes about the week's episodes and putting them up on the VH1 website.

28 Most candid reality shows end the season with an onscreen party, always justified as an event hosted by a particular cast member. In this case, it was to celebrate Jennifer Williams's birthday.

29 Warner, "They Gon' Think You Loud," 133.

30 *Love & Hip Hop Atlanta* is a particularly high ratings performer for the network. See Bellino, "VH1 Announces Stevie J and Joseline Spinoff and New Season of *K. Michelle: My Life*."

31 The notable exception to this is cast member Cardi B (born Belcalis Almanzar), a former exotic dancer whose self-awareness, humor, and general likability made her the breakout star of the sixth season of *Love & Hip Hop*. Coming onto the show with a strong social media following already, Cardi B translated her large fan base and reality television popularity (not to mention her own musical talent) into success in the music industry: she became the first solo woman rapper in nineteen years to score a number one hit on the Billboard 100 chart with her single "Bodak Yellow." Gary Trust, "Cardi B 'Moves' to No. 1 on Billboard Hot 100 with 'Bodak Yellow,' Post Malone Debuts at No. 2 with 'Rockstar,'" *Billboard*, September 25, 2017, http://www.billboard.com/articles/columns/chart-beat/7973958/cardi-b-no-1-hot-100-post-malone-portugal-the-man.

32 Susan Murray and Laurie Ouellette, "Introduction," in *Reality TV: Remaking Television Culture*, ed. Susan Murray and Laurie Ouellette (New York: New York University Press, 2009), 8.

33 Kathleen Billman, "Pastoral Care as an Art of Community," in *The Arts of Ministry: Feminist-Womanist Approaches*, ed. Christie Cozad Neuger (Louisville, KY: Westminster John Knox Press, 1996), 35.

34 Nicole Fleetwood, *Troubling Vision: Performance, Visuality, and Blackness* (Chicago: University of Chicago Press, 2011), Kindle edition, location 211.

35 The term can be found on Urban Dictionary at http://Bravo.urbandictionary.com/define.php?term=some%20type%20of%20way.

36 King, "Multiple Jeopardy, Multiple Consciousness."

37 Lauren Berlant, *The Female Complaint: The Unfinished Business of Sentimentality in American Culture* (Durham, NC: Duke University Press, 2008), Kindle edition, location 2058.

38 Nicholas Robinson, "Joe Budden Accused of Domestic Violence by Video Vixen," *Rolling Out*, May 10, 2011, http://rollingout.com/music/joe-budden-accused-of-domestic-violence-by-video-vixen/.

39 Berlant, *Female Complaint*, 181.

40 See Ralph Richard Banks, *Is Marriage for White People? How the African American Marriage Decline Affects Everyone* (New York: Penguin, 2012), and the dating website OK

Cupid's "How Your Race Affects the Messages You Get," September 30, 2009, https://theblog.okcupid.com/how-your-race-affects-the-messages-you-get-39c68771b99e.

41 Mena and Santana break up in the next season. At the time of this writing, Santana is dating Joe Budden and the two are expecting their first child.

42 Veronica Wells, "'We're Not Lesbians': Erica Mena and Cyn Santana Discuss Their Relationship on Hot 97," *Madame Noire*, January 16, 2014, http://madamenoire.com/341575/erica-mena-and-cyn-santana-discuss-their-relationship-on-hot-97/.

43 Damian Bellino, "Chris Candidly Explains His Gender Identity and Clarifies What a 'Touch-Me-Not' Is," VH1.com, April 11, 2016.

44 "Three Way, No Way," *Love & Hip Hop*, VH1, June 23, 2014.

45 I refer to Kalenna Harper's husband, Tony, by his first name here for clarity, given that the couple share the same last name.

46 Megan Saad, "Q&A: Erica Mena Dismisses Rumors That She's Bisexual for Male Attention, Talks Coming Out to Her Family," *Vibe*, October 30, 2013, http://www.vibe.com/article/erica-mena-bisexual-talks-coming-out-her-family.

47 E. Patrick Johnson, "'Quare' Studies, or (Almost) Everything I Know about Queer Studies I Learned from My Grandmother," in *Black Queer Studies*, ed. E. Patrick Johnson and Mae G. Henderson (Durham, NC: Duke University Press, 2005), 130.

48 Johnson, "'Quare' Studies," 130.

49 *Love & Hip Hop* continued its representations of black queer identity in the second season of its *Hollywood* series, which featured a gay male couple.

50 Alexander Doty, *Making Things Perfectly Queer: Interpreting Mass Culture* (Minneapolis: University of Minnesota Press, 1993), 3.

51 Gates, "Keeping It Real(ity) Television," 150.

52 Lee Edelman, *No Future: Queer Theory and the Death Drive* (Durham, NC: Duke University Press, 2004), Kindle edition, locations 261–263.

53 Edelman, *No Future*, locations 206–209.

54 Edelman, *No Future*, locations 505–509.

55 Boyce Watkins, "7 Ways VH1 Is Destroying the Black Community," *Financial Juneteenth*, April 22, 2014, http://financialjuneteenth.com/dr-boyce-watkins-7-ways-vh1-is-destroying-the-black-community/.

56 Senator Daniel Patrick Moynihan released a highly controversial 1965 report, *The Negro Family: The Case for National Action*, which cited family structure (specifically, matriarchal households) as the cause of the worsening situation of African Americans in urban areas. Moynihan did, however, single out the black middle class as a group that had managed to escape the pitfalls of their ghetto-dwelling brethren. According to Hortense Spillers and other critics of the report, Moynihan's praise of the black middle class stemmed from what he identified as its similarities to the white middle class, which he unquestioningly positioned as the norm in terms of gender roles and family structure. In doing so, he ignored the myriad other social and structural factors that contributed to black poverty or black success. In the 1980s, Ronald Reagan famously invoked the specter of a "welfare queen" who enjoyed a lavish, work-free lifestyle at the hands of taxpayers.

57 Watkins, "7 Ways."

58 Olivia Cole, "Joy, Fear, and Twerking: The Glory of Amber Rose," *Huffington Post*, September 4, 2014, http://www.huffingtonpost.com/olivia-cole/joy-fear-and -twerking-the_b_5760482.html.

59 Gates, "Keeping It Real(ity) Television," 142.

60 Andreas Hale, "Why Aren't VH1's *Basketball Wives* Actual Wives?," Dr.Jays.com, December 22, 2010, http://live.drjays.com/index.php/2010/12/22/why-arent-vh1s -basketball-wives-actual-wives/.

61 Frantz Fanon, *Black Skin, White Masks* (London: Pluto Press, 1986), 145.

Conclusion

Epigraphs: *Empire*, "Die But Once," FOX, March 18, 2015. "False Imposition," *Empire*, FOX, January 28, 2015. "Joseline Claims Cookie from 'Empire' Is Based on Her," clip, VH1, February 10, 2015, http://www.vh1.com/shows/love_and_hip_hop _atlanta/joseline-claims-cookie-from-empire-is-based-on-her/1166158/video/.

1 Anthony Crupi, "One Tough Cookie: 'Empire' Finale Smashes Ratings Records," *Ad Age*, March 19, 2015, http://adage.com/article/media/empire-finale-smashes-ratings -records/297681/.

2 Crupi, "One Tough Cookie."

3 Nellie Andreeva, "Pilots 2015: The Year of Ethnic Castings," *Deadline*, March 24, 2015, http://deadline.com/2015/03/tv-pilots-ethnic-casting-trend-backlash-1201386511/.

4 Debra Birnbaum, "'Empire' Revels in Diverse Dynamic in the Writers' Room," *Variety*, January 8, 2015, http://variety.com/2015/tv/news/diversity-authenticity-key -to-assembling-writing-crew-for-foxs-empire-1201393872/.

5 Keith Caulfield, "'Empire' Soundtrack Debuts at No. 1 on Billboard 200 Chart, Madonna Arrives at No. 2," *Billboard*, March 17, 2015, http://www.billboard.com /articles/columns/chart-beat/6502441/empire-soundtrack-number-one-madonna -number-two.

6 Boyce Watkins, "Dr. Boyce Watkins: Why I Refuse to Support the Coonery of the Show, 'Empire,'" *Financial Juneteenth*, March 1, 2015, http://financialjuneteenth .com/dr-boyce-watkins-why-i-refuse-to-support-the-coonery-of-the-show-empire/.

7 Don Lemon, "I Hate *Empire*," *Tom Joyner Morning Show*, streaming radio, February 17, 2015.

8 "*Empire* Rules the Ratings," CNN *Tonight*, March 18, 2015.

9 Watkins, "Dr. Boyce Watkins."

10 Lemon, "I Hate *Empire*," emphasis added.

11 "Joseline Claims Cookie from 'Empire' Is Based on Her."

12 In yet another area of overlap between *Empire* and the "ratchet reality shows," Snoop Dogg makes a cameo on the season one finale of *Empire* as well as one of the last episodes of the third season of *Love & Hip Hop Atlanta*.

13 This is in spite of the fact that FOX gained a foothold among the other major networks by promoting black-oriented programming in the early 1990s. See Krystal Brent Zook, *The FOX Network and the Revolution in Black Television* (New York: Oxford University Press, 1999).

14 Birnbaum, "'Empire' Revels in Diverse Dynamic."

15 Chaiken also neglected to acknowledge shows like the medical drama *City of Angels* (CBS, 2000) and the FOX network's own comedy-drama hybrid *Roc* (FOX, 1991–1994).

16 Author conversation with Kristen Warner.

17 To my mention of Bravo and VH1 shows, I would also add Tyler Perry's soap opera, *The Haves and the Have Nots*, which airs on the Oprah Winfrey Network (OWN).

Abad-Santos, Alex. "The Only Gay Story Hollywood Is Telling Is One That Belongs to White Men." *Vox*, November 1, 2014.

Adorno, Theodor W. *The Culture Industry: Selected Essays on Mass Culture*. New York: Routledge, 1991.

"Alex Haley's Epic Drama 'Queen' Stars Halle Berry as Mulatto Struggling with Her Identity in Six-Hour Mini-Series." *Jet*, February 15, 1995.

Andreeva, Nellie. "Pilots 2015: The Year of Ethnic Castings." *Deadline*, March 24, 2015.

Babington, Bruce, and Peter Evans. *Blue Skies and Silver Linings: Aspects of the Hollywood Musical*. Dover, NH: Manchester University Press, 1985.

Banks, Ralph Richard. *Is Marriage for White People? How the African American Marriage Decline Affects Everyone*. New York: Penguin, 2012.

Baudrillard, Jean. *Simulations*. New York: Semiotext(e), 1983.

Bellino, Damian. "Chris Candidly Explains His Gender Identity and Clarifies What a 'Touch-Me-Not' Is." vH1.com, April 11, 2016.

———. "vH1 Announces Stevie J and Joseline Spinoff and New Season of *K. Michelle: My Life*." vH1.com, August 27, 2015.

Benjamin, Walter. *The Work of Art in the Age of Mechanical Reproduction*. New York: Classic Books America, 2009.

Berlant, Lauren. *The Female Complaint: The Unfinished Business of Sentimentality in American Culture*. Durham, NC: Duke University Press, 2008.

"Bill Cosby Returns to TV in Family Series." *Jet*, August 13, 1984.

Billman, Kathleen. "Pastoral Care as an Art of Community." In *The Arts of Ministry: Feminist-Womanist Approaches*, edited by Christie Cozad Neuger. Louisville, KY: Westminster John Knox Press, 1996. 10–38.

Birnbaum, Debra. "'Empire' Revels in Diverse Dynamic in the Writers' Room." *Variety*, January 8, 2015.

"Black Film Issue." *Black American Literature Forum* 25, no. 2 (Summer 1991).

Bogle, Donald. *Bright Boulevards, Bold Dreams: The Story of Black Hollywood*. New York: One World Ballantine Books, 2005.

———. *Toms, Coons, Mulattoes, Mammies, and Bucks: An Interpretive History of African Americans in American Films*. 4th ed. New York: Continuum, 2001.

Bourdieu, Pierre. *Distinction: A Social Critique of the Judgment of Taste*. Cambridge, MA: Harvard University Press, 1984.

Boyar, Jay. "Star's Get-Up Is Only Funny Thing in *The Associate*." *Orlando Sentinel*, October 25, 1996.

Brooks, Daphne A. *Bodies in Dissent: Spectacular Performances of Race and Freedom, 1850–1910*. Durham, NC: Duke University Press, 2006.

Canby, Vincent. "African Prince in Queens." *New York Times*, June 29, 1988.

Carbado, Devon. "Privilege." In *Black Queer Studies: A Critical Anthology*, edited by E. Patrick Johnson and Mae Henderson. Durham, NC: Duke University Press, 2005. 190–212.

Carbado, Devon W., and Mitu Gulati. *Acting White? Rethinking Race in Post-racial America*. New York: Oxford University Press, 2013.

Caulfield, Keith. "'Empire' Soundtrack Debuts at No. 1 on Billboard 200 Chart, Madonna Arrives at No. 2." *Billboard*, March 17, 2015.

"Character Building: The Many Faces of Rick Baker." Special feature, *Coming to America*. Dir. John Landis. Burbank, CA: Warner Home Video, 2007. DVD.

Chude-Sokei, Louis. *The Last "Darky": Bert Williams, Black-on-Black Minstrelsy, and the African Diaspora*. Durham, NC: Duke University Press, 2006.

Coignet, Rémi. "Une conversation avec Adam Broomberg and Oliver Chanarin." *Le Monde*, October 2013.

Cole, Olivia. "Joy, Fear, and Twerking: The Glory of Amber Rose." *Huffington Post*, September 4, 2014.

Collier, Aldore. "Why I Will Never Marry Again." *Ebony*, August 2004.

Collins, Patricia Hill. "Shifting the Center: Race, Class, and Feminist Theorizing about Motherhood." In *Mothering: Ideology, Experience and Agency*, edited by Evelyn Nakano Glenn, Grace Chang, and Linda Rennie Forcey. New York: Routledge. 45–65.

Corey, Mary. "Hair Like Halle: A Cut above the Rest." *Baltimore Sun*, August 21, 1992.

Cornelius, Ray. "Up Close with 'Love & Hip Hop's' Mona Scott Young." RayCornelius .com, April 1, 2013.

Crenshaw, Kimberlé. "Demarginalizing the Intersection of Race and Sex: A Black Feminist Critique of Antidiscrimination Doctrine, Feminist Theory and Antiracist Politics." *University of Chicago Legal Forum* 1989, no. 1: 139–167.

Crunk Feminist Collective. "Disrespectability Politics: On Jay-Z's Bitch, Beyonce's 'Fly' Ass, and Black Girl Blue." *Crunk Feminist Collective*, January 19, 2012.

Crupi, Anthony. "One Tough Cookie: 'Empire' Finale Smashes Ratings Records." *Ad Age*, March 19, 2015.

Demby, Gene. "*All My Babies' Mamas* Won't Be Happening, But What If It Had?" NPR, January 17, 2013.

Diawara, Manthia. *In Search of Africa*. Cambridge, MA: Harvard University Press, 1998.

Doty, Alexander. *Making Things Perfectly Queer: Interpreting Mass Culture*. Minneapolis: University of Minnesota Press, 1993.

Ebert, Roger. "*The Associate*." *Chicago Sun-Times*, October 25, 1996.

———. "Review of *Monster's Ball*." RogerEbert.com, February 1, 2002.

"Eddie Murphy on His Legacy, the Oscars, and 'Saturday Night Live.'" *Rolling Stone*, October 26, 2011.

"Eddie Murphy Signs Five-Film Contract." *New York Times*, June 28, 1983.

"Eddie Murphy Signs Pact with Paramount." *New York Times*, August 27, 1987.

Edelman, Lee. *No Future: Queer Theory and the Death Drive*. Durham, NC: Duke University Press, 2004.

Ely, Melvin Patrick. *The Adventures of Amos 'n' Andy: A Social History of an American Phenomenon*. Charlottesville: University of Virginia Press, 1991.

Ferrell, Pamela. *Let's Talk Hair: Every Black Woman's Personal Consultation for Healthy Growing Hair*. Washington, DC: Cornrows and Co., 1996.

"Fit for Akeem: The Costumes of *Coming to America*." Special feature, *Coming to America*. Dir. John Landis. Burbank, CA: Warner Home Video, 2007. DVD.

Fleetwood, Nicole. *Troubling Vision: Performance, Visuality, and Blackness*. Chicago: University of Chicago Press, 2011.

French, Phillip. "*Monster's Ball*—Review." *Observer*, June 8, 2002.

Gamson, Joshua. *Freaks Talk Back: Tabloid Talk Shows and Sexual Nonconformity*. Chicago: University of Chicago Press, 1999.

Gates, Henry Louis, Jr. *The Signifying Monkey: A Theory of Afro-American Literary Criticism*. New York: Oxford University Press, 1988.

Gates, Racquel. "Activating the Negative Image." *Television & New Media* 16, no. 7 (2015): 616–630. https://doi.org/10.1177/1527476415569363.

———. "Bringing the Black: Eddie Murphy and African American Humor on *Saturday Night Live*." In *Saturday Night Live and American TV*, edited by Ron Becker, Nick Marx, and Matt Sienkiewicz. Bloomington: Indiana University Press, 2013. 151–172.

———. "Keeping It Real(ity) Television." In *Watching while Black: Centering the Television of Black Audiences*, edited by Beretta Smith-Shomade. New Brunswick, NJ: Rutgers University Press, 2013. 141–156.

———. "Subverting Hollywood from the Inside Out: Melvin Van Peebles's *Watermelon Man*." *Film Quarterly* 68, no. 1 (Fall 2014): 9–21.

———. "What Snooki and Joseline Taught Me about Race, Motherhood, and Reality TV." *Los Angeles Review of Books*, October 21, 2017.

———. "You Can't Turn a Ho into a Housewife: *Basketball Wives* and the Politics of Wifedom." *In Media Res*, September 26, 2011. http://mediacommons .futureofthebook.org/imr/2011/09/26/you-cant-turn-ho-housewife-basketball-wives -and-politics-wifedom.

George, Nelson. *Post-soul Nation: The Explosive, Contradictory, Triumphant, and Tragic 1980s as Experienced by African Americans (Previously Known as Blacks and before That Negroes)*. New York: Viking, 2004.

Gordon, Lewis. "Existential Dynamics of Theorizing Black Invisibility." In *Existence in Black: An Anthology of Black Existential Philosophy*, edited by Lewis Gordon. New York: Routledge, 1997. 69–80.

Grant, Drew. "10 Year Time Capsule: When Reality TV Took Over." *Salon*, April 26, 2011.

Gray, Herman. *Cultural Moves: African Americans and the Politics of Representation*. Berkeley: University of California Press, 2005.

————. *Watching Race: Television and the Struggle for "Blackness."* Minneapolis: University of Minnesota Press, 1995.

Grey, Ian. "Love and Death: *Monster's Ball* Takes Its Characters into Hell." *Baltimore City Paper*, February 13, 2002.

Grindstaff, Laura. *The Money Shot: Trash, Class, and the Making of TV Talk Shows.* Chicago: University of Chicago Press, 2002.

Guerrero, Ed. *Framing Blackness: The African American Image in Film.* Culture and the Moving Image. Philadelphia: Temple University Press, 1993.

Haggins, Bambi. *Laughing Mad: The Black Comic Persona in Post-soul America.* New Brunswick, NJ: Rutgers University Press, 2007.

Hale, Andreas. "Why Aren't VH1's *Basketball Wives* Actual Wives?" Dr.Jays.com, December 22, 2010.

Hall, Stuart. "The Spectacle of the 'Other.'" In *Representation: Cultural Representations and Signifying Practices*, edited by Stuart Hall. London: Sage, 2003. 225–279.

————. "What Is This 'Black' in Black Popular Culture?" In *Black Popular Culture*, edited by Gina Dent and Michele Wallace. New York: New Press, 1998. 21–33.

"Halle Berry." *People*, May 4, 1992.

Harper, Phillip Brian. "The Evidence of Felt Intuition: Minority Evidence, Everyday Life, and Critical Speculative Knowledge." In *Black Queer Studies*, edited by E. Patrick Johnson and Mae G. Henderson. Durham, NC: Duke University Press, 2005. 106–123.

Harris, Fredrick C. "The Rise of Respectability Politics." *Dissent* 61, no. 1 (Winter 2014): 33–37.

Harris, Keith M. *Boys, Boyz, Bois: An Ethics of Black Masculinity in Film and Popular Media.* Studies in African American History and Culture. New York: Routledge, 2006.

Hartmann, Jon. "The Trope of Blaxploitation in Critical Responses to 'Sweetback.'" *Film History* 6, no. 3 (Autumn 1994): 382–404.

Hinson, Hal. "*Strictly Business*." *Washington Post*, November 8, 1991.

Holden, Stephen. "Whoopi Goldberg's Turn to Try a Gender Bender." *New York Times*, October 25, 1996.

hooks, bell. *Black Looks: Race and Representation.* New York: Routledge, 1992.

Hornaday, Anne. "'12 Years a Slave,' 'Mother of George,' and the Aesthetic Politics of Filming Black Skin." *Washington Post*, October 17, 2013.

Jenkins, Henry. *What Made Pistachio Nuts? Early Sound Comedy and the Vaudeville Aesthetic.* New York: Columbia University Press, 1992.

Jhally, Sut, and Justin Lewis. *"Enlightened" Racism: "The Cosby Show," Audiences, and the Myth of the American Dream.* Boulder, CO: Westview, 1992.

Johnson, E. Patrick. "'Quare' Studies, or (Almost) Everything I Know about Queer Studies I Learned from My Grandmother." In *Black Queer Studies*, edited by E. Patrick Johnson and Mae G. Henderson. Durham, NC: Duke University Press, 2005. 124–160.

Johnson, Malcolm. "Goldberg Does the Guy Thing in *The Associate*." *Courant*, October 25, 1996.

Jones, Lisa. "The Blacker the Berry." *Essence*, June 1994.

Jordan, Tina. "In 'Queen,' Alex Haley's Roots Are Showing." *Entertainment Weekly*, May 14, 1993.

Joseph, Ralina. *Transcending Blackness: From the New Millennium Mulatta to the Exceptional Multiracial*. Durham, NC: Duke University Press, 2012.

"'Julia': Television Network Introduces First Black Family Series." *Ebony*, November 1968.

Kael, Pauline. "Trash, Art, and the Movies." *Harper's Magazine*, February 1969.

Kaplan, Carla. *Zora Neale Hurston: A Life in Letters*. New York: Doubleday, 2002.

Keeling, Kara. *The Witch's Flight: The Cinematic, the Black Femme, and the Image of Common Sense*. Durham, NC: Duke University Press, 2007.

King, Deborah K. "Multiple Jeopardy, Multiple Consciousness: The Context of a Black Feminist Ideology." *Signs* 14, no. 1 (Autumn 1988): 42–72.

Lazarus, Judith. "The Woman Who Would Be Queen." *Los Angeles Times*, February 14, 1993.

Leonard, Suzanne. *Fatal Attraction*. Malden, MA: Wiley-Blackwell, 2009.

Levine, Lawrence W. *Black Culture and Black Consciousness: Afro-American Folk Thought from Slavery to Freedom*. Oxford: Oxford University Press, 1978.

Lott, Eric. *Love and Theft: Blackface Minstrelsy and the American Working Class*. Race and American Culture. New York: Oxford University Press, 1993.

Lott, Tommy. "A No-Theory Theory of Contemporary Black American Cinema." *Black American Literature Forum* 25, no. 2 (Summer 1991): 221–237.

Love & Hip Hop: Reality Check. Episode 211. VH1, February 8, 2012.

Lubiano, Wahneema. "But Compared to What? Reading Realism, Representation, and Essentialism in *School Daze, Do the Right Thing*, and the Spike Lee Discourse." *Black American Literature Forum* 25, no. 2 (Summer 1991): 253–282.

Lucas, Bob. "A 'Salt Pork and Collard Greens' TV Show." *Ebony*, June 1974.

MacDonald, J. Fred. *Blacks and White TV: Afro-Americans in Television since 1948*. Chicago: Nelson-Hall, 1983.

Martin, Cybel. "The Art of Lighting Dark Skin for Film and HD." *Shadow and Act*, February 4, 2014.

Martin, Stefan, and Walt Wolfram. "The Sentence in African American Vernacular English." In *African-American English: Structure, History, and Use*, edited by Salikoko S. Mufwene, John R. Rickford, Guy Bailey, and John Baugh. New York: Routledge, 1998. 11–36.

Mask, Mia. *Divas on Screen: Black Women in American Film*. Champaign: University of Illinois Press, 2009.

Maslin, Janet. "Nick Nolte and Eddie Murphy in *48 Hours*." *New York Times*, December 8, 1982.

———. "The Tables Are Turned on a Smug, Sweet-Talking Don Juan." *New York Times*, July 1, 1992.

McAllister, Marvin. *White People Do Not Know How to Behave at Entertainments Designed for Ladies and Gentlemen of Colour: William Brown's African and American Theater*. Chapel Hill: University of North Carolina Press, 2003.

———. *Whiting Up: Whiteface Minstrels and Stage Europeans in African American Performance*. Chapel Hill: University of North Carolina Press, 2014.

McBride, Dwight A. *Why I Hate Abercrombie and Fitch: Essays on Race and Sexuality.* New York: New York University Press, 2005.

McBride, James. "Eddie Murphy Comes Clean." *People,* August 8, 1988.

McDowell, Jeanne. "Strikers on the Catwalk." *Time,* July 27, 2006.

McFadden, Syreeta. "Teaching the Camera to See My Skin: Navigating Photography's Inherited Bias against Dark Skin." *Buzzfeed,* April 2, 2014.

Membis, Liane. "It's Time to Bury the Ratchet." *Clutch Magazine,* December 2012.

Mifflin, Lawrie. "Black Protest Delays Sitcom Episode." *New York Times,* October 3, 1998.

Mills, Quincy T. *Cutting across the Color Line: Black Barbers and Barbershops in America.* Philadelphia: University of Pennsylvania Press, 2013.

Mims, Sergio. "Star Jones Calls for Boycott of 'Basketball Wives' and Other Reality Shows." *Shadow and Act,* April 27, 2012.

Mitchell, Elvis. "Spike Lee: The *Playboy* Interview" (July 1991). In *Spike Lee: Interviews,* edited by Cynthia Fuchs. Jackson: University Press of Mississippi, 2002. 35–64.

Mull, Martin, and Allen Rucker. *The History of White People in America.* New York: Putnam, 1985.

Mulvey, Laura. "Visual Pleasure and Narrative Cinema." In *Film Theory and Criticism: Introductory Readings,* edited by Leo Braudy and Marshall Cohen. New York: Oxford University Press. 833–844.

Murphy, Mekado. "Talking Comedy with John Landis." *New York Times,* November 21, 2011.

Murray, Susan, and Laurie Ouellette. "Introduction." In *Reality TV: Remaking Television Culture,* edited by Susan Murray and Laurie Ouellette. New York: New York University Press, 2009. 1–22.

Ndounou, Monica. *Shaping the Future of African American Film: Color-Coded Economics and the Story behind the Numbers.* New Brunswick, NJ: Rutgers University Press, 2014.

Neal, Mark Anthony. *Soul Babies: Black Popular Culture and the Post-soul Aesthetic.* New York: Routledge, 2002.

Obenson, Tambay A. "When Paramount Withheld *Coming to America* from the Press, Not Knowing What They Had." *Shadow and Act,* March 29, 2016.

O'Connell, Michael. "Race and Reality: The Quiet Success of the Black Unscripted Boom." *Hollywood Reporter,* April 3, 2014.

Paskin, Willa. "Shonda Rhimes: 'Calling a Show a "Guilty Pleasure"—It's Like Saying It's a Piece of Crap.'" *Salon,* February 10, 2013.

Petersen, Anne Helen. "Scandals of Classic Hollywood: Dorothy Dandridge vs. the World." *Hairpin,* June 20, 2012.

"Pharrell Williams." *Oprah Prime.* OWN, April 13, 2014.

Piper, Adrian. *Out of Order, Out of Sight.* Cambridge, MA: MIT Press, 1996.

Pozner, Jennifer L. *Reality Bites Back: The Troubling Truth about Guilty Pleasure TV.* Berkeley, CA: Seal Press, 2010.

"President Obama Speaks at the National Urban League Convention." White House, July 25, 2012.

Randolph, Laura B. "Halle Berry: Hollywood's Hottest Black Actress Has a New Husband, a New Home and a New Attitude." *Ebony,* April 1993.

The Real Housewives of Atlanta Reunion Part II. Season 5, episode 22. Bravo, April 14, 2013.

Reeves, Jimmie Lynn, and Richard Campbell. *Cracked Coverage: Television News, the Anti-cocaine Crusade, and the Reagan Legacy.* Durham, NC: Duke University Press, 1994.

Rensin, David. "Playboy Interview: Eddie Murphy." *Playboy,* February 1990.

Robinson, Nicholas. "Joe Budden Accused of Domestic Violence by Video Vixen." *Rolling Out,* May 10, 2011.

Roediger, David. *The Wages of Whiteness: Race and the Making of the American Working Class.* London: Verso, 2007.

Rogin, Michael. *Blackface, White Noise: Jewish Immigrants in the Hollywood Melting Pot.* Berkeley: University of California Press, 1996.

Roth, Lorna. "Looking at Shirley, the Ultimate Norm: Colour Balance, Image Technologies, and Cognitive Equity." *Canadian Journal of Communication* 34 (2009): 111–136.

Saad, Megan. "Q&A: Erica Mena Dismisses Rumors That She's Bisexual for Male Attention, Talks Coming Out to Her Family." *Vibe,* October 30, 2013.

Samuels, Allison. "Angela's Fire." *Newsweek,* June 30, 2002.

Saturday Night Live. Season 1, episode 7. NBC, December 13, 1975.

——. Season 6, episode 3. NBC, December 6, 1980.

Schaeffer, Eric. *Bold! Daring! Shocking! True: A History of Exploitation Films, 1919–1959.* Durham, NC: Duke University Press, 1999.

Schickel, Richard. "Review of *48 Hours*." *Time,* December 20, 1982.

Sconce, Jeffrey. "Introduction." In *Sleaze Artists: Cinema at the Margins of Taste, Style, and Politics,* edited by Jeffrey Sconce. Durham, NC: Duke University Press, 2007. 1–16.

——. "'Trashing' the Academy: Taste, Excess, and an Emerging Politics of Cinematic Style." *Screen* 36, no. 4 (Winter 1995): 371–393.

Scott, A. O. "Courtesy and Decency Play Sneaky with a Tough Guy." *New York Times,* December 26, 2001.

——. "Not-So-Cuddly Cat: This One Packs a Mean Whip." *New York Times,* July 22, 2004.

Shales, Tom, and James Andrew Miller. *Live from New York: An Uncensored History of Saturday Night Live.* New York: Little, Brown, 2002.

Smith, Valerie. *Not Just Race, Not Just Gender: Black Feminist Readings.* New York: Routledge, 1998.

Stevens, David. *Queen.* First draft. April 19, 1991. UCLA Film and Television Archive, Los Angeles, CA.

——. *Queen.* Second draft. January 17, 1992. UCLA Film and Television Archive, Los Angeles, CA.

Stewart, Jacqueline. *Migrating to the Movies: Cinema and Black Urban Modernity.* Berkeley: University of California Press, 2005.

Streeter, Caroline. "Faking the Funk: Mariah Carey, Alicia Keys, and (Hybrid) Black Celebrity." In *Black Cultural Traffic: Crossroads in Global Performance and Popular Culture,* edited by Harry Justin Elam and Kennell A. Jackson. Ann Arbor: University of Michigan Press, 2005. 185–207.

Sue, Derald Wing, Christina M. Capodilupo, Gina C. Torino, Jennifer M. Bucceri, Aisha M. B. Holder, Kevin L. Nadal, and Marta Esquilin. "Racial Microaggressions in Everyday Life: Implications for Clinical Practice." *American Psychologist* 62, no. 4 (May–June 2007): 271–286.

Taylor, Yuval, and Jake Austen. *Darkest America: Black Minstrelsy from Slavery to Hip-Hop*. New York: W. W. Norton, 2012.

"Three Way, No Way." *Love & Hip Hop*. VH1, June 23, 2014.

Tinkcom, Matthew. *Working Like a Homosexual: Camp, Capital, Cinema*. Durham, NC: Duke University Press, 2002.

Trust, Gary. "Cardi B 'Moves' to No. 1 on Billboard Hot 100 with 'Bodak Yellow,' Post Malone Debuts at No. 2 with 'Rockstar.'" *Billboard*, September 25, 2017.

"Tyler Perry to Spike Lee: 'Go Straight to Hell.'" *Huffington Post*, April 20, 2011.

Vecsey, George. "Sports of the Times: Quotas Wrong for School Sports." *New York Times*, December 3, 1980.

Wald, Gayle Freda. *Crossing the Line: Racial Passing in Twentieth-Century U.S. Literature and Culture*. Durham, NC: Duke University Press, 2000.

Walker, Alice. *In Search of Our Mothers' Gardens: Womanist Prose*. Orlando: Harcourt, 2004.

Warner, Kristen J. "A Black Cast Doesn't Make a Black Show: City of Angels and the Plausible Deniability of Color-Blindness." In *Watching While Black: Centering the Television of Black Audiences*, edited by Beretta E. Smith-Shomade. New Brunswick, NJ: Rutgers University Press, 2012. 49–62.

———. *The Cultural Politics of Colorblind TV Casting*. Routledge Transformations in Race and Media. New York: Routledge, 2015.

———. "They Gon' Think You Loud Regardless: Ratchetness, Reality Television, and Black Womanhood." *Camera Obscura* 30, no. 1 (2015): 129–153.

Watkins, Boyce. "7 Ways VH1 Is Destroying the Black Community." *Financial Juneteenth*, April 22, 2014.

———. "Dr. Boyce Watkins: Why I Refuse to Support the Coonery of the Show, 'Empire.'" *Financial Juneteenth*, March 1, 2015.

Watkins, Mel. *On the Real Side: Laughing, Lying, and Signifying—the Underground Tradition of African-American Humor That Transformed American Culture, from Slavery to Richard Pryor*. New York: Simon and Schuster, 1994.

Weintraub, Steve. "The Collider Interview: John Landis, Part II." *Collider*, September 2, 2005.

Wells, Veronica. "'We're Not Lesbians': Erica Mena and Cyn Santana Discuss Their Relationship on Hot 97." *Madame Noire*, January 16, 2014.

White, Armond. *The Resistance: Ten Years of Pop Culture That Shocked the World*. Woodstock, NY: Overlook, 1995.

Widdicombe, Lizzie. "Perfect Pitching: Bethenny Frankel and the New Breed of Celebrity Entrepreneur." *New Yorker*, September 21, 2015.

Williams, Linda. *Playing the Race Card: Melodramas of Black and White from Uncle Tom to O.J. Simpson*. Princeton, NJ: Princeton University Press, 2001.

Williams, Raymond. *Marxism and Literature*. Oxford: Oxford University Press, 1977.

Wright, Richard. "Between Laughter and Tears." *New Masses*, October 5, 1937.

Zook, Krystal Brent. *The FOX Network and the Revolution in Black Television*. New York: Oxford University Press, 1999.

Zurawik, David. "'Queen' for a Day—or Three: Miniseries Star Halle Berry Likes Exposure as Opinions Surface about Haley Saga." *Baltimore Sun*, February 17, 1993.

Page numbers in *italics* refer to illustrations.

around-the-way girl, 115, 116–120, 135

Ashley, on *Love & Hip Hop in Atlanta*, 172–173, *173*

Asian Americans, 156. *See also* women of color

assimilation, 33, 83, 90, 105

Associate, The (Petrie, 1996), 20, 33, 82, 113, 200n25; intersectionality in, 103–112; Laurel Ayres in, 88, 105–112, *107, 109*; plotlines of, 105–106; reviews of, 105, 107–108, 111

Atlanta, 25, 146, 148, 154, 192n13

Aubry, Gabriel, 116

audience, audiences, 9, 12, 118, 148; engagement of, 31, 153–154. *See also* black audiences

auteurist-focused analyses, 13; of *Coming to America*, 38, 57–58

authenticity, 113, 149; racial, 120, 133. *See also* black cultural authenticity and specificity

authorship, film, 54–55

Ava DuVernay Barbie, 13, *14*

avant-garde, 27

Aykroyd, Dan, *41, 42*

Babington, Bruce, 66–67

Bachelor, The, 2

background, 75, 138; in *The Cosby Show*, 68, 70, 201n35. *See also* foreground

Bailey, Cynthia, 155

Baker, Rick, 53–54, 196n2

Bakhtin, Mikhail, 30

Banks, Tyra, 148

BAPS (Townsend, 1995), 135

Barbie dolls, 13, *14*

Basketball Wives (VH1), 16, 34, 150, 154, 156, 167–168, 181, 189; audiences of, 148; boycott of, 25, 175; conflict on, 153, 159–161; story lines of, 159–161; title of, 177–178; wives and women on, *162*, 178–179, 186

Bassett, Angela, 137, 140

Beals, Jennifer, 124, 125, 202n12, 202–203n14

Beatty, Warren, 52, 135

Behan, Brendan, *The Quare Fellow*, 174

behavior, 60, 103, 191–192n5; of Flav, 1–2, 4; gendered, 92, 105, 193n23; racial code of,

4, 18, 21, 30, 94, 95, 97, 111, 125; on reality television, 143–146, 159, 174, 179, 180, 206n17; social norms of, 12, 151, 177

Benét, Eric, 141

Benjamin, Walter, 27

Benny, Jack, 73

Ben's Chili Bowl (Washington, DC), 9

Berlant, Lauren, 166, 167, 168, 170

Berry, Halle, 127, 140, 204n35; Academy Award of, 116, 135, 140, 187, 204n39; "around-the-way girl" trope and, 115, 116–120; as beauty queen, 115, 116–117, 122; biraciality of, 124, 127, 128, 203n22; in *Boomerang*, *118, 119*, 135; career and films of, 115, 132, 134, 135, 140; in *Catwoman*, 140–141; circumstantial negativity of, 114–141; as crossover star, 26, 33, 140, 141; Dandridge and, 121–122, 202n9; Goldberg and, 110, 137–138, 201n34; hairstyle of, 120–121, 202n8; *Monster's Ball* and, 116, 137, 138, 139, *139*, 140, 187; mother of, 127, 128; passing and, 116, 202n13; persona of, 123, 140, 141; in *Queen* and, 116, 122–134, *126, 134*, 202n13; as race traitor, 116, 141; selling out by, 139, 140, 141; in *Strictly Business*, 89, 91–92, *93*; "tragic mulatto" trope and, 115, 123, 124–128, 125; "white man's whore" trope and, 115, 134–140

BET network, 183, 189

Beulah (ABC), 24

Beverly Hills Cop (Brest, 1984), 52–53

Beverly Hills Cop II (Scott, 1987), 59

Billboard charts, 183, 207n31

Billman, Kathleen, 167

biraciality, 132; of Beals, 124, 203n14; of Berry, 122, 124–125, 127–128, 201n34, 203n22

Birnbaum, Debra, 183

Birth of a Nation, The (Griffith, 1915), 2, 28, 137

bisexuality and bisexual identity, 172, 173

black audiences, 30, 84, 136, 148, 166, 189; of *Coming to America*, 39, 57, 68; of *The Cosby Show*, 68, 70

Black Awareness Rally, in *Coming to America*, 67–68

black barbershops, 36, 196n4; in *Coming to America*, 35–36, 39, 67, 69, 71, 79

black-cast films, 124, 127, 135

black-cast reality television, 147–148, 149, 154, 166, 167

black church, 39, 71, 79

black comedy, comedians, 6, 9, 30, 43, 48–49, 55, 192n10, 197n25, 205n5; black humor and, 30, 43, 48, 66, 70, 71; buffoonery and coonery, 2–3, 11, 24, 40, 42, 43, 46, 191n1; sellout films and, 33, 82, 88

black community, 2, 11, 29, 89, 103, 177, 203n15; destruction of, 175, 184; in sellout films, 97, 103; Williams and, 6, 9

black cultural authenticity and specificity, 23–25, 87, 88, 90, 120, 151; in *Coming to America*, 65, 77, 79; of Murphy and Pryor, 46–47, 48

black culture, 20, 21, 27, 79, 113, 114, 129, 191n3; *Coming to America* and, 63, 71, 80; *The Cosby Show* and, 68, 70; traditions of, 7–8

blackface, 32, 110. *See also* blackface minstrelsy; whiteface

blackface minstrelsy, 175; Bert Williams and, 18–19; Jews and, 36–37, 53

black film, films, 30, 86, 114, 116, 133, 199n3; of the 1990s, 84–87; *Coming to America*, 31, 39, 57–58; definition of, 38, 195n58

black identity, 45, 83, 97, 98, 114; in sellout films, 89, 112–113

black-ish (ABC), 183

black media, 15, 24–25, 86, 166

black music, 111–112, 199n3. *See also* hip hop music; rap groups and rappers; rap music industry

blackness, 12, 63, 87, 92, 114, 118, 125, 135–136, 144, 191n3; acting, 4, 130; aesthetic of, 9, 29, 88, 112; authentic, 33, 46–47, 201n34; of Berry, 124, 127; coding of, 202–203n14, 203n15; on *The Cosby Show*, 45, 201n35; cultural, 47, 74, 75, 90, 97; *Empire* and, 183–184; femininity and, 115, 121, 181, 200n25; idea of, 28–29, 105, 180; media as

threat to, 97–101; perceptions of, 11, 14, 18, 25, 47; in *Queen*, 131, 133; in sellout films, 33, 103, 111–112; society and, 4, 191n4; stereotypes of, 5, 9, 11, 191–192n5

black popular culture, 9, 21, 23, 28–29, 48, 133, 195n63, 205n5; *Coming to America* and, 29, 31, 67, 73–80. *See also* black film, films; black media; black music

black queer identity, 26, 34, 208n49

blacks: empowerment of, 2, 103; as film directors, 13, 29, 85, 124; niggas vs., 3–4; survival strategies of, 102–103; vernacular and slang of, 9, 20, 37, 90, 97. *See also* African Americans; African American women; black women; women of color

black vernacular. *See* AAVE (African American Vernacular English)

black women, 13, 14, 133, 140, 150, 155, 177; Berry as, 124, 127, 128; erasure and invisibility of, 105, 112, 178; hip hop industry and, 163–164; in Hollywood, 121, 141; intersectionality of, 112, 168; labor of, 152–166; marriage and, 171, 179; reality television shows and, 145, 146, 150, 179, 180, 186. *See also* African American women; women of color

black youth, 85, 86, 88

blaxploitation, 9, 192n11; films of, 7, 23–24, 68, 84, 85, 98, 99

Blige, Mary J., 187

bling culture, 7

Bobby, in *Strictly Business*, 89, 90, 91, 94, 95

Bodyguard, The (Jackson, 1992), 138–139

Bogle, Donald, 42, 46, 85, 125, 199n3, 202n12, 202–203n14; on crossover comedy, 66, 197n24

Boomerang (Hudlin, 1992), 202n8; Berry and, 33, 115, 117, 122, 124; Murphy in, 53, 115; plotlines of, 38, 118; stills from, *118*, *119*

Bourdieu, Pierre, 19, 20, 27

Bowfinger (Oz, 1999), 53

Boyar, Kay, 107

Boyz n the Hood (Singleton, 1991), 23, 33, 82, 85, *86*, 88, 89 branding, 157, 162

Bravo network, 147, 159, 161, 189, 210n17; *The Real Housewives* on, 22, 75; spinoffs on, 148, 157; store of, 162, *163*

Braxton, Toni, 202n8

Bride, The (Roddam, 1985), 203n14

Bring the Pain, 3

Broadway, 157–158

Brown, James, 54, 191n1

Brown, Venel, 120

Buddafly, Amina, 164, 165

Budden, Joe, 164, 168–171, *171*, 208n41

Bullock, Sandra, 204n35

Bulworth (Beatty, 1998), 135, 140

Burruss, Kandi, 33, 75, 77, 155

Bury the Ratchet campaign, 25

Bush, George W., 140

business ventures, of women on reality television shows, 152, 153, 156–157, 161–162, 164–166

Busta Rhymes, 195n63

Butler, Judith, 102

Butler, The (Daniels, 2013), 187

cakewalk, 197n26

camp, 18, 193n30, 206n16

Campbell, Richard, 44

Campbell, Tisha, 38

Canby, Vincent, 57, 72

canon, 23, 26, 30, 33

Cantor, Eddie, 53

capitalism and materialism, 85, 91, 113

Carbado, Devon W., 6, 108

Cardi B (Belcalis Almanzar), 158, 207n31

Carey, Mariah, 203n15

Carmen Jones (Preminger, 1954), 121–122

carnivalesque, 30, 200n25

Carroll, Diahann, 24

Carson, Terrence "T. C.," 97

Car Wash (Schultz, 1976), 99

casting, 123, 135, 137; auditions and, 121–122, 124–125; of *Coming to America*, 38, 58, 70

categorization: of positivity and negativity, 11, 15; of race, 5, 16–17

catharsis, 21; in ratchet reality shows, 167, 180

Catwoman (2004), 140–141

celebrities, 158; Berry, 33, 116; blacks and, 6, 110; Murphy, 40, 50, 52, 58, 74, 81

Chaiken, Ilene, 189, 210n15

Chanel, 162

Chappelle, Dave, 180

Chicago, 183

Chicago (musical), 158

Chong, Rae Dawn, 124, 202n12

Chuck D, 2, 191n1

Chude-Sokei, Louis, 19

Cinderella, 157

cinema verité style, 138, 169

City of Angels (CBS), 210n15

civil rights movement and protests, 20, 184

Clair Huxtable, on *The Cosby Show*, 180

Clarence, in *Coming to America*, 39, 67, 70, 71–72, 77, 79

class, 16, 19, 26, 95, 146; gender and sexuality and, 174, 201n36; race and, 102, 201n36

Clay, Cassius (Muhammad Ali), 36, 67, 71

Clockers (Lee, 1998), 85

CNN (Cable News Network), 184

coding, codes, 88, 91–92, 156; of biracial women, 117–118, 203n15; racial, 44, 63, 111; switching of, 130, 132

Cohen, Andy, 154–155

Cohen, Cathy, 174

Cole, Olivia, 178

Collins, Patricia Hill, 156

color-blindness and -muteness, 15, 16, 135; in *The Associate*, 106, 108; of *Coming to America*, 70, 74; Landis and, 55, 57, 63, 74

comedy, comedians, 3, 66, 197n24, 200n25

Comedy Central, 11, 180

Coming to America (Landis, 1988), 31–32, 36, 39, 57, 62, 68, 74, 81, 196n2; authorship of, 54–55; as black cult classic, 28, 31; as black cultural text, 37, 80; in black popular culture, 29, 73–80, 195n63; casting of, 38, 58; closing credits of, 36, 72–73; as collection of sketches, 66, 68, 75; engagement scene in, 75, 77; formal negativity and, 35–80; Hall in, 36, 38, 55, 63, 67, 72, 199n68; Landis's relationship with Murphy and, 53–63; Murphy and, 17, 60, 61; Murphy's multiple roles in, 48–49, 70–71, 78; as negative text, 26, 80; plotlines of, 32, 55, 57, 67, 68, 70, 73, 75, 77; reviews of, 70–72; as romantic comedy, 65–66, 70, 82; Saul in, 36–37, 37, 53, 72–73, 196n4, 200n20; shadows of, 63–73; stills from, 37, 64, 69, 76; supporting characters in, 67–68, 77, 79; tensions on set of, 61–62, 198n41

common sense, 7, 40, 192n12

consciousness, double, 3

conservative right, 44, 175, 177, 199n63

context, 4, 6, 13

Cookie Lyon, on *Empire*, 183, 186–187, *188*, 189, 190

Cooley High (Schultz, 1975), 99

Cooper, Brittney, 21

Corey, Mary, 120, 122

Corrina, Corrina (Nelson, 1994), 111

Cosby, Bill, 24, 43, 46, 174. See also *Cosby Show, The*

Cosby Show, The (NBC), 28, 123, 180, 195n63; blackness in, 86, 201n35; crossover appeal of, 68, 70; as positive intervention, 24–25; racially coded discourse and, 44–45

cosmopolitanism, of Rock, 6, 7, 192n9

Costner, Kevin, 138–139

crack cocaine, 84, 85, 135

Crain, William, 98

Crenshaw, Kimberlé, 112

Cronin, Mark, 2

crossover films and stars, 42; in the 1980s, 45, 66, 68, 84; Berry, 127, 134–136, 139, 140, 141; Jackie Robinson, 136; Michael Jackson, 62; Murphy, 44–45, 49, 52, 73

Crowley, James, 5–6

cult status, 28, 195n58

culture, 19, 29, 97; high, 27, 195n58; low, 27, 195n58; mass, 27; popular, 27, 28–29, 30, 42, 47, 170, 171; race and, 27–28, 30, 44; theory of, 27. *See also* hegemony, cultural

Cypress Hill, 85

Dallas, 184

Dancing with the Stars, 157

Dandridge, Dorothy, 121–122, 202n9, 204n39

Daniels, Lee, 183, 186, 187

Danson, Ted, 110, 111

Darryl Brown, in *True Identity*, 102

Daryl, in *Coming to America*, 63

Dash, Julie, 132

David, in *Strictly Business*, 94, 95–96, *96*

Davidson, Tommy, in *Strictly Business*, 89

Davis, Michaela Angela, 25, 34, 146

Deadline, 183

DeGeneres, Ellen, 158

Devil in a Blue Dress (Franklin, 1995), 203n14

Dexter Jackson, in *Livin' Large*, 88, 97–101, *99, 100*, 103, 105

Diawara, Manthia, 192n9

Die Another Day (Tamahori, 2002), 140

Diedre, in *Strictly Business*, 91–92, *93*

diegeses, 138, 183; of reality television shows, 152, 153, 159, 169

Different World, A, 123, 195n63

directors, film, 57; black, 29, 98; black women, 13, *14*; white, 20, 29, 58

discrimination, 108; reverse, 44, 72, 96, 199n63

Distinguished Gentleman, The (Lynn, 1992), 53, 73

diversity: of *Empire*, 183, 189; at FOX, 187

Do the Right Thing (Lee, 1989), 17; *Coming to America* and, 39, 81, 82; race relations in, 32–33

Doty, Alexander, 174

double negative: in AAVE, 18; ratchet reality shows as, 151

Doughboy, in *Boyz n the Hood*, 85

drag, Goldberg in, 106

Drayton, William. *See* Flavor Flav

Dr. Black and Mr. Hyde (Crain, 1976), 98

Dreamgirls (Condon, 2006), 53

drug addicts and dealers, 7, 143. *See also* crack cocaine

Du Bois, W. E. B., 3, 22

"Duffle Bag Boy" (Playaz Circle), 7

DuVernay, Ava, 13, *14*
Dynasty, 183, 184, 186

Ebert, Roger, 55, 57, 74, 108, 139
Eddie Murphy Productions, 40, 54–55, 59–60
Eddie Murphy: Raw (Townsend, 1987), 59–60
Edelman, Lee, 175–176
Ellen DeGeneres Show, The, 158
Elliott, Sam, 111
empathy, 144, 167
Empire (FOX), 34, 209n12; as false negative
     representation, 182–192; *Love & Hip Hop*
     and, 30, 189; nuance and, 185, 186; success
     of, 182, 183, 190
English, American, 18, 142. *See also* AAVE (Afri-
     can American Vernacular English)
Entertainment Tonight, 184
Erman, John, 132
Estelle, *Empire* and, 187
Evans, Peter William, 66–67
Everson, Kevin Jerome, 68
exceptionalism, 5, 12
excess: on *Love & Hip Hop*, 145, 186; ratchet-
     ness and, 144, 174, 177

Facebook, 164
Falcon Crest, 184
false negatives, 34; *Empire* as, 182–190
family: African Americans and, *126*, 208n56;
     values of, 175
Fanon, Frantz, 21, 180, 191n4
Fashion Police, 158
Fatal Beauty (Holland, 1987), 111
Faust, Mimi, 142, 143, 172
feeling some type of way, 166–171
female complaint, 170
female empowerment, 34
femininity: black, 115, 121, 152, 200n25;
     conventional models of, 150, 151; hairstyles
     and, 120; middle class and, 178
feminism, feminists, 20, 166, 170, 171; black,
     156, 201n36
Ferguson, Missouri, 184
51 Minds Entertainment, 2

film, films, 13, 27, 33, 99, 137; cameos in, 103,
     104, 187, 209n12; closing credits of, 32,
     36, 72–73, 89; critics of, 92, 96, 97, 138,
     140–141. *See also* Hollywood films; hood
     films; sellout films of the 1990s; *and specific
     films*
Financial Juneteenth, 184
First Wives Club, The (Wilson, 1996),
     107
Fizz, 164–165, 172
Flashdance (Lyne, 1983), 203n14
Flavor Flav, 2, 192n16; behavior and persona
     of, 1–2, 4; Comedy Central roast of, 11; as
     negative representation, 1–4, 17; Public
     Enemy and, 1–2, 191n1; wardrobe of,
     1, 3, 5
Flavor of Love, The, 2, 3, 17
Fleetwood, Nicole, 167
Flintsones, The (Levant, 1994), 135
flipping of the script, 37
foreground, 68, 70, 75, 111, 112, 170, 201n35.
     See also background
formal negativity, 37
Forster, Marc, 137, 138, 139
48 Hours (Hill, 1982), Murphy in, 40, 41, 47,
     49, 52, 59, 65
fourth wall, breaking of, 150, 154
Fox, Michael J., 62
FOX Network, 184, 189, 209n13, 210n15; *Em-
     pire* and, 34, 182, 184, 187
Frankel, Bethenny, 156, 157, 158, 161
Frank La Motta, in *True Identity*, 102
free speech, 71, 110
French, Phillip, 138
Fresh Off the Boat (ABC), 183
Fruity, 61–62
funk music, 191n1
futurism, 176

Gamson, Joshua, 25
gangs, gangsta, 89, 183, 184
Gardner, Ava, 202n13
Gary O'Hara, in *Strictly Business*, 94, 95–96,
     96

Lee, Spike, 24, 57; as black director, 82, 85; *Do the Right Thing* and, 17, 32, 39, 82; *Malcolm X*, 113; Murphy and, 43, 50

Leland Carver, in *True Identity*, 101

Lemon, Don, 184, 185

Leonard, Suzanne, 91–92

lesbian identity, 172, 173

Leticia, in *Monster's Ball*, 137–138

Levine, Elana, 151, 205n5

Levine, Lawrence, 30

Lewis, Jerry, *The Nutty Professor*, 73

Lewis, Justin, 45, 68, 70

LGBTQ rights, 175

Life (Demme, 1999), 53

Lil Wayne, 7

linguistics and language, 18, 20, 103, 129–131, 197n20. *See also* AAVE (African American Vernacular English)

Liotta, Ray, 111

Lisa, in *Coming to America*, 68, 69, 77

Live with Kelly and Michael, 158

Livin' Large (Schultz, 1991), 33, 82, 108, 113; Dexter in, 88, 103, 105; media and blackness in, 97–101

LL Cool J, "Around-the-Way Girl," 117

Lockhart, Calvin, 29

London, 7

Los Angeles, 192n13; 1992 riots in, 84; South Central, 86, 88, 89

Losing Isaiah (Gyllenhaal, 1995), 135

Lost Boundaries (Werker, 1949), 125

Louis, Joe, 71–72

Love, Courtney, 187

Love & Hip Hop (VH1), 16, 34, 142, 150, 153–154, 156, 167, 171, 180–181, 184, 189, 207n31; audience of, 148; *Empire* and, 30, 189; music on, 163–164; proposal scene on, 168–171, *171*; queer sexuality on, 20, 26, 172; ratchetness of, 144, 185; soap opera elements of, 151; story lines of, 164, 172; women and, 168, 186

Love & Hip Hop Atlanta (VH1), 171, 209n12; Hernandez on, 142–145, 187, *188*; queer sexuality on, 172–173

Love & Hip Hop Hollywood (VH1), 171, 208n49; Mudarris on, *165*, 165–166; plotlines of, 164–166, 172

Lozada, Evelyn, 186, 189; on *Basketball Wives*, 153, *162*; Roman vs., 159–161, 178

Lubiano, Wahneema, 87–88, 192n12

Lucious, on *Empire*, 183, 185

Lyne, Adrian, 203n14

Lyon family, on *Empire*, 182

MacDonald, J. Fred, 40

Mack, The (Campus, 1973), 7, 192n14

Made in America (Benjamin, 1993), 111

Madonna, 183

Mafia mobsters, 101–102, 103

magazines: *Ebony*, 24, 33, 52, 110, 128, 141; *Entertainment Weekly*, 124–125; *Essence*, 128; *Jet*, 33, 133; *Newsweek*, 137; *People*, 62, 116–117, 141; *Rolling Stone*, 63; *Slate*, 183; *Time*, 70–71; *Variety*, 183, 189; *Vibe*, 173

mainstream: Berry and, 121, 134, 140; culture of, 27, 30, 85, 87; media of, 84–85, 98, 166, 189; as white, 7, 25–26, 115

makeup, 19, 132; in *Coming to America*, 19, 37, 53–54, 58, 196n2; makeup artists and, 54, 88, 108, 125, 196n2; whiteface, 102–103, *104*. *See also* blackface; blackface minstrelsy

Malcolm X, 49

Malcolm X (Lee, 1992), 113

maleness and masculinity, 105, 177; black, 17, 18, 186; in sellout films, 91, 113; white, 106, 108, 200n25

Mama Morton, in *Chicago*, 157–158

mammy trope, 24, 115

Marciano, Rocky, 72

Marcus, in *Boomerang*, 118, 120

marriage, 172, 178; in reality television shows, 164, 170; women of color and, 170, 179

Marriott Hotels, 202n7

Martin, Stefan, 18

Martin, Trayvon, 184

Martinez, Olivier, 116

Marx Brothers, 66

Mask, Mia, 118, 200n25, 202n9, 203n22

Maslin, Janet, 65

Mattel, Ava DuVernay Barbie by, 13, *14*

Mayfield, Curtis, 85

McBride, Dwight, 96, 199n63

McDaniel, Hattie, 51

McDowell, Jeanne, 149

McKee, Lonette, 125, *132*, *134*, 203n16

media, 12, 17, 21, 23, 101, 167; black, 15; blackness and, 97–101, 176; mainstream, 84–85, 98, 166, 189; popular, 105, 146; power and, 23, 99; race and, 11, 132; white normativity in, 27, 43, 135; women of color in, 112, 145, 179. *See also* magazines; newspapers; television

Melissa Harris-Perry Show, The, 13

melodrama, 30, 34, 170, 206n16; *Empire* and, 185, 189; in reality television, 150, 159, 180

Mena, Erica, 172, 173–174, 208n41

Menace II Society (Hughes Brothers, 1993), 33, 82, 85, 89, 112

meta discourse, 20, 31, 132

"me-tooism," 72

Micheaux, Oscar, 28

middle class, 7, 87, 118, 168, 179; black, 103, 120–121, 175, 195n63, 208n56; femininity and, 178, 179; white, 12, 21, 26, 156, 179, 208n56; women of, 120, 156

Miles Pope, in *True Identity*, 88, 101–103, *104*, 200n23

mimicry, 54–55

minstrelsy, 23, 175; Murphy's *SNL* performances as, 40, 42. *See also* blackface minstrelsy

mise-en-scènes, 32, 161, 164, 201n35

"Mister Robinson's Neighborhood," Murphy's *SNL* sketch of, 45–46

Monster's Ball (Forster, 2001), 187; Berry and, 116, 136–140, 204n39

Morehouse College, 89

Morris, in *Coming to America*, 67, 77, 79

motherhood, 34

motherwork, 156, 159

Motown, 45

Moynihan, Daniel Patrick, 177; *The Negro Family*, 179, 208n56

Mr. Drake, in *Strictly Business*, 94, 95

Mrs. Doubtfire (Columbus, 1993), 107, 200n25

MTV, 28

Mudarris, Nikki, *165*, 165–166, 172

mulatto and mulatta, 133, 136; trope of tragic, 115, 116, 123, 124–128

multiculturalism, 86, 199n63

multiracial category, in U.S. Census, 136

Murphy, Eddie, 6, 42, 46, 47, 121, 192n10; Academy Awards speech (1988) of, 50–52, *52*; arrogance of, 60, 62; as blockbuster star, 38, 59, 60–61; in *Boomerang*, 38, 115, 117, *118*, 135; business sense of, 59–60; as comedic sidekick to white leads, 40, 42, 52–53; comedic work and talents of, 70, 72, 73; *Coming to America* and, 17, 28, 29, 35–80, 60, 82; as crossover star, 33, 42, 44–45, 49, 73; "entourage" of, 61–62, 63; in *48 Hours*, *41*, 65; as Gumby, 45, 54, 56; Landis and, 53–63, 61–62, 198n41; as matinee idol, 39–53, 50; multiple roles of, in *Coming to America*, 36, 48–49, 67, 70–71, *78*, 196n2; nonconfrontational style of, 51–52; political agenda of, 49, 50; production company of, 40, 54–55, 59–60; as Saul in *Coming to America*, 36, 38, 53–54, 70, 71, 72–73, 200n20; as sellout, 43–44; on *SNL*, 38, 43–44, 45, 54, 56, 71, 199n61; tokenism and, 32, 49; in *Trading Places*, *41*, 46, 59; in *White Like Me*, 43–44, 54, 56, 71, 199n61

Murphy, Mekado, 65

Murphy, Ryan, 157

Murray, Susan, 166

music industry, 139, 163, 171

NAACP (National Association for the Advancement of Colored People): *Amos 'n' Andy* and, 24, 28, 174; *The Birth of a Nation* and, 28, 137

narratives, 32; of black success, 82; realism of, 88

Natalie, in *Strictly Business*, 89, 91–92, *93*, 95, 97

National Association of Broadcasters, 148

Native Americans, 156

Naughty by Nature, 85

Ndounou, Monica, 50, 63, 74–75, 89, 198n52

Neal, Mark Anthony, 100, 103, 105, 114, 192n9, 205n5

negative, negativity, 26, 31, 151, 193n22; categorization of, 11, 32–34; circumstantial, 33, 114–141; comparative, 32–33; concept of, 17–20; perceptions and, 4, 18; performativity of, 12–16; photographic, 17–18; productive use of, 16–17; relational, 32–33, 81–113; space and, 73, 80; trash and, 26–28

negative images, representations, and texts, 4, 17, 22, 27, 81, 98, 137, 138, 166; agency and, 28–30; complexity of, 19, 31; *Empire* as, 183–184; false, 182–192; Flavor Flav and, 1–3; positive vs., 23–25, 187; power of, 18, 30; ratchetness and, 34, 151, 174–175; reality television and, 145–152, 167, 205n5; work of, 25–26

neighborhoods, 15. *See also* hood

neoliberalism, 21, 166

New Jack City (Van Peebles, 1991), 85

New Jersey, 157, 172

Newman, Michael Z., 151, 205n5

New Normal, The, 157

newspapers: *Baltimore Sun*, 125; *Los Angeles Times*, 125, 127; *Washington Post*, 96. See also *New York Times*

New York City, 7, 36, 66; Times Square, 169, 171

New York Times, 57, 59, 60, 65; reviews in, 72, 107, 108, 115

"nigga"/"nigger," 50, 99; "black" vs., 3–4; as n-word, 11; as pejorative, 131, 192n15; used by Williams, 5, 9, 11, 192n15

Nina, in *Bulworth*, 135

9 to 5 (Higgins, 1980), 200n25

Nolte, Nick, *41*, 42, 65

nonnormativity, in ratchet reality shows, 150, 175, 177

Norbit (Robbins, 2007), 6, 53

normalization, of whiteness, 132, 135, 205n9

"Nude by Nikki" product line, 165

Nutty Professor, The (Shadyac, 1996), 53, 73

Obama, Barack, 3, 6, 9, 11, 17, 113, 192n6; beer summit of, 5–6; black respectability and, 17–18; drops microphone, 77, *78*; on hard work, 22, 34; whites and, 4–5

O'Connell, Michael, 148

Olivia Pope, on *Scandal*, 180, 189

O'Neal, Shaunie, 159

Oscars. *See* Academy Awards

Othello, 102, 103, 200n23

Ouellette, Laurie, 166, 205n5

Outkast, with UGK, 9

overdetermination, 4, 191n4

OWN (Oprah Winfrey Network), 210n17

Oyin Handmade, 77, 79

Paramount Pictures: *Coming to America* and, 29, 32, 40, 54, 58, 74, 75; executives of, 60, 61, 65, 74; Murphy's deals with, 59, 60

Parks, Phaedra, 155–156

parody, 4, 48, 197n26

Passing (Larsen), 168

passing, 33, 102, 202n13; of Berry in *Queen*, 116, 123, 124, 130, 131; in *Illusions*, 132–133; *Queen* and, 132, 133

Pearman, Raven-Symoné, 123

Peele, Jordan, 192n6

performance, performances, 7, 11, 101–103, 130, 134, 161; agency and, 144–145; of identity, 12, 150; of labor, 152–166; performativity and, 132, 144, 200n25; racial, 4, 123, 125, 127, 132

Perry, Tyler, 24, 210n17

Persian Gulf war, 84

persona, of Berry, 33, 116, 121, 123, 125, 140, 141

Petersen, Anne Helen, 121

Petrie, Donald, 20, 33, 107

Phillips, Joseph C., 89

photonegative, as metaphor, 17–18

pimping, pimps, 7, 47, 102, 103, 192n11

Pinky (Kazan, 1949), 125, 202n13

Piper, Adrian, 131

Playaz Circle, "Duffle Bag Boy," 7

plotlines and story lines: of *The Associate*,
105–106; of *Boomerang*, 118; of *Coming to
America*, 31, 32, 37–38, 55, 57, 67, 70, 73,
75, 77; of *Empire*, 183, 185; of hood films,
89; of *Love & Hip Hop Hollywood*, 164–165;
of *Monster's Ball*, 137; of reality television
shows, 153, 158–161, 164, 172–173; of sellout
films, 83, 90; of *Strictly Business*, 89, 95, 97;
of *True Identity*, 101

Poitier, Sidney, 42, 51

police and law enforcement, 2, 5–6, 192n13

political correctness, 44

politics, 12, 44, 191n1

positivity, 5, 11; negativity vs., 12–16, 187;
performativity of, 12–16; positive images
and texts and, 17, 21, 23–25, 31, 187

postblack films, 102

postsoul aesthetic and films, 102, 103,
105

power and power structure, 4, 23, 30

Pozner, Jennifer L., 146, 166

Precious (Daniels, 2009), 187

Preminger, Otto, 121

Pretty Woman (Marshall, 1990), 92

Prince Akeem, in *Coming to America*, 35, 57,
67–68, 70, 76, 82

privilege, 105, 156, 172, 179; white, 43–44, 92,
95, 96; of white males, 108, 110

Production Code, 138, 204n42

profanity, of Williams, 6, 9

Professor Griff, 2

prostitution, prostitutes, 47, 137, 138, 143. *See
also* pimping, pimps

Pryor, Richard, 43, 49; black authenticity of,
46–47, 48

Public Enemy, 1–2; Flavor Flav and, 4,
191n1

quality, 13, 151, 186, 187; ratchet reality shows
and, 152, 169

quare, 174. *See also* queerness and queer
identity

Queen: language of, 129–131; in *Queen*, 122,
126, *134*

Queen. See *Alex Haley's Queen*

Queens, New York, 36, 66

queerness and queer identity, 20, 173, 176;
camp and, 193n30, 206n16; genderqueer,
172; queers of color and, 20, 26, 166,
171–179

Questlove, 77

race, 19, 21, 38, 43, 108, 155, 184, 203n15;
Berry and, 135–136; betrayal to, 116, 141; in
Coming to America, 36–37; culture and taste
and, 27–28, 30; discourses and narratives
of, 12, 146; gender and sexuality and, 114,
174, 201n36; norms of, 16, 110, 167; Obama
and, 5–6; performativity of, 101–103, 130,
132, 134; politics of, 133, 205n9; relations of,
32–33; society and, 17, 175

racial diversity, 15, 36, 86; of *Empire*, 183,
187–188, 189

racial identity, 17, 21, 86, 97, 124, 125, 129, 147;
of Berry, 26, 33, 140, 141; in *Strictly Business*,
91, 92

racism, 30, 108, 131, 136; in American culture, 15, 44, 62–63; of conservative right,
96, 175; Hollywood and, 13, 32, 38, 42–44,
62, 82, 95, 96, 137; microaggressions
and, 83, 95, 192n16; racial oppression
and, 15, 97; sexism and, 105, 112; structural, 4, 15, 44, 176; television and, 2, 11,
146, 147

Randy Watson: in *Coming to America*, 67, 70;
drops microphone, 77, *78*

Randy Watson Experience, 77

rape, in *Queen*, 130, 132

rap groups and rappers, 1, 7, 28, 77, 85, 117, 121,
139–140, 187, 192n9, 207n31; *Empire* and,
183, 185; *Love & Hip Hop* and, 163–165, 168;
rap songs and, 9, 25, 111–112, 167

rap music industry, 139, 163, 171. See also
Empire

ratchetness, 12, 16, 144, 151, 162, 165, 174, 181,
187

violence, 89, 165, 169; in *Boyz n the Hood*, 86, *86*

Vulture, 183

Wachs, Robert, 59

Waiting to Exhale (Whitaker, 1995), 57

Walker, Alice, 201n36

Wallace, Tara, 164

Wall Street, 105, 106

wardrobe: of Dandridge, 121–122; of Dexter in *Livin' Large*, 99; of Rock and Williams, 6–7, 9; significance of, 192n10, 192n11

Warner, Kristen, 135, 174, 195n58, 205n5; on ratchetness, 16, 34, 144, 162

Washington, DC, 10, 202n7; as Chocolate City, 7, 9

Washington, Denzel, 137, 140, 203n14

Washington, Fredi, 124, 202n13

Washington, Kerry, 189

WASPS, 101, 102

Watermelon Man (Melvin Van Peebles, 1970), 103

Watkins, Boyce, 175, 176–178, 184, 185

Watkins, Mel, 46, 48, 71, 175, 197n25, 205n5

Wayans, Keenen Ivory, 50

Waymon Tinsdale III, in *Strictly Business*, 88–95, *91*, *93*, 97

Wedding, The (Burnett, 1998), 135

Weintraub, Steve, 47

welfare queens, 44, 208n56

West Africa, 197n25

white, acting, 94–95, 103, 113, 131; in *Boomerang*, 118, 120; in *Strictly Business*, 96, 118

White, Armond, 92

white audiences, 118, 148, 194n40; of *Coming to America*, 65, 68; of *The Cosby Show*, 68, 70. *See also* crossover films and stars

white-cast films, color-blind casting in, 135

White Chicks (Wayans, 2004), 106

whiteface, 101, 105–106; of Murphy in *Coming to America*, 36, 53; sellout films and, 98–99, 103

white hegemony, 17, 20, 196n4

white identity, 101–102, 200n20

White Like Me short on SNL (Murphy), 43–44, 54, 56, 71, 199n61

white man's whore trope, Berry and, 115, 134–140

whiteness, 2, 5, 20, 28, 97, 103, 117, 132, 136, 199n63, 200n25; of *Coming to America*, 39, 70; Hollywood films and, 38, 71; media and, 27, 99, 135; normativity of, 63, 135, 189, 205n9; sellout films and, 89, 98, 101, 105, 108, 113; in *Strictly Business*, 90, 92, 94–96; television and, 46–47, 189; white privilege and, 43–44, 94, 105

whites, 72, 154; as movie directors, 20, 29, 82; Obama and, 4–5

Whitfield, Sheree, 162, 163

Why Do Fools Fall in Love (Nava, 1999), 135

Williams, Bert, blackface minstrelsy and, 18–19

Williams, Jennifer, 153, 159, 178–179, 207n28

Williams, Katt, 17, 192n5, 192n10, 192n11, 192n13, 192n15; Flavor Flav and, 11, 192n16; *It's Pimpin' Pimpin'* and, 4–7, 10; wardrobe of, 6–7

Williams, Linda, 15, 28

Williams, Pharrell, 21

Williams, Raymond, 27

Williams, Vanessa, 125

Wilson, Flip, 49

Wilson, Woodrow, 28

Winfrey, Oprah, 74, 135, 210n17

Witherspoon, Chris, 184

wives, as term, 178, 179

Wolfram, Walt, 18

women, 34, 118, 170, 179, 200n25, 207n31; coding of, 91–92; as mothers, 154, 155–156; on reality television shows, 144, 152–153, 166, 177; whiteface and, 105–106

women of color, 156; biracial, 122, 201n34, 203n14, 203n15; black, 155, 201n36; womanism and, 201n36. *See also* African American women; black women

Wonder, Stevie, 54, 55

work: labor and, 152, 206n16; on reality television, 152–166

Working Girl (Nichols, 1988), 91, 94, 200n12, 200n25

Wright, Richard, 23

writers, television, 148–149

Writers Guild, 149; 2001 strike of, 148

Young, Mona Scott, 151, 154

YouTube, 164, 184

Zolciak, Kim, 154–155